BOOKS

SERBIAN
VOCABULARY

FOR ENGLISH SPEAKERS

ENGLISH-SERBIAN

The most useful words
To expand your lexicon and sharpen
your language skills

9000 words

Serbian vocabulary for English speakers - 9000 words

By Andrey Taranov

T&P Books vocabularies are intended for helping you learn, memorize and review foreign words. The dictionary is divided into themes, covering all major spheres of everyday activities, business, science, culture, etc.

The process of learning words using T&P Books' theme-based dictionaries gives you the following advantages:

- Correctly grouped source information predetermines success at subsequent stages of word memorization
- Availability of words derived from the same root allowing memorization of word units (rather than separate words)
- Small units of words facilitate the process of establishing associative links needed for consolidation of vocabulary
- Level of language knowledge can be estimated by the number of learned words

T&P Books Publishing
www.tpbooks.com

ISBN: 978-1-78071-814-9

This book is also available in E-book formats.
Please visit www.tpbooks.com or the major online bookstores.

SERBIAN VOCABULARY
for English speakers

T&P Books vocabularies are intended to help you learn, memorize, and review foreign words. The vocabulary contains over 9000 commonly used words arranged thematically.

- Vocabulary contains the most commonly used words
- Recommended as an addition to any language course
- Meets the needs of beginners and advanced learners of foreign languages
- Convenient for daily use, revision sessions, and self-testing activities
- Allows you to assess your vocabulary

Special features of the vocabulary

- Words are organized according to their meaning, not alphabetically
- Words are presented in three columns to facilitate the reviewing and self-testing processes
- Words in groups are divided into small blocks to facilitate the learning process
- The vocabulary offers a convenient and simple transcription of each foreign word

The vocabulary has 256 topics including:

Basic Concepts, Numbers, Colors, Months, Seasons, Units of Measurement, Clothing & Accessories, Food & Nutrition, Restaurant, Family Members, Relatives, Character, Feelings, Emotions, Diseases, City, Town, Sightseeing, Shopping, Money, House, Home, Office, Working in the Office, Import & Export, Marketing, Job Search, Sports, Education, Computer, Internet, Tools, Nature, Countries, Nationalities and more …

TABLE OF CONTENTS

PRONUNCIATION GUIDE

Letter	Serbian example	T&P phonetic alphabet	English example

Vowels

Letter	Serbian example	T&P phonetic alphabet	English example
А а	авлија	[a]	shorter than in ask
Е е	ексер	[e]	elm, medal
И и	излаз	[i]	shorter than in feet
О о	очи	[o]	pod, John
У у	ученик	[u]	book

Consonants

Letter	Serbian example	T&P phonetic alphabet	English example
Б б	брег	[b]	baby, book
В в	вода	[ʋ]	vase, winter
Г г	глава	[g]	game, gold
Д д	дим	[d]	day, doctor
Ђ ђ	ђак	[ʥ]	jeans, gene
Ж ж	жица	[ʒ]	forge, pleasure
З з	зец	[z]	zebra, please
Ј ј	мој	[j]	yes, New York
К к	киша	[k]	clock, kiss
Л л	лептир	[l]	lace, people
Љ љ	љиљан	[ʎ]	daily, million
М м	мајка	[m]	magic, milk
Н н	нос	[n]	name, normal
Њ њ	књига	[ɲ]	canyon, new
П п	праг	[p]	pencil, private
Р р	рука	[r]	rice, radio
С с	слово	[s]	city, boss
Т т	тело	[t]	tourist, trip
Ћ ћ	ћуран	[tɕ]	cheer
Ф ф	фењер	[f]	face, food
Х х	хлеб	[h]	home, have
Ц ц	цео	[ts]	cats, tsetse fly
Ч ч	чизме	[tʃ]	church, French

Letter	Serbian example	T&P phonetic alphabet	English example
Џ џ	џбун	[dʒ]	joke, general
Ш ш	шах	[ʃ]	machine, shark

ABBREVIATIONS
used in the vocabulary

English abbreviations

ab.	-	about
adj	-	adjective
adv	-	adverb
anim.	-	animate
as adj	-	attributive noun used as adjective
e.g.	-	for example
etc.	-	et cetera
fam.	-	familiar
fem.	-	feminine
form.	-	formal
inanim.	-	inanimate
masc.	-	masculine
math	-	mathematics
mil.	-	military
n	-	noun
pl	-	plural
pron.	-	pronoun
sb	-	somebody
sing.	-	singular
sth	-	something
v aux	-	auxiliary verb
vi	-	intransitive verb
vi, vt	-	intransitive, transitive verb
vt	-	transitive verb

Serbian abbreviations

ж	-	feminine noun
ж мн	-	feminine plural
м	-	masculine noun
м мн	-	masculine plural
м, ж	-	masculine, feminine
мн	-	plural
нг	-	intransitive verb

нг, пг	-	intransitive, transitive verb
пг	-	transitive verb
с	-	neuter
с мн	-	neuter plural

BASIC CONCEPTS

Basic concepts. Part 1

1. Pronouns

I, me	**ja**	ja
you	**ти**	ti
he	**он**	on
she	**она**	óna
it	**оно**	óno
we	**ми**	mi
you (to a group)	**ви**	vi
they (masc.)	**они**	óni
they (fem.)	**оне**	óne

2. Greetings. Salutations. Farewells

Hello! (fam.)	**Здраво!**	Zdrávo!
Hello! (form.)	**Добар дан!**	Dóbar dan!
Good morning!	**Добро јутро!**	Dóbro jútro!
Good afternoon!	**Добар дан!**	Dóbar dan!
Good evening!	**Добро вече!**	Dóbro véče!
to say hello	**поздрављати** (пг)	pózdravljati
Hi! (hello)	**Здраво!**	Zdrávo!
greeting (n)	**поздрав** (м)	pózdrav
to greet (vt)	**поздрављати** (пг)	pózdravljati
How are you? (form.)	**Како сте?**	Káko ste?
How are you? (fam.)	**Како си?**	Káko si?
What's new?	**Шта је ново?**	Šta je nóvo?
Goodbye!	**Довиђења!**	Doviđénja!
Bye!	**Здраво!**	Zdrávo!
See you soon!	**Видимо се ускоро!**	Vídimo se úskoro!
Farewell!	**Збогом!**	Zbógom!
to say goodbye	**опраштати се**	opráštati se
So long!	**Ћао! Здраво!**	Ćáo! Zdrávo!

| Thank you! | Хвала! | Hvála! |
| Thank you very much! | Хвала лепо! | Hvála lépo! |

You're welcome	Изволите	Izvólite
Don't mention it!	Нема на чему!	Néma na čému!
It was nothing	Нема на чему	Néma na čému

Excuse me! (fam.)	Извини!	Izvíni!
Excuse me! (form.)	Извините!	Izvínite!
to excuse (forgive)	извињавати (пг)	izvinjávati

to apologize (vi)	извињавати се	izvinjávati se
My apologies	Извињавам се	Izvinjávam se
I'm sorry!	Извините!	Izvínite!

to forgive (vt)	опраштати (пг)	opráštati
It's okay! (that's all right)	Ништа страшно!	Níšta strášno!
please (adv)	молим	mólim

Don't forget!	Не заборавите!	Ne zabóravite!
Certainly!	Наравно!	Náravno!
Of course not!	Наравно да не!	Náravno da ne!
Okay! (I agree)	Слажем се!	Slážem se!
That's enough!	Доста!	Dósta!

3. How to address

Excuse me, …	Извините, …	Izvínite, …
mister, sir	господине	gospódine
ma'am	госпођо	góspođo
miss	госпођице	góspođice
young man	младићу	mládiću
young man (little boy, kid)	дечко	déčko
miss (little girl)	девојчица	devójčica

4. Cardinal numbers. Part 1

0 zero	нула (ж)	núla
1 one	један	jédan
2 two	два	dva
3 three	три	tri
4 four	четири	čétiri

5 five	пет	pet
6 six	шест	šest
7 seven	седам	sédam
8 eight	осам	ósam
9 nine	девет	dévet

10 ten	десет	déset
11 eleven	једанаест	jedánaest
12 twelve	дванаест	dvánaest
13 thirteen	тринаест	trínaest
14 fourteen	четрнаест	četŕnaest
15 fifteen	петнаест	pétnaest
16 sixteen	шеснаест	šésnaest
17 seventeen	седамнаест	sedámnaest
18 eighteen	осамнаест	osámnaest
19 nineteen	деветнаест	devétnaest
20 twenty	двадесет	dvádeset
21 twenty-one	двадесет и један	dvádeset i jédan
22 twenty-two	двадесет и два	dvádeset i dva
23 twenty-three	двадесет и три	dvádeset i tri
30 thirty	тридесет	trídeset
31 thirty-one	тридесет и један	trídeset i jédan
32 thirty-two	тридесет и два	trídeset i dva
33 thirty-three	тридесет и три	trideset i tri
40 forty	четрдесет	četrdéset
41 forty-one	четрдесет и један	četrdéset i jédan
42 forty-two	четрдесет и два	četrdéset i dva
43 forty-three	четрдесет и три	četrdéset i tri
50 fifty	педесет	pedéset
51 fifty-one	педесет и један	pedéset i jédan
52 fifty-two	педесет и два	pedéset i dva
53 fifty-three	педесет и три	pedéset i tri
60 sixty	шездесет	šezdéset
61 sixty-one	шездесет и један	šezdéset i jédan
62 sixty-two	шездесет и два	šezdéset i dva
63 sixty-three	шездесет и три	šezdéset i tri
70 seventy	седамдесет	sedamdéset
71 seventy-one	седамдесет и један	sedamdéset i jédan
72 seventy-two	седамдесет и два	sedamdéset i dva
73 seventy-three	седамдесет и три	sedamdéset i tri
80 eighty	осамдесет	osamdéset
81 eighty-one	осамдесет и један	osamdéset i jédan
82 eighty-two	осамдесет и два	osamdéset i dva
83 eighty-three	осамдесет и три	osamdéset i tri
90 ninety	деведесет	devedéset
91 ninety-one	деведесет и један	devedéset i jédan
92 ninety-two	деведесет и два	devedéset i dva
93 ninety-three	деведесет и три	devedéset i tri

5. Cardinal numbers. Part 2

100 one hundred	сто	sto
200 two hundred	двеста	dvésta
300 three hundred	триста	trísta
400 four hundred	четиристо	čétiristo
500 five hundred	петсто	pétsto
600 six hundred	шестсто	šéststo
700 seven hundred	седамсто	sédamsto
800 eight hundred	осамсто	ósamsto
900 nine hundred	деветсто	dévetsto
1000 one thousand	хиљада (ж)	híljada
2000 two thousand	две хиљаде	dve híljade
3000 three thousand	три хиљаде	tri híljade
10000 ten thousand	десет хиљада	déset híljada
one hundred thousand	сто хиљада	sto híljada
million	милион (м)	milíon
billion	милијарда (ж)	milíjarda

6. Ordinal numbers

first (adj)	први	pŕvi
second (adj)	други	drúgi
third (adj)	трећи	tréći
fourth (adj)	четврти	čétvrti
fifth (adj)	пети	péti
sixth (adj)	шести	šésti
seventh (adj)	седми	sédmi
eighth (adj)	осми	ósmi
ninth (adj)	девети	déveti
tenth (adj)	десети	déseti

7. Numbers. Fractions

fraction	разломак (м)	rázlomak
one half	једна половина	jédna pólovina
one third	једна трећина (ж)	jédna trećína
one quarter	једна четвртина	jédna četvrtina
one eighth	једна осмина (ж)	jédna osmína
one tenth	једна десетина	jédna désetina
two thirds	две трећине	dve trećíne
three quarters	три четвртине	tri četvŕtine

8. Numbers. Basic operations

subtraction	одузимање (c)	oduzímanje
to subtract (vi, vt)	одузимати (nr)	odúzimati
division	дељење (c)	déljenje
to divide (vt)	делити (nr)	déliti
addition	сабирање (c)	sabíranje
to add up (vt)	сабрати (nr)	sábrati
to add (vi, vt)	сабирати (nr)	sábirati
multiplication	множење (c)	mnóženje
to multiply (vt)	множити (nr)	mnóžiti

9. Numbers. Miscellaneous

digit, figure	цифра (ж)	cífra
number	број (м)	broj
numeral	број (м)	broj
minus sign	минус (м)	mínus
plus sign	плус (м)	plus
formula	формула (ж)	fórmula
calculation	израчунавање (c)	izračunávanje
to count (vi, vt)	бројати (nr)	brójati
to count up	бројати (nr)	brójati
to compare (vt)	упоређивати (nr)	upoređívati
How much?	Колико?	Kolíko?
sum, total	збир (м)	zbir
result	резултат (м)	rezúltat
remainder	остатак (м)	ostátak
a few (e.g., ~ years ago)	неколико	nékoliko
little (I had ~ time)	мало	málo
the rest	остало (c)	óstalo
one and a half	један и по	jédan i po
dozen	туце (c)	túce
in half (adv)	напола	nápola
equally (evenly)	на равне делове	na rávne délove
half	половина (ж)	polóvina
time (three ~s)	пут (м)	put

10. The most important verbs. Part 1

to advise (vt)	саветовати (nr)	sávetovati
to agree (say yes)	слагати се	slágati se

to answer (vi, vt)	одговарати (нг, пг)	odgovárati
to apologize (vi)	извињавати се	izvinjávati se
to arrive (vi)	стизати (нг)	stízati
to ask (~ oneself)	питати (пг)	pítati
to ask (~ sb to do sth)	молити (пг)	móliti
to be (vi)	бити (нг, пг)	bíti
to be afraid	плашити се	plášiti se
to be hungry	бити гладан	bíti gládan
to be interested in ...	интересовати се	ínteresovati se
to be needed	бити потребан	bíti pótreban
to be surprised	чудити се	čúditi se
to be thirsty	бити жедан	bíti žédan
to begin (vt)	почињати (нг, пг)	póčinjati
to belong to ...	припадати (нг)	prípadati
to boast (vi)	хвалисати се	hválisati se
to break (split into pieces)	ломити (пг)	lómiti
to call (~ for help)	звати (пг)	zváti
can (v aux)	моћи (нг)	móći
to catch (vt)	ловити (пг)	lóviti
to change (vt)	променити (пг)	proméniti
to choose (select)	бирати (пг)	bírati
to come down (the stairs)	спуштати се	spúštati se
to compare (vt)	упоређивати (пг)	uporeðívati
to complain (vi, vt)	жалити се	žáliti se
to confuse (mix up)	бркати (пг)	bŕkati
to continue (vt)	настављати (пг)	nástavljati
to control (vt)	контролисати (пг)	kontrólisati
to cook (dinner)	кувати (пг)	kúvati
to cost (vt)	коштати (нг)	kóštati
to count (add up)	рачунати (пг)	račúnati
to count on ...	рачунати на ...	račúnati na ...
to create (vt)	створити (пг)	stvóriti
to cry (weep)	плакати (нг)	plákati

11. The most important verbs. Part 2

to deceive (vi, vt)	обмањивати (пг)	obmanjívati
to decorate (tree, street)	украшавати (пг)	ukrašávati
to defend (a country, etc.)	штитити (пг)	štítiti
to demand (request firmly)	захтевати, тражити	zahtévati, trážiti
to dig (vt)	копати (пг)	kópati
to discuss (vt)	расправљати (пг)	ráspravljati
to do (vt)	радити (пг)	ráditi

to doubt (have doubts)	сумњати (нг)	súmnjati
to drop (let fall)	испуштати (пг)	ispúštati
to enter (room, house, etc.)	ући, улазити (нг)	úći, úlaziti
to excuse (forgive)	извињавати (пг)	izvinjávati
to exist (vi)	постојати (нг)	póstojati
to expect (foresee)	предвиђати (пг)	predvíđati
to explain (vt)	објашњавати (пг)	objašnjávati
to fall (vi)	падати (нг)	pádati
to find (vt)	наћи (пг)	náći
to finish (vt)	завршавати (пг)	završávati
to fly (vi)	летети (нг)	léteti
to follow ... (come after)	пратити (пг)	prátiti
to forget (vi, vt)	заборављати (нг, пг)	zabóravljati
to forgive (vt)	опраштати (пг)	opráštati
to give (vt)	давати (пг)	dávati
to give a hint	дати миг	dáti mig
to go (on foot)	ићи (нг)	íći
to go for a swim	купати се	kúpati se
to go out (for dinner, etc.)	изаћи (нг)	ízaći
to guess (the answer)	погодити (пг)	pogóditi
to have (vt)	имати (пг)	ímati
to have breakfast	доручковати (нг)	dóručkovati
to have dinner	вечерати (нг)	véčerati
to have lunch	ручати (нг)	rúčati
to hear (vt)	чути (нг, пг)	čúti
to help (vt)	помагати (пг)	pomágati
to hide (vt)	крити (пг)	kríti
to hope (vi, vt)	надати се	nádati se
to hunt (vi, vt)	ловити (пг)	lóviti
to hurry (vi)	журити се	žúriti se

12. The most important verbs. Part 3

to inform (vt)	информисати (пг)	infórmisati
to insist (vi, vt)	инсистирати (нг)	insistírati
to insult (vt)	вређати (пг)	vréđati
to invite (vt)	позивати (пг)	pozívati
to joke (vi)	шалити се	šáliti se
to keep (vt)	чувати (пг)	čúvati
to keep silent, to hush	ћутати (нг)	ćútati
to kill (vt)	убијати (нг)	ubíjati
to know (sb)	знати (пг)	znáti

to know (sth)	знати (пг)	znáti
to laugh (vi)	смејати се	sméjati se
to liberate (city, etc.)	ослобађати (пг)	oslobáđati
to like (I like …)	свиђати се	svíđati se
to look for … (search)	тражити (пг)	trážiti
to love (sb)	волети (пг)	vóleti
to make a mistake	грешити (нг)	gréšiti
to manage, to run	руководити (пг)	rukovóditi
to mean (signify)	значити (нг)	znáčiti
to mention (talk about)	спомињати (пг)	spóminjati
to miss (school, etc.)	пропуштати (пг)	propúštati
to notice (see)	запажати (пг)	zapážati
to object (vi, vt)	приговарати (нг)	prigovárati
to observe (see)	посматрати (нг)	posmátrati
to open (vt)	отварати (пг)	otvárati
to order (meal, etc.)	наручивати (пг)	naručívati
to order (mil.)	наређивати (пг)	naređívati
to own (possess)	поседовати (пг)	pósedovati
to participate (vi)	учествовати (нг)	účestvovati
to pay (vi, vt)	платити (нг, пг)	plátiti
to permit (vt)	дозвољавати (нг, пг)	dozvoljávati
to plan (vt)	планирати (пг)	planírati
to play (children)	играти (нг)	ígrati
to pray (vi, vt)	молити се	móliti se
to prefer (vt)	преферирати (пг)	preferírati
to promise (vt)	обећати (пг)	obéćati
to pronounce (vt)	изговарати (пг)	izgovárati
to propose (vt)	предлагати (пг)	predlágati
to punish (vt)	кажњавати (пг)	kažnjávati

13. The most important verbs. Part 4

to read (vi, vt)	читати (нг, пг)	čítati
to recommend (vt)	препоручивати (пг)	preporučívati
to refuse (vi, vt)	одбијати се	odbíjati se
to regret (be sorry)	жалити (нг)	žáliti
to rent (sth from sb)	изнајмити (пг)	iznájmiti
to repeat (say again)	понављати (пг)	ponávljati
to reserve, to book	резервисати (пг)	rezervísati
to run (vi)	трчати (нг)	tŕčati
to save (rescue)	спасавати (пг)	spasávati
to say (~ thank you)	рећи (пг)	réći
to scold (vt)	грдити (пг)	gŕditi
to see (vt)	видети (пг)	vídeti

to sell (vt)	продавати (nr)	prodávati
to send (vt)	слати (nr)	sláti
to shoot (vi)	пуцати (нг)	púcati

to shout (vi)	викати (нг)	víkati
to show (vt)	показивати (nr)	pokazívati
to sign (document)	потписивати (nr)	potpisívati
to sit down (vi)	седати (нг)	sédati

to smile (vi)	осмехивати се	osmehívati se
to speak (vi, vt)	говорити (нг)	govóriti
to steal (money, etc.)	красти (nr)	krásti
to stop (for pause, etc.)	заустављати се	zaústavljati se
to stop (please ~ calling me)	прекидати (nr)	prekídati

to study (vt)	студирати (nr)	studírati
to swim (vi)	пливати (нг)	plívati
to take (vt)	узети (nr)	úzeti
to think (vi, vt)	мислити (нг)	mísliti
to threaten (vt)	претити (нг)	prétiti

to touch (with hands)	дирати (nr)	dírati
to translate (vt)	преводити (nr)	prevóditi
to trust (vt)	веровати (nr)	vérovati
to try (attempt)	пробати (нг)	próbati
to turn (e.g., ~ left)	скретати (нг)	skrétati

to underestimate (vt)	подцењивати (nr)	podcenjívati
to understand (vt)	разумевати (nr)	razumévati
to unite (vt)	уједињавати (nr)	ujedinjávati
to wait (vt)	чекати (нг, nr)	čékati

to want (wish, desire)	хтети (nr)	htéti
to warn (vt)	упозоравати (nr)	upozorávati
to work (vi)	радити (нг)	ráditi
to write (vt)	писати (nr)	písati
to write down	записивати (nr)	zapisívati

14. Colors

color	боја (ж)	bója
shade (tint)	нијанса (ж)	nijánsa
hue	тон (м)	ton
rainbow	дуга (ж)	dúga

white (adj)	бео	béo
black (adj)	црн	crn
gray (adj)	сив	siv
green (adj)	зелен	zélen

yellow (adj)	жут	žut
red (adj)	црвен	cȓven
blue (adj)	плав	plav
light blue (adj)	светло плав	svétlo plav
pink (adj)	ружичаст	rúžičast
orange (adj)	наранџаст	nárandžast
violet (adj)	љубичаст	ljúbičast
brown (adj)	браон	bráon
golden (adj)	златан	zlátan
silvery (adj)	сребрнаст	srébrnast
beige (adj)	беж	bež
cream (adj)	боје крем	bóje krem
turquoise (adj)	тиркизан	tírkizan
cherry red (adj)	боје вишње	bóje víšnje
lilac (adj)	лила	líla
crimson (adj)	боје малине	bóje máline
light (adj)	светао	svétao
dark (adj)	таман	táman
bright, vivid (adj)	јарки	járki
colored (pencils)	обојен	óbojen
color (e.g., ~ film)	у боји	u bóji
black-and-white (adj)	црно-бели	cȓno-béli
plain (one-colored)	једнобојан	jédnobojan
multicolored (adj)	разнобојан	ráznobojan

15. Questions

Who?	Ко?	Ko?
What?	Шта?	Šta?
Where? (at, in)	Где?	Gde?
Where (to)?	Куда?	Kúda?
From where?	Одакле? Откуд?	Ódakle? Ótkud?
When?	Када?	Káda?
Why? (What for?)	Зашто?	Zášto?
Why? (~ are you crying?)	Зашто?	Zášto?
What for?	За шта? Због чега?	Zá šta? Zbog čéga?
How? (in what way)	Како?	Káko?
What? (What kind of ...?)	Какав?	Kákav?
Which?	Који?	Kóji?
To whom?	Коме?	Kóme?
About whom?	О коме?	O kóme?
About what?	О чему?	O čému?
With whom?	Са ким?	Sa kim?

How many? How much?	Колико?	Kolíko?
Whose?	Чији?	Číji?
Whose? (fem.)	Чија?	Číja?
Whose? (pl)	Чије?	Číje?

16. Prepositions

with (accompanied by)	с, са	s, sa
without	без	bez
to (indicating direction)	у	u
about (talking ~ …)	о	o
before (in time)	пре	pre
in front of …	испред	íspred

under (beneath, below)	испод	íspod
above (over)	изнад	íznad
on (atop)	на	na
from (off, out of)	из	iz
of (made from)	од	od

| in (e.g., ~ ten minutes) | за | za |
| over (across the top of) | преко | préko |

17. Function words. Adverbs. Part 1

Where? (at, in)	Где?	Gde?
here (adv)	овде	óvde
there (adv)	тамо	támo

| somewhere (to be) | негде | négde |
| nowhere (not in any place) | нигде | nígde |

| by (near, beside) | код | kod |
| by the window | поред прозора | póred prózora |

Where (to)?	Куда?	Kúda?
here (e.g., come ~!)	овамо	óvamo
there (e.g., to go ~)	тамо	támo
from here (adv)	одавде	ódavde
from there (adv)	оданде	ódande

| close (adv) | близу | blízu |
| far (adv) | далеко | daléko |

near (e.g., ~ Paris)	близу, у близини	blízu, u blizíni
nearby (adv)	у близини	u blízini
not far (adv)	недалеко	nédaleko
left (adj)	леви	lévi

| on the left | слева | sléva |
| to the left | лево | lévo |

right (adj)	десни	désni
on the right	десно	désno
to the right	десно	désno

in front (adv)	спреда	spréda
front (as adj)	предњи	prédnji
ahead (the kids ran ~)	напред	nápred

behind (adv)	иза	íza
from behind	отпозади	otpozádi
back (towards the rear)	назад, унатраг	názad, unátrag

| middle | средина (ж) | sredína |
| in the middle | у средини | u sredíni |

at the side	са стране	sa stráne
everywhere (adv)	свуда	svúda
around (in all directions)	око	óko

from inside	изнутра	iznútra
somewhere (to go)	некуда	nékuda
straight (directly)	право	právo
back (e.g., come ~)	назад	názad

| from anywhere | однекуд | ódnekud |
| from somewhere | однекуд | ódnekud |

firstly (adv)	прво	pŕvo
secondly (adv)	друго	drúgo
thirdly (adv)	треће	tréće

suddenly (adv)	изненада	íznenada
at first (in the beginning)	у почетку	u počétku
for the first time	први пут	pŕvi put
long before …	много пре …	mnógo pre …
anew (over again)	поново	pónovo
for good (adv)	заувек	záuvek

never (adv)	никад	níkad
again (adv)	опет	ópet
now (at present)	сада	sáda
often (adv)	често	čésto
then (adv)	тада	táda
urgently (quickly)	хитно	hítno
usually (adv)	обично	óbično

by the way, …	узгред, …	úzgred, …
possibly	могуће	móguće
probably (adv)	вероватно	vérovatno

maybe (adv)	можда	móžda
besides ...	осим тога ...	ósim tóga ...
that's why ...	дакле ..., због тога ...	dákle ..., zbog toga ...
in spite of ...	без обзира на ...	bez óbzira na ...
thanks to ...	захваљујући ...	zahváljujući ...
what (pron.)	шта	šta
that (conj.)	да	da
something	нешто	néšto
anything (something)	нешто	néšto
nothing	ништа	níšta
who (pron.)	ко	ko
someone	неко	néko
somebody	неко	néko
nobody	нико	níko
nowhere (a voyage to ~)	никуд	níkud
nobody's	ничији	níčiji
somebody's	нечији	néčiji
so (I'm ~ glad)	тако	táko
also (as well)	такође	takóđe
too (as well)	такође	takóđe

18. Function words. Adverbs. Part 2

Why?	Зашто?	Zášto?
for some reason	из неког разлога	iz nékog rázloga
because ...	јер ..., зато што ...	jer ..., záto što ...
for some purpose	из неког разлога	iz nékog rázloga
and	и	i
or	или	íli
but	али	áli
for (e.g., ~ me)	за	za
too (~ many people)	сувише, превише	súviše, préviše
only (exclusively)	само	sámo
exactly (adv)	тачно	táčno
about (more or less)	око	óko
approximately (adv)	приближно	príbližno
approximate (adj)	приближан	príbližan
almost (adv)	скоро	skóro
the rest	остало (c)	óstalo
the other (second)	други	drúgi
other (different)	други	drúgi
each (adj)	свак	svak

any (no matter which)	било који	bílo kóji
many, much (a lot of)	много	mnógo
many people	многи	mnógi
all (everyone)	сви	svi

in return for ...	у замену за ...	u zámenu za ...
in exchange (adv)	у замену	u zámenu
by hand (made)	ручно	rúčno
hardly (negative opinion)	тешко да, једва да	téško da, jédva da

probably (adv)	вероватно	vérovatno
on purpose (intentionally)	намерно	námerno
by accident (adv)	случајно	slúčajno

very (adv)	врло	vŕlo
for example (adv)	на пример	na prímer
between	између	ízmeđu
among	међу	méđu
so much (such a lot)	толико	tolíko
especially (adv)	нарочито	náročito

Basic concepts. Part 2

19. Opposites

| rich (adj) | богат | bógat |
| poor (adj) | сиромашан | sirómašan |

| ill, sick (adj) | болестан | bólestan |
| well (not sick) | здрав | zdrav |

| big (adj) | велик | vélik |
| small (adj) | мали | máli |

| quickly (adv) | брзо | bŕzo |
| slowly (adv) | споро | spóro |

| fast (adj) | брз | bŕz |
| slow (adj) | спор | spor |

| glad (adj) | весео | véseo |
| sad (adj) | тужан | túžan |

| together (adv) | заједно | zájedno |
| separately (adv) | одвојено | ódvojeno |

| aloud (to read) | наглас | náglas |
| silently (to oneself) | у себи | u sébi |

| tall (adj) | висок | vísok |
| low (adj) | низак | nízak |

| deep (adj) | дубок | dúbok |
| shallow (adj) | плитак | plítak |

| yes | да | da |
| no | не | ne |

| distant (in space) | далек | dálek |
| nearby (adj) | близак | blízak |

| far (adv) | далеко | daléko |
| nearby (adv) | близу | blízu |

long (adj)	дуг, дугачак	dug, dúgačak
short (adj)	кратак	krátak
good (kindhearted)	добар	dóbar

evil (adj)	зао	záo
married (adj)	ожењен	óuženjen
single (adj)	неожењен	neóženjen
to forbid (vt)	забранити (пг)	zábraniti
to permit (vt)	дозволити (нг, пг)	dozvóliti
end	крај (м)	kraj
beginning	почетак (м)	počétak
left (adj)	леви	lévi
right (adj)	десни	désni
first (adj)	први	pŕvi
last (adj)	последњи	póslednji
crime	злочин (м)	zlóčin
punishment	казна (ж)	kázna
to order (vt)	наредити (пг)	naréditi
to obey (vi, vt)	подчинити се	podčíniti se
straight (adj)	прав	prav
curved (adj)	крив	kriv
paradise	рај (м)	raj
hell	пакао (м)	pákao
to be born	родити се	róditi se
to die (vi)	умрети (нг)	úmreti
strong (adj)	снажан	snážan
weak (adj)	слаб	slab
old (adj)	стар	star
young (adj)	млад	mlad
old (adj)	стар	star
new (adj)	нов	nov
hard (adj)	чврст	čvŕst
soft (adj)	мек, мекан	mek, mékan
warm (tepid)	топао	tópao
cold (adj)	хладан	hládan
fat (adj)	дебео	débeo
thin (adj)	танак, мршав	tának, mŕšav
narrow (adj)	узак	úzak
wide (adj)	широк	šírok
good (adj)	добар	dóbar

bad (adj)	лош	loš
brave (adj)	храбар	hrábar
cowardly (adj)	кукавички	kúkavički

20. Weekdays

Monday	понедељак (м)	ponédeljak
Tuesday	уторак (м)	útorak
Wednesday	среда (ж)	sréda
Thursday	четвртак (м)	četvŕtak
Friday	петак (м)	pétak
Saturday	субота (ж)	súbota
Sunday	недеља (ж)	nédelja

today (adv)	данас	dánas
tomorrow (adv)	сутра	sútra
the day after tomorrow	прекосутра	prékosutra
yesterday (adv)	јуче	júče
the day before yesterday	прекјуче	prékjuče

day	дан (м)	dan
working day	радни дан (м)	rádni dan
public holiday	празничан дан (м)	prázničan dan
day off	слободан дан (м)	slóbodan dan
weekend	викенд (м)	víkend

all day long	цео дан	céo dan
the next day (adv)	следећег дана, сутра	slédećeg dána, sútra
two days ago	пре два дана	pre dva dána
the day before	уочи	úoči
daily (adj)	свакодневан	svákodnevan
every day (adv)	свакодневно	svákodnevno

week	недеља (ж)	nédelja
last week (adv)	прошле недеље	próšle nédelje
next week (adv)	следеће недеље	slédeće nédelje
weekly (adj)	недељни	nédeljni
every week (adv)	недељно	nédeljno
twice a week	два пута недељно	dva púta nédeljno
every Tuesday	сваког уторка	svákog útorka

21. Hours. Day and night

morning	јутро (с)	jútro
in the morning	ујутру	újutru
noon, midday	подне (с)	pódne
in the afternoon	поподне	popódne
evening	вече (с)	véče

in the evening	увече	úveče
night	ноћ (ж)	noć
at night	ноћу	nóću
midnight	поноћ (ж)	pónoć

second	секунд (м)	sékund
minute	минут (ж)	mínut
hour	сат (м)	sat
half an hour	пола сата	póla sáta
a quarter-hour	четврт сата	četvrt sáta
fifteen minutes	петнаест минута	pétnaest minúta
24 hours	двадесет четири сата	dvádeset četiri sáta

sunrise	излазак (м) сунца	ízlazak súnca
dawn	свануће (с)	svanúće
early morning	рано јутро (с)	ráno jútro
sunset	залазак (м) сунца	zálazak súnca

early in the morning	рано ујутру	ráno újutru
this morning	јутрос	jútros
tomorrow morning	сутра ујутру	sútra újutru

this afternoon	овог поподнева	óvog popódneva
in the afternoon	поподне	popódne
tomorrow afternoon	сутра поподне	sútra popódne

| tonight (this evening) | вечерас | večéras |
| tomorrow night | сутра увече | sútra úveče |

at 3 o'clock sharp	тачно у три сата	táčno u tri sáta
about 4 o'clock	око четири сата	óko četiri sáta
by 12 o'clock	до дванаест сати	do dvánaest sáti

in 20 minutes	за двадесет минута	za dvádeset minúta
in an hour	за сат времена	za sat vrémena
on time (adv)	навреме	návreme

a quarter to ...	четвртина до	četvŕtina do
within an hour	за сат времена	za sat vrémena
every 15 minutes	сваких петнаест минута	svákih pétnaest minúta
round the clock	дан и ноћ	dan i noć

22. Months. Seasons

January	јануар (м)	jánuar
February	фебруар (м)	fébruar
March	март (м)	mart
April	април (м)	ápril
May	мај (м)	maj
June	јун, јуни (м)	jun, júni

July	јули (м)	júli
August	август (м)	ávgust
September	септембар (м)	séptembar
October	октобар (м)	óktobar
November	новембар (м)	nóvembar
December	децембар (м)	décembar

spring	пролеће (с)	próleće
in spring	у пролеће	u próleće
spring (as adj)	пролећни	prólećni

summer	лето (с)	léto
in summer	лети	léti
summer (as adj)	летни	létni

fall	јесен (ж)	jésen
in fall	у јесен	u jésen
fall (as adj)	јесењи	jésenji

winter	зима (ж)	zíma
in winter	зими	zími
winter (as adj)	зимски	zímski

month	месец (м)	mésec
this month	овог месеца	óvog méseca
next month	следећег месеца	slédećeg méseca
last month	прошлог месеца	próšlog méseca

a month ago	пре месец дана	pre mésec dána
in a month (a month later)	за месец дана	za mésec dána
in 2 months (2 months later)	за два месеца	za dva méseca
the whole month	цео месец	céo mésec
all month long	цео месец	céo mésec

monthly (~ magazine)	месечни	mésečni
monthly (adv)	месечно	mésečno
every month	сваког месеца	svákog méseca
twice a month	два пута месечно	dva púta mésečno

year	година (ж)	gódina
this year	ове године	óve gódine
next year	следеће године	slédeće gódine
last year	прошла година	próšla gódina

a year ago	пре годину дана	pre gódinu dána
in a year	за годину дана	za gódinu dána
in two years	за две године	za dve gódine
the whole year	цела година	céla gódina
all year long	цела година	céla gódina
every year	сваке године	sváke gódine
annual (adj)	годишњи	gódišnji

| annually (adv) | годишње | gódišnje |
| 4 times a year | четири пута годишње | četiri púta gódišnje |

date (e.g., today's ~)	датум (м)	dátum
date (e.g., ~ of birth)	датум (м)	dátum
calendar	календар (м)	kaléndar

half a year	пола године	póla gódine
six months	полугодиште (с)	polugódište
season (summer, etc.)	сезона (ж)	sezóna
century	век (м)	vek

23. Time. Miscellaneous

time	време (с)	vréme
moment	часак, тренутак (м)	čásak, trenútak
instant (n)	тренутак (м)	trenútak
instant (adj)	тренутан	trénutan
lapse (of time)	раздобље (с)	rázdoblje
life	живот (м)	žívot
eternity	вечност (ж)	véčnost

epoch	епоха (ж)	epóha
era	ера (ж)	éra
cycle	циклус (м)	cíklus
period	период (м)	períod
term (short-~)	рок (м)	rok

the future	будућност (ж)	budúćnost
future (as adj)	будући	búdući
next time	следећи пут	slédeći put
the past	прошлост (ж)	próšlost
past (recent)	прошли	próšli
last time	прошлог пута	próšlog púta

later (adv)	касније	kásnije
after (prep.)	после	pósle
nowadays (adv)	сада	sáda
now (at this moment)	сада	sáda
immediately (adv)	одмах	ódmah
soon (adv)	ускоро	úskoro
in advance (beforehand)	унапред	unápred

a long time ago	одавно	ódavno
recently (adv)	недавно	nédavno
destiny	судбина (ж)	súdbina
memories (childhood ~)	сећање (с)	séćanje
archives	архив (м)	árhiv
during …	за време …	za vréme …
long, a long time (adv)	дуго	dúgo

not long (adv)	кратко	krátko
early (in the morning)	рано	ráno
late (not early)	касно	kásno
forever (for good)	заувек	záuvek
to start (begin)	почињати (нг, пг)	póčinjati
to postpone (vt)	одгодити (пг)	odgóditi
at the same time	истовремено	istóvremeno
permanently (adv)	стално	stálno
constant (noise, pain)	константан	konstántan
temporary (adj)	привремен	prívremen
sometimes (adv)	понекад	pónekad
rarely (adv)	ретко	rétko
often (adv)	често	čésto

24. Lines and shapes

square	квадрат (м)	kvádrat
square (as adj)	квадратни	kvádratni
circle	круг (м)	krug
round (adj)	округли	ókrugli
triangle	троугао (м)	tróugao
triangular (adj)	троугласти	tróuglasti
oval	овал (м)	óval
oval (as adj)	овалан	óvalan
rectangle	правоугаоник (м)	pravougaónik
rectangular (adj)	правоугаони	pravoúgaoni
pyramid	пирамида (ж)	piramída
rhombus	ромб (м)	romb
trapezoid	трапез (м)	trápez
cube	коцка (ж)	kócka
prism	призма (ж)	prízma
circumference	кружница (ж)	krúžnica
sphere	сфера (ж)	sféra
ball (solid sphere)	кугла (ж)	kúgla
diameter	пречник (м)	préčnik
radius	полупречник (м)	polupréčnik
perimeter (circle's ~)	периметар (м)	perímetar
center	центар (м)	céntar
horizontal (adj)	хоризонталан	hórizontalan
vertical (adj)	вертикалан	vértikalan
parallel (n)	паралела (ж)	paraléla
parallel (as adj)	паралелан	paralélan
line	линија (ж)	línija

stroke	црта (ж)	cŕta
straight line	права линија (ж)	práva línija
curve (curved line)	крива (ж)	kríva
thin (line, etc.)	танак	tának
contour (outline)	контура (ж)	kóntura

intersection	пресек (м)	prések
right angle	прав угао (м)	prav úgao
segment	сегмент (м)	ségment
sector (circular ~)	сектор (м)	séktor
side (of triangle)	страна (ж)	strána
angle	угао (м)	úgao

25. Units of measurement

weight	тежина (ж)	težína
length	дужина (ж)	dužína
width	ширина (ж)	šírina
height	висина (ж)	vísina
depth	дубина (ж)	dubína
volume	запремина (ж)	zápremina
area	површина (ж)	póvršina

gram	грам (м)	gram
milligram	милиграм (м)	míligram
kilogram	килограм (м)	kílogram
ton	тона (ж)	tóna
pound	фунта (ж)	fúnta
ounce	унца (ж)	únca

meter	метар (м)	métar
millimeter	милиметар (м)	mílimetar
centimeter	сантиметар (м)	santimétar
kilometer	километар (м)	kílometar
mile	миља (ж)	mílja

inch	палац (м)	pálac
foot	стопа (ж)	stópa
yard	јард (м)	jard

| square meter | квадратни метар (м) | kvádratni métar |
| hectare | хектар (м) | héktar |

liter	литар (м)	lítar
degree	степен (м)	stépen
volt	волт (м)	volt
ampere	ампер (м)	ámper
horsepower	коњска снага (ж)	kónjska snága
quantity	количина (ж)	količína
a little bit of ...	мало ...	málo ...

half	половина (ж)	polóvina
dozen	туце (с)	túce
piece (item)	комад (м)	kómad

| size | величина (ж) | veličína |
| scale (map ~) | размер (м) | rázmer |

minimal (adj)	минималан	mínimalan
the smallest (adj)	најмањи	nájmanji
medium (adj)	средњи	srédnji
maximal (adj)	максималан	máksimalan
the largest (adj)	највећи	nájveći

26. Containers

canning jar (glass ~)	тегла (ж)	tégla
can	лименка (ж)	límenka
bucket	ведро (с)	védro
barrel	буре (с)	búre

wash basin (e.g., plastic ~)	лавор (м)	lávor
tank (100L water ~)	резервоар (м)	rezervóar
hip flask	чутурица (ж)	čúturica
jerrycan	канта (ж) за гориво	kánta za górivo
tank (e.g., tank car)	цистерна (ж)	cistérna

mug	кригла (ж)	krígla
cup (of coffee, etc.)	шоља (ж)	šólja
saucer	тацна (ж)	tácna
glass (tumbler)	чаша (ж)	čáša
wine glass	чаша (ж) за вино	čáša za víno
stock pot (soup pot)	шерпа (ж), лонац (м)	šerpa, lónac

| bottle (~ of wine) | боца, флаша (ж) | bóca, fláša |
| neck (of the bottle, etc.) | врат (м) | vrat |

carafe (decanter)	бокал (м)	bókal
pitcher	крчаг (м)	kŕčag
vessel (container)	суд (м)	sud
pot (crock, stoneware ~)	лонац (м)	lónac
vase	ваза (ж)	váza

flacon, bottle (perfume ~)	боца (ж)	bóca
vial, small bottle	бочица (ж)	bóčica
tube (of toothpaste)	туба (ж)	túba

sack (bag)	џак (м)	džak
bag (paper ~, plastic ~)	кеса (ж)	késa
pack (of cigarettes, etc.)	паковање (с)	pákovanje
box (e.g., shoebox)	кутија (ж)	kútija

| crate | сандук (м) | sánduk |
| basket | корпа (ж) | kórpa |

27. Materials

material	материјал (м)	materíjal
wood (n)	дрво (с)	dŕvo
wood-, wooden (adj)	дрвен	dŕven

| glass (n) | стакло (с) | stáklo |
| glass (as adj) | стаклен | stáklen |

| stone (n) | камен (м) | kámen |
| stone (as adj) | камени | kámeni |

| plastic (n) | пластика (ж) | plástika |
| plastic (as adj) | пластичан | plástičan |

| rubber (n) | гума (ж) | gúma |
| rubber (as adj) | гумен | gúmen |

| cloth, fabric (n) | тканина (ж) | tkánina |
| fabric (as adj) | од тканине | od tkaníne |

| paper (n) | папир (м) | pápir |
| paper (as adj) | папирни | pápirni |

| cardboard (n) | картон (м) | kárton |
| cardboard (as adj) | картонски | kártonski |

polyethylene	полиетилен (м)	poliétilen
cellophane	целофан (м)	celófan
linoleum	линолеум (м)	linoléum
plywood	шперплоча (ж)	špérploča

porcelain (n)	порцелан (м)	porcélan
porcelain (as adj)	порцелански	porcélanski
clay (n)	глина (ж)	glína
clay (as adj)	глинени	glíneni
ceramic (n)	керамика (ж)	kerámika
ceramic (as adj)	керамички	kerámički

28. Metals

metal (n)	метал (м)	métal
metal (as adj)	металан	métalan
alloy (n)	легура (ж)	legúra
gold (n)	злато (с)	zláto

gold, golden (adj)	златан	zlátan
silver (n)	сребро (c)	srébro
silver (as adj)	сребрен	srébren
iron (n)	гвожђе (c)	gvóžđe
iron-, made of iron (adj)	гвозден	gvózden
steel (n)	челик (м)	čélik
steel (as adj)	челични	čélični
copper (n)	бакар (м)	bákar
copper (as adj)	бакарни, бакрени	bákarni, bákreni
aluminum (n)	алуминијум (м)	alumínijum
aluminum (as adj)	алуминијумски	alumínijumski
bronze (n)	бронза (ж)	brónza
bronze (as adj)	бронзан	brónzan
brass	месинг (м), мјед (ж)	mésing, mjed
nickel	никл (м)	nikl
platinum	платина (ж)	plátina
mercury	жива (ж)	žíva
tin	калај (м)	kálaj
lead	олово (c)	ólovo
zinc	цинк (м)	cink

HUMAN BEING

Human being. The body

human being	человек (м)	čóvek
man (adult male)	мушкарац (м)	muškárac
woman	жена (ж)	žéna
child	дете (с)	déte
girl	девојчица (ж)	devójčica
boy	дечак (м)	déčak
teenager	тинејџер (м)	tinéjdžer
old man	старац (м)	stárac
old woman	старица (ж)	stárica

organism (body)	организам (м)	organízam
heart	срце (с)	sŕce
blood	крв (ж)	kŕv
artery	артерија (ж)	árterija
vein	вена (ж)	véna
brain	мозак (м)	mózak
nerve	живац (м)	žívac
nerves	живци (мн)	žívci
vertebra	кичмени пршљен (м)	kíčmeni pŕšljen
spine (backbone)	кичма (ж)	kíčma
stomach (organ)	желудац (м)	žéludac
intestines, bowels	црева (мн)	créva
intestine (e.g., large ~)	црево (с)	crévo
liver	јетра (ж)	jétra
kidney	бубрег (м)	búbreg
bone	кост (ж)	kost
skeleton	костур (м)	kóstur
rib	ребро (с)	rébro
skull	лобања (ж)	lóbanja
muscle	мишић (м)	míšić
biceps	бицепс (м)	bíceps

triceps	трицепс (м)	tríceps
tendon	тетива (ж)	tetíva
joint	зглоб (м)	zglob
lungs	плућа (мн)	plúća
genitals	полни органи (мн)	pólni orgáni
skin	кожа (ж)	kóža

31. Head

head	глава (ж)	gláva
face	лице (с)	líce
nose	нос (м)	nos
mouth	уста (мн)	ústa

eye	око (с)	óko
eyes	очи (мн)	óči
pupil	зеница (ж)	zénica
eyebrow	обрва (ж)	óbrva
eyelash	трепавица (ж)	trépavica
eyelid	капак (м), веђа (ж)	kápak, véđa

tongue	језик (м)	jézik
tooth	зуб (м)	zub
lips	усне (мн)	úsne
cheekbones	јагодице (мн)	jágodice
gum	десни (мн)	désni
palate	непце (с)	népce

nostrils	ноздрве (мн)	nózdrve
chin	брада (ж)	bráda
jaw	вилица (ж)	vílica
cheek	образ (м)	óbraz

forehead	чело (с)	čélo
temple	слепоочница (ж)	slepoóčnica
ear	ухо (с)	úho
back of the head	потиљак (м)	pótiljak
neck	врат (м)	vrat
throat	грло (с)	gŕlo

hair	коса (ж)	kósa
hairstyle	фризура (ж)	frizúra
haircut	фризура (ж)	frizúra
wig	перика (ж)	périka

mustache	брркови (мн)	bŕkovi
beard	брада (ж)	bráda
to have (a beard, etc.)	носити (пг)	nósiti
braid	плетеница (ж)	pleténica
sideburns	зулуфи (мн)	zulúfi

red-haired (adj)	риђ	riđ
gray (hair)	сед	sed
bald (adj)	ћелав	ćelav
bald patch	ћела (ж)	ćéla
ponytail	реп (м)	rep
bangs	шишке (мн)	šíške

32. Human body

hand	шака (ж)	šáka
arm	рука (ж)	rúka
finger	прст (м)	pŕst
toe	ножни прст (м)	nóžni pŕst
thumb	палац (м)	pálac
little finger	мали прст (м)	máli pŕst
nail	нокат (м)	nókat
fist	песница (ж)	pésnica
palm	длан (м)	dlan
wrist	зглоб (м), запешће (с)	zglob, zápešće
forearm	подлактица (ж)	pódlaktica
elbow	лакат (м)	lákat
shoulder	раме (с)	ráme
leg	нога (ж)	nóga
foot	стопало (с)	stópalo
knee	колено (с)	kóleno
calf (part of leg)	лист (м)	list
hip	кук (м)	kuk
heel	пета (ж)	péta
body	тело (с)	télo
stomach	трбух (м)	tŕbuh
chest	прса (мн)	pŕsa
breast	груди (мн)	grúdi
flank	бок (м)	bok
back	леђа (мн)	léđa
lower back	крста (ж)	kŕsta
waist	струк (м)	struk
navel (belly button)	пупак (м)	púpak
buttocks	стражњица (ж)	strážnjica
bottom	задњица (ж)	zádnjica
beauty mark	младеж (м)	mládež
birthmark (café au lait spot)	белег, младеж (м)	béleg, mládež
tattoo	тетоважа (ж)	tetováža
scar	ожиљак (м)	óžiljak

Clothing & Accessories

33. Outerwear. Coats

clothes	одећа (ж)	ódeća
outerwear	горња одећа (ж)	górnja ódeća
winter clothing	зимска одећа (ж)	zímska ódeća
coat (overcoat)	капут (м)	káput
fur coat	бунда (ж)	búnda
fur jacket	кратка бунда (ж)	krátka búnda
down coat	перјана јакна (ж)	pérjana jákna
jacket (e.g., leather ~)	јакна (ж)	jákna
raincoat (trenchcoat, etc.)	кишни мантил (м)	kíšni mántil
waterproof (adj)	водоотпоран	vodoótporan

34. Men's & women's clothing

shirt (button shirt)	кошуља (ж)	kóšulja
pants	панталоне (мн)	pantalóne
jeans	фармерке (мн)	fármerke
suit jacket	сако (м)	sáko
suit	одело (с)	odélo
dress (frock)	хаљина (ж)	háljina
skirt	сукња (ж)	súknja
blouse	блуза (ж)	blúza
knitted jacket (cardigan, etc.)	џемпер (м)	džémper
jacket (of woman's suit)	жакет (м)	žáket
T-shirt	мајица (ж)	májica
shorts (short trousers)	шорц, шортс (м)	šorc, šorts
tracksuit	спортски костим (м)	spórtski kóstim
bathrobe	баде мантил (м)	báde mántil
pajamas	пиџама (ж)	pidžáma
sweater	џемпер (м)	džémper
pullover	пуловер (м)	pulóver
vest	прслук (м)	pŕsluk
tailcoat	фрак (м)	frak
tuxedo	смокинг (м)	smóking

uniform	униформа (ж)	úniforma
workwear	радна одећа (ж)	rádna ódeća
overalls	комбинезон (м)	kombinézon
coat (e.g., doctor's smock)	мантил (м)	mántil

35. Clothing. Underwear

underwear	доње рубље (с)	dónje rúblje
boxers, briefs	мушке гаће (мн)	múške gáće
panties	гаћице (мн)	gáćice
undershirt (A-shirt)	мајица (ж)	májica
socks	чарапе (мн)	čárape

nightdress	спаваћица (ж)	spaváćica
bra	грудњак (м)	grúdnjak
knee highs	доколенице (мн)	dokolénice
(knee-high socks)		

pantyhose	хулахопке (мн)	húlahopke
stockings (thigh highs)	чарапе (мн)	čárape
bathing suit	купаћи костим (м)	kúpaći kóstim

36. Headwear

hat	капа (ж)	kápa
fedora	шешир (м)	šéšir
baseball cap	бејзбол качкет (м)	béjzbol káčket
flatcap	енглеска капа (ж),	éngleska kápa,
	качкет (м)	káčket

beret	берета, беретка (ж)	beréta, beretka
hood	капуљача (ж)	kapúljača
panama hat	панама-шешир (м)	panáma-šéšir
knit cap (knitted hat)	плетена капа (ж)	plétena kápa
headscarf	марама (ж)	márama
women's hat	женски шешир (м)	žénski šéšir

hard hat	кацига (ж), шлем (м)	káciga, šlem
garrison cap	титовка (ж)	títovka
helmet	шлем (м)	šlem
derby	полуцилиндар (м)	pólucilindar
top hat	цилиндар (м)	cilíndar

37. Footwear

| footwear | обућа (ж) | óbuća |
| shoes (men's shoes) | ципеле (мн) | cípele |

shoes (women's shoes)	ципеле (мн)	cípele
boots (e.g., cowboy ~)	чизме (мн)	čízme
slippers	папуче (мн)	pápuče

tennis shoes (e.g., Nike ~)	патике (мн)	pátike
sneakers (e.g., Converse ~)	патике (мн)	pátike
sandals	сандале (мн)	sandále

cobbler (shoe repairer)	обућар (м)	óbućar
heel	потпетица (ж)	pótpetica
pair (of shoes)	пар (м)	par

shoestring	пертла (ж)	pértla
to lace (vt)	шнирати (пг)	šnírati
shoehorn	кашика (ж) за ципеле	kášika za cípele
shoe polish	крема (ж) за обућу	kréma za óbuću

38. Textile. Fabrics

cotton (n)	памук (м)	pámuk
cotton (as adj)	памучан	pámučan
flax (n)	лан (м)	lan
flax (as adj)	од лана	od lána

silk (n)	свила (ж)	svíla
silk (as adj)	свилен	svílen
wool (n)	вуна (ж)	vúna
wool (as adj)	вунен	vúnen

velvet	плиш, сомот (м)	pliš, sómot
suede	антилоп (м)	ántilop
corduroy	сомот (м)	sómot

nylon (n)	најлон (м)	nájlon
nylon (as adj)	од најлона	od nájlona
polyester (n)	полиестер (м)	poliéster
polyester (as adj)	од полиестра	od poliéstra

leather (n)	кожа (ж)	kóža
leather (as adj)	од коже	od kóže
fur (n)	крзно (с)	kŕzno
fur (e.g., ~ coat)	крзнени	kŕzneni

39. Personal accessories

| glasses (eyeglasses) | наочаре (мн) | náočare |
| frame (eyeglass ~) | оквир (м) | ókvir |

gloves	рукавице (мн)	rukávice
mittens	рукавице (мн) с једним прстом	rukávice s jednim prstom
scarf (muffler)	шал (м)	šal
umbrella	кишобран (м)	kíšobran
walking stick	штап (м)	štap
hairbrush	четка (ж) за косу	čétka za kósu
fan	лепеза (ж)	lepéza
tie (necktie)	краватa (ж)	kraváta
bow tie	лептир машна (ж)	léptir mášna
suspenders	трегери (мн)	trégeri
handkerchief	џепна марамица (ж)	džépna máramica
comb	чешаљ (м)	čéšalj
barrette	шнала (ж)	šnála
hairpin	укосница (ж)	úkosnica
buckle	копча (ж)	kópča
belt	каиш (м)	káiš
shoulder strap	каиш (м)	káiš
bag (handbag)	торба (ж)	tórba
purse	ташна (ж)	tášna
backpack	ранац (м)	ránac

40. Clothing. Miscellaneous

fashion	мода (ж)	móda
in vogue (adj)	модеран	móderan
fashion designer	модни креатор (м)	módni kreátor
collar	овратник (м)	óvratnik
pocket	џеп (м)	džep
pocket (as adj)	џепни	džépni
sleeve	рукав (м)	rúkav
hanging loop	вешалица (ж)	véšalica
fly (on trousers)	шлиц (м)	šlic
zipper (fastener)	рајсфершлус (м)	rájsferšlus
fastener	копча (ж)	kópča
button	дугме (с)	dúgme
buttonhole	рупица (ж)	rúpica
to come off (ab. button)	откинути се	ótkinuti se
to sew (vi, vt)	шити (нг, пг)	šíti
to embroider (vi, vt)	вести (нг, пг)	vésti
embroidery	вез (м)	vez
sewing needle	игла (ж)	ígla
thread	конац (м)	kónac

seam	шав (м)	šav
to get dirty (vi)	испрљати се	ispŕljati se
stain (mark, spot)	мрља (ж)	mŕlja
to crease, crumple (vi)	изгужвати се	izgúžvati se
to tear, to rip (vt)	цепати (пг)	cépati
clothes moth	мољац (м)	móljac

41. Personal care. Cosmetics

toothpaste	паста (ж) за зубе	pásta za zúbe
toothbrush	четкица (ж) за зубе	čétkica za zúbe
to brush one's teeth	прати зубе	práti zúbe
razor	бријач (м)	bríjač
shaving cream	крема (ж) за бријање	kréma za bríjanje
to shave (vi)	бријати се	bríjati se
soap	сапун (м)	sápun
shampoo	шампон (м)	šámpon
scissors	маказе (мн)	mákaze
nail file	турпија (ж) за нокте	túrpija za nokte
nail clippers	грицкалица (ж) за нокте	gríckalica za nókte
tweezers	пинцета (ж)	pincéta
cosmetics	козметика (ж)	kozmétika
face mask	маска (ж)	máska
manicure	маникир (м)	mánikir
to have a manicure	радити маникир	ráditi mánikir
pedicure	педикир (м)	pédikir
make-up bag	козметичка торбица (ж)	kozmétička tórbica
face powder	пудер (м)	púder
powder compact	пудријера (ж)	pudrijéra
blusher	руменило (с)	ruménilo
perfume (bottled)	парфем (м)	párfem
toilet water (lotion)	тоалетна вода (ж)	tóaletna vóda
lotion	лосион (м)	lósion
cologne	колоњска вода (ж)	kólonjska vóda
eyeshadow	сенка (ж) за очи	sénka za óči
eyeliner	оловка (ж) за очи	ólovka za óči
mascara	маскара (ж)	máskara
lipstick	кармин (м)	kármin
nail polish, enamel	лак (м) за нокте	lak za nókte
hair spray	лак (м) за косу	lak za kósu
deodorant	дезодоранс (м)	dezodórans
cream	крема (ж)	kréma

face cream	крема (ж) за лице	kréma za líce
hand cream	крема (ж) за руке	kréma za rúke
anti-wrinkle cream	крема (ж) против бора	kréma prótiv bóra
day cream	дневна крема (ж)	dnévna kréma
night cream	ноћна крема (ж)	nóćna kréma
day (as adj)	дневни	dnévni
night (as adj)	ноћни	nóćni
tampon	тампон (м)	támpon
toilet paper (toilet roll)	тоалет-папир (м)	toálet-pápir
hair dryer	фен (м)	fen

42. Jewelry

jewelry, jewels	накит (м)	nákit
precious (e.g., ~ stone)	драгоцен	dragócen
hallmark stamp	жиг (м)	žig
ring	прстен (м)	pŕsten
wedding ring	бурма (ж)	búrma
bracelet	наруквица (ж)	nárukvica
earrings	минђуше (мн)	mínđuše
necklace (~ of pearls)	огрлица (ж)	ógrlica
crown	круна (ж)	krúna
bead necklace	огрлица (ж) од перли	ógrlica od pérli
diamond	дијамант (м)	dijámant
emerald	смарагд (м)	smáragd
ruby	рубин (м)	rúbin
sapphire	сафир (м)	sáfir
pearl	бисер (м)	bíser
amber	ћилибар (м)	ćilíbar

43. Watches. Clocks

watch (wristwatch)	сат (м)	sat
dial	бројчаник (м)	brojčánik
hand (of clock, watch)	казаљка (ж)	kázaljka
metal watch band	наруквица (ж)	nárukvica
watch strap	каиш (м) за сат	káiš za sat
battery	батерија (ж)	báterija
to be dead (battery)	испразнити се	isprázniti se
to change a battery	заменити батерију	zaméniti batériju
to run fast	журити (нг)	žúriti
to run slow	заостајати (нг)	zaóstajati
wall clock	зидни сат (м)	zídni sat

hourglass	пешчани сат (м)	péščani sat
sundial	сунчани сат (м)	súnčani sat
alarm clock	будилник (м)	búdilnik
watchmaker	часовничар (м)	čásovničar
to repair (vt)	поправљати (пг)	pópravljati

Food. Nutricion

44. Food

meat	месо (c)	méso
chicken	пилетина, кокош (ж)	píletina, kokoš
Rock Cornish hen (poussin)	пиле (c)	píle
duck	патка (ж)	pátka
goose	гуска (ж)	gúska
game	дивљач (ж)	dívljač
turkey	ћуретина (ж)	ćurétina
pork	свињетина (ж)	svínjetina
veal	телетина (ж)	téletina
lamb	јагњетина (ж)	jágnjetina
beef	говедина (ж)	góvedina
rabbit	зец (м)	zec
sausage (bologna, etc.)	кобасица (ж)	kobásica
vienna sausage (frankfurter)	виршла (ж)	víršla
bacon	сланина (ж)	slánina
ham	шунка (ж)	šúnka
gammon	шунка (ж)	šúnka
pâté	паштета (ж)	paštéta
liver	џигерица (ж)	džígerica
hamburger (ground beef)	млевено месо (c)	mléveno méso
tongue	језик (м)	jézik
egg	јаје (c)	jáje
eggs	јаја (мн)	jája
egg white	беланце (c)	belánce
egg yolk	жуманце (c)	žumánce
fish	риба (ж)	ríba
seafood	морски плодови (мн)	mórski plódovi
crustaceans	ракови (мн)	rákovi
caviar	кавијар (м)	kávijar
crab	краба (ж)	krába
shrimp	шкамп (м)	škamp
oyster	острига (ж)	óstriga
spiny lobster	јастог (м)	jástog
octopus	хоботница (ж)	hóbotnica

squid	лигња (ж)	lígnja
sturgeon	јесетра (ж)	jésetra
salmon	лосос (м)	lósos
halibut	пацифички лист (м)	pacífički list

cod	бакалар (м)	bakálar
mackerel	скуша (ж)	skúša
tuna	туњевина (ж)	túnjevina
eel	јегуља (ж)	jégulja

trout	пастрмка (ж)	pástrmka
sardine	сардина (ж)	sardína
pike	штука (ж)	štúka
herring	харинга (ж)	háringa

bread	хлеб (м)	hleb
cheese	сир (м)	sir
sugar	шећер (м)	šéćer
salt	со (ж)	so

rice	пиринач (м)	pírinač
pasta (macaroni)	макарони (мн)	mákaroni
noodles	резанци (мн)	rezánci

| butter | маслац (м) | máslac |
| vegetable oil | зејтин (м) | zéjtin |

| sunflower oil | сунцокретово уље (с) | súncokretovo úlje |
| margarine | маргарин (м) | margárin |

| olives | маслине (мн) | másline |
| olive oil | маслиново уље (с) | máslinovo úlje |

milk	млеко (с)	mléko
condensed milk	кондензовано млеко (с)	kondenzóvano mléko
yogurt	јогурт (м)	jógurt

| sour cream | кисела павлака (ж) | kísela pávlaka |
| cream (of milk) | павлака (ж) | pávlaka |

| mayonnaise | мајонез (м), мајонеза (ж) | majonéz, majonéza |
| buttercream | крем (м) | krem |

groats (barley ~, etc.)	житарице (мн)	žitárice
flour	брашно (с)	brášno
canned food	конзерве (мн)	konzérve

| cornflakes | кукурузне пахуљице (мн) | kukúruzne pahúljice |

honey	мед (м)	med
jam	џем (м), мармелада (ж)	džem, marmeláda
chewing gum	гума (ж) за жвакање	gúma za žvákanje

45. Drinks

water	вода (ж)	vóda
drinking water	питка вода (ж)	pítka vóda
mineral water	кисела вода (ж)	kísela vóda
still (adj)	негазиран	negazíran
carbonated (adj)	gazíran	gazíran
sparkling (adj)	газиран	gazíran
ice	лед (м)	led
with ice	са ледом	sa lédom
non-alcoholic (adj)	безалкохолан	bézalkoholan
soft drink	безалкохолно пиће (с)	bézalkoholno píće
refreshing drink	освежавајући напитак (м)	osvežávajući nápitak
lemonade	лимунада (ж)	limunáda
liquors	алкохолна пића (мн)	álkoholna píća
wine	вино (с)	víno
white wine	бело вино (с)	bélo víno
red wine	црно вино (с)	cŕno víno
liqueur	ликер (м)	líker
champagne	шампањац (м)	šampánjac
vermouth	вермут (м)	vérmut
whiskey	виски (м)	víski
vodka	вотка (ж)	vótka
gin	џин (м)	džin
cognac	коњак (м)	kónjak
rum	рум (м)	rum
coffee	кафа (ж)	káfa
black coffee	црна кафа (ж)	cŕna káfa
coffee with milk	кафа (ж) са млеком	káfa sa mlékom
cappuccino	капучино (м)	kapučíno
instant coffee	инстант кафа (ж)	ínstant káfa
milk	млеко (с)	mléko
cocktail	коктел (м)	kóktel
milkshake	милкшејк (м)	mílkšejk
juice	сок (м)	sok
tomato juice	сок (м) од парадајза	sok od parádajza
orange juice	сок (м) од наранџе	sok od nárandže
freshly squeezed juice	свеже цеђени сок (м)	svéže céđeni sok
beer	пиво (с)	pívo
light beer	светло пиво (с)	svétlo pívo
dark beer	тамно пиво (с)	támno pívo

tea	чај (м)	čaj
black tea	црни чај (м)	cŕni čaj
green tea	зелени чај (м)	zéleni čaj

46. Vegetables

| vegetables | поврће (с) | póvrće |
| greens | зелен (ж) | zélen |

tomato	парадајз (м)	parádajz
cucumber	краставац (м)	krástavac
carrot	шаргарепа (ж)	šargarépa
potato	кромпир (м)	krómpir
onion	црни лук (м)	cŕni luk
garlic	бели лук (м)	béli luk

cabbage	купус (м)	kúpus
cauliflower	карфиол (м)	karfíol
Brussels sprouts	прокељ (м)	prókelj
broccoli	брокуле (мн)	brókule

beet	цвекла (ж)	cvékla
eggplant	патлиџан (м)	patlidžán
zucchini	тиквица (ж)	tíkvica
pumpkin	тиква (ж)	tíkva
turnip	репа (ж)	répa

parsley	першун (м)	péršun
dill	мироћија (ж)	miróđija
lettuce	зелена салата (ж)	zélena saláta
celery	целер (м)	céler
asparagus	шпаргла (ж)	špárgla
spinach	спанаћ (м)	spánać

pea	грашак (м)	grášak
beans	махунарке (мн)	mahúnarke
corn (maize)	кукуруз (м)	kukúruz
kidney bean	пасуљ (м)	pásulj

bell pepper	паприка (ж)	páprika
radish	ротквица (ж)	rótkvica
artichoke	артичока (ж)	artičóka

47. Fruits. Nuts

fruit	воће (с)	vóće
apple	јабука (ж)	jábuka
pear	крушка (ж)	krúška

lemon	лимун (м)	límun
orange	наранџа (ж)	nárandža
strawberry (garden ~)	јагода (ж)	jágoda

mandarin	мандарина (ж)	mandarína
plum	шљива (ж)	šljíva
peach	бресква (ж)	bréskva
apricot	кајсија (ж)	kájsija
raspberry	малина (ж)	málina
pineapple	ананас (м)	ánanas

banana	банана (ж)	banána
watermelon	лубеница (ж)	lubénica
grape	грожђе (с)	gróžđe
sour cherry	вишња (ж)	víšnja
sweet cherry	трешња (ж)	tréšnja
melon	диња (ж)	dínja

grapefruit	грејпфрут (м)	gréjpfrut
avocado	авокадо (м)	avokádo
papaya	папаја (ж)	papája
mango	манго (м)	mángo
pomegranate	нар (м)	nar

redcurrant	црвена рибизла (ж)	crvéna ríbizla
blackcurrant	црна рибизла (ж)	cŕna ríbizla
gooseeberry	огрозд (м)	ógrozd
bilberry	боровница (ж)	boróvnica
blackberry	купина (ж)	kupína

raisin	суво грожђе (с)	súvo gróžđe
fig	смоква (ж)	smókva
date	урма (ж)	úrma

peanut	кикирики (м)	kikiríki
almond	бадем (м)	bádem
walnut	орах (м)	órah
hazelnut	лешник (м)	léšnik
coconut	кокосов орах (м)	kókosov órah
pistachios	пистаћи (мн)	pistáći

48. Bread. Candy

bakers' confectionery (pastry)	посластице (мн)	póslastice
bread	хлеб (м)	hleb
cookies	колачић (м)	koláčić

| chocolate (n) | чоколада (ж) | čokoláda |
| chocolate (as adj) | чоколадни | čókoladni |

candy (wrapped)	бомбона (ж)	bombóna
cake (e.g., cupcake)	колач (м)	kólač
cake (e.g., birthday ~)	торта (ж)	tórta

| pie (e.g., apple ~) | пита (ж) | píta |
| filling (for cake, pie) | надев (м) | nádev |

jam (whole fruit jam)	слатко (с)	slátko
marmalade	мармелада (ж)	marmeláda
wafers	облатне (мн)	óblatne
ice-cream	сладолед (м)	sládoled
pudding	пудинг (м)	púding

49. Cooked dishes

course, dish	јело (с)	jélo
cuisine	кухиња (ж)	kúhinja
recipe	рецепт (м)	récept
portion	порција (ж)	pórcija

| salad | салата (ж) | saláta |
| soup | супа (ж) | súpa |

clear soup (broth)	буљон (м)	búljon
sandwich (bread)	сендвич (м)	séndvič
fried eggs	пржена јаја (мн)	pržena јája

| hamburger (beefburger) | хамбургер (м) | hámburger |
| beefsteak | бифтек (м) | bíftek |

side dish	прилог (м)	prílog
spaghetti	шпагете (мн)	špagéte
mashed potatoes	кромпир пире (м)	krómpir píre
pizza	пица (ж)	píca
porridge (oatmeal, etc.)	каша (ж)	káša
omelet	омлет (м)	ómlet

boiled (e.g., ~ beef)	кувани	kúvani
smoked (adj)	димљени	dímljeni
fried (adj)	пржени	prženi
dried (adj)	сув	suv
frozen (adj)	замрзнут	zámrznut
pickled (adj)	маринирани	marinírani

sweet (sugary)	сладак	sládak
salty (adj)	слан	slan
cold (adj)	хладан	hládan
hot (adj)	врућ	vruć
bitter (adj)	горак	górak
tasty (adj)	укусан	úkusan

to cook in boiling water	барити (пг)	báriti
to cook (dinner)	кувати (пг)	kúvati
to fry (vt)	пржити (пг)	pŕžiti
to heat up (food)	подгревати (пг)	podgrévati
to salt (vt)	солити (пг)	sóliti
to pepper (vt)	биберити (пг)	bíberiti
to grate (vt)	рендати (пг)	réndati
peel (n)	кора (ж)	kóra
to peel (vt)	љуштити (пг)	ljúštiti

50. Spices

salt	со (ж)	so
salty (adj)	слан	slan
to salt (vt)	солити (пг)	sóliti
black pepper	црни бибер (м)	cŕni bíber
red pepper (milled ~)	црвени бибер (м)	cŕveni bíber
mustard	сенф (м)	senf
horseradish	рен, хрен (м)	ren, hren
condiment	зачин (м)	záčin
spice	зачин (м)	záčin
sauce	сос (м)	sos
vinegar	сирће (с)	sírće
anise	анис (м)	ánis
basil	босиљак (м)	bósiljak
cloves	каранфил (м)	karánfil
ginger	ђумбир (м)	đúmbir
coriander	коријандер (м)	korijánder
cinnamon	цимет (м)	címet
sesame	сусам (м)	súsam
bay leaf	ловор (м)	lóvor
paprika	паприка (ж)	páprika
caraway	ким (м)	kim
saffron	шафран (м)	šáfran

51. Meals

food	храна (ж)	hrána
to eat (vi, vt)	јести (нг, пг)	jésti
breakfast	доручак (м)	dóručak
to have breakfast	доручковати (нг)	dóručkovati

lunch	ручак (м)	rúčak
to have lunch	ручати (нг)	rúčati
dinner	вечера (ж)	véčera
to have dinner	вечерати (нг)	véčerati

appetite	апетит (м)	apétit
Enjoy your meal!	Пријатно!	Príjatno!

to open (~ a bottle)	отварати (пр)	otvárati
to spill (liquid)	пролити (пр)	próliti
to spill out (vi)	пролити се	próliti se

to boil (vi)	кључати (нг)	kljúčati
to boil (vt)	кључати (пр)	kljúčati
boiled (~ water)	кувани	kúvani
to chill, cool down (vt)	охладити (пр)	ohláditi
to chill (vi)	охлађивати се	ohlađivati se

taste, flavor	укус (м)	úkus
aftertaste	укус (м)	úkus

to slim down (lose weight)	смршати (нг)	smŕšati
diet	дијета (ж)	dijéta
vitamin	витамин (м)	vitámin
calorie	калорија (ж)	kalórija

vegetarian (n)	вегетаријанац (м)	vegetarijánac
vegetarian (adj)	вегетаријански	vegetaríjanski

fats (nutrient)	масти (мн)	másti
proteins	беланчевине (мн)	belánčevine
carbohydrates	угљени хидрати (мн)	úgljeni hidráti

slice (of lemon, ham)	парче (с)	párče
piece (of cake, pie)	комад (м)	kómad
crumb (of bread, cake, etc.)	мрва (ж)	mŕva

52. Table setting

spoon	кашика (ж)	kášika
knife	нож (м)	nož
fork	виљушка (ж)	víljuška

cup (e.g., coffee ~)	шоља (ж)	šólja
plate (dinner ~)	тањир (м)	tánjir

saucer	тацна (ж)	tácna
napkin (on table)	салвета (ж)	salvéta
toothpick	чачкалица (ж)	čáčkalica

53. Restaurant

restaurant	ресторан (м)	restóran
coffee house	кафић (м), кафана (ж)	káfić, kafána
pub, bar	бар (м)	bar
tearoom	чајџиница (ж)	čájdžinica
waiter	конобар (м)	kónobar
waitress	конобарица (ж)	konobárica
bartender	бармен (м)	bármen
menu	јеловник (м)	jélovnik
wine list	винска карта (ж)	vínska kárta
to book a table	резервисати сто	rezervísati sto
course, dish	јело (с)	jélo
to order (meal)	наручити (пг)	narúčiti
to make an order	наручити	narúčiti
aperitif	аперитив (м)	áperitiv
appetizer	предјело (с)	prédjelo
dessert	десерт (м)	désert
check	рачун (м)	ráčun
to pay the check	платити рачун	plátiti ráčun
to give change	вратити кусур	vrátiti kúsur
tip	бакшиш (м)	bákšiš

Family, relatives and friends

name (first name)	име (с)	íme
surname (last name)	презиме (с)	prézime
date of birth	датум (м) рођења	dátum rođénja
place of birth	место (с) рођења	mésto rođénja
nationality	националност (ж)	nacionálnost
place of residence	пребивалиште (с)	prébivalište
country	земља (ж)	zémlja
profession (occupation)	професија (ж)	profésija
gender, sex	пол (м)	pol
height	раст (м)	rast
weight	тежина (ж)	težína

mother	мајка (ж)	májka
father	отац (м)	ótac
son	син (м)	sin
daughter	кћи (ж)	kći
younger daughter	млађа кћи (ж)	mláđa kći
younger son	млађи син (м)	mláđi sin
eldest daughter	најстарија кћи (ж)	nájstarija kći
eldest son	најстарији син (м)	nájstariji sin
brother	брат (м)	brat
elder brother	старији брат (м)	stáriji brat
younger brother	млађи брат (м)	mláđi brat
sister	сестра (ж)	séstra
elder sister	старија сестра (ж)	stárija séstra
younger sister	млађа сестра (ж)	mláđa séstra
cousin (masc.)	рођак (м)	róđak
cousin (fem.)	рођака (ж)	róđaka
mom, mommy	мама (ж)	máma
dad, daddy	тата (м)	táta
parents	родитељи (мн)	róditelji
child	дете (с)	déte
children	деца (мн)	déca

grandmother	бака (ж)	báka
grandfather	деда (м)	déda
grandson	унук (м)	únuk
granddaughter	унука (ж)	únuka
grandchildren	унуци (мн)	únuci
uncle	ујак, стриц (м)	újak, stric
aunt	ујна, стрина (ж)	újna, strína
nephew	нећак, сестрић (м)	nécak, séstrić
niece	нећакиња, сестричина (ж)	nećákinja, séstričina
mother-in-law (wife's mother)	ташта (ж)	tášta
father-in-law (husband's father)	свекар (м)	svékar
son-in-law (daughter's husband)	зет (м)	zet
stepmother	маћеха (ж)	máćeha
stepfather	очух (м)	óćuh
infant	беба (ж)	béba
baby (infant)	беба (ж)	béba
little boy, kid	мало дете (с), беба (ж)	málo déte, béba
wife	жена (ж)	žéna
husband	муж (м)	muž
spouse (husband)	супруг (м)	súprug
spouse (wife)	супруга (ж)	súpruga
married (masc.)	ожењен	óženjen
married (fem.)	удата	údata
single (unmarried)	неожењен	neóženjen
bachelor	нежења (м)	néženja
divorced (masc.)	разведен	razvéden
widow	удовица (ж)	udóvica
widower	удовац (м)	údovac
relative	рођак (м)	róđak
close relative	блиски рођак (м)	blíski róđak
distant relative	даљи рођак (м)	dálji róđak
relatives	рођаци (мн)	róđaci
orphan (boy or girl)	сироче (с)	siróče
guardian (of a minor)	старатељ (м)	stáratelj
to adopt (a boy)	усвојити (пг)	usvójiti
to adopt (a girl)	усвојити (пг)	usvójiti

56. Friends. Coworkers

| friend (masc.) | пријатељ (м) | príjatelj |
| friend (fem.) | пријатељица (ж) | prijatéljica |

| friendship | пријатељство (c) | prijatéljstvo |
| to be friends | дружити се | drúžiti se |

buddy (masc.)	пријатељ (м)	príjatelj
buddy (fem.)	пријатељица (ж)	prijatéljica
partner	партнер (м)	pártner

chief (boss)	шеф (м)	šef
superior (n)	начелник (м)	náčelnik
owner, proprietor	власник (м)	vlásnik
subordinate (n)	потчињени (м)	pótčinjeni
colleague	колега (м)	koléga

acquaintance (person)	познаник (м)	póznanik
fellow traveler	сапутник (м)	sáputnik
classmate	школски друг (м)	škólski drug

neighbor (masc.)	комшија (м)	kómšija
neighbor (fem.)	комшиница (ж)	kómšinica
neighbors	комшије (мн)	kómšije

57. Man. Woman

woman	жена (ж)	žéna
girl (young woman)	девојка (ж)	dévojka
bride	млада, невеста (ж)	mláda, névesta

beautiful (adj)	лепа	lépa
tall (adj)	висока	vísoka
slender (adj)	витка	vítka
short (adj)	ниска	níska

| blonde (n) | плавуша (ж) | plávuša |
| brunette (n) | црнка (ж) | cŕnka |

ladies' (adj)	дамски	dámski
virgin (girl)	девица (ж)	dévica
pregnant (adj)	трудна	trúdna

man (adult male)	мушкарац (м)	muškárac
blond (n)	плавушан (м)	plávušan
brunet (n)	бринет (м)	brínet
tall (adj)	висок	vísok
short (adj)	низак	nízak

rude (rough)	груб	grub
stocky (adj)	здепаст	zdépast
robust (adj)	јак	jak
strong (adj)	снажан	snážan
strength	снага (ж)	snága

stout, fat (adj)	дебео	débeo
swarthy (adj)	тамнопут, гарав	támnoput, gárav
slender (well-built)	витак	vítak
elegant (adj)	елегантан	elegántan

58. Age

age	узраст (м), старост (ж)	úzrast, stárost
youth (young age)	младост (ж)	mládost
young (adj)	млад	mlad
younger (adj)	млађи	mláđi
older (adj)	старији	stáriji
young man	младић (м)	mládić
teenager	тинејџер (м)	tinéjdžer
guy, fellow	момак (м)	mómak
old man	старац (м)	stárac
old woman	старица (ж)	stárica
adult (adj)	одрасла особа (ж)	ódrasla ósoba
middle-aged (adj)	средовјечни	srédovječni
elderly (adj)	постарији	póstariji
old (adj)	стар	star
retirement	пензија (ж)	pénzija
to retire (from job)	отићи у пензију	ótići u pénziju
retiree	пензионер (м)	penzióner

59. Children

child	дете (с)	déte
children	деца (мн)	déca
twins	близанци (мн)	blizánci
cradle	колевка (ж)	kólevka
rattle	звечка (ж)	zvéčka
diaper	пелена (ж)	pélena
pacifier	цуцла (ж)	cúcla
baby carriage	дечија колица (мн)	déčija kolíca
kindergarten	обданиште (с)	óbdanište
babysitter	дадиља (ж)	dádilja
childhood	детињство (с)	detínjstvo
doll	лутка (ж)	lútka
toy	играчка (ж)	ígračka

construction set (toy)	конструктор (м)	konstrúktor
well-bred (adj)	васпитан	váspitan
ill-bred (adj)	неваспитан	neváspitan
spoiled (adj)	размажен	rázmažen

to be naughty	бити несташан	bíti néstašan
mischievous (adj)	несташан	néstašan
mischievousness	несташлук (м)	néstašluk
mischievous child	несташко (м)	néstaško

| obedient (adj) | послушан | póslušan |
| disobedient (adj) | непослушан | néposlušan |

docile (adj)	паметан, послушан	pámetan, póslušan
clever (smart)	паметан	pámetan
child prodigy	вундеркинд (м)	vúnderkind

60. Married couples. Family life

to kiss (vt)	љубити (нг)	ljúbiti
to kiss (vi)	љубити се	ljúbiti se
family (n)	породица (ж)	pórodica
family (as adj)	породични	pórodični
couple	пар (м)	par
marriage (state)	брак (м)	brak
hearth (home)	домаће огњиште (с)	domáće ógnjište
dynasty	династија (ж)	dinástija

| date | сусрет (м) | súsret |
| kiss | пољубац (м) | póljubac |

love (for sb)	љубав (ж)	ljúbav
to love (sb)	волети (нг)	vóleti
beloved	вољени	vóljeni

tenderness	нежност (ж)	néžnost
tender (affectionate)	нежан	néžan
faithfulness	верност (ж)	vérnost
faithful (adj)	веран	véran
care (attention)	брига (ж)	bríga
caring (~ father)	брижан	brížan

newlyweds	младенци (мн)	mládenci
honeymoon	медени месец (м)	médeni mésec
to get married (ab. woman)	удати се	údati se
to get married (ab. man)	женити се	žéniti se

| wedding | свадба (ж) | svádba |
| golden wedding | златна свадба (ж) | zlátna svádba |

anniversary	годишњица (ж)	gódišnjica
lover (masc.)	љубавник (м)	ljúbavnik
mistress (lover)	љубавница (ж)	ljúbavnica
adultery	превара (ж)	prévara
to cheat on … (commit adultery)	преварити (пг)	prévariti
jealous (adj)	љубоморан	ljúbomoran
to be jealous	бити љубоморан	bíti ljúbomoran
divorce	развод (м)	rázvod
to divorce (vi)	развести се	rázvesti se
to quarrel (vi)	свађати се	sváđati se
to be reconciled (after an argument)	мирити се	míriti se
together (adv)	заједно	zájedno
sex	секс (м)	seks
happiness	срећа (ж)	sréća
happy (adj)	срећан	sréćan
misfortune (accident)	несрећа (ж)	nésreća
unhappy (adj)	несрећан	nésrećan

Character. Feelings. Emotions

61. Feelings. Emotions

feeling (emotion)	осећај (м)	ósećaj
feelings	осећања (мн)	ósećanja
to feel (vt)	осећати (нг)	ósećati
hunger	глад (ж)	glád
to be hungry	бити гладан	bíti gládan
thirst	жеђ (ж)	žeđ
to be thirsty	бити жедан	bíti žédan
sleepiness	поспаност (ж)	póspanost
to feel sleepy	бити поспан	bíti póspan
tiredness	умор (м)	úmor
tired (adj)	уморан	úmoran
to get tired	уморити се	umóriti se
mood (humor)	расположење (с)	raspoložénje
boredom	досада (ж)	dósada
to be bored	досађивати се	dosađívati se
seclusion	самоћа (ж)	samóća
to seclude oneself	усамити се	usámiti se
to worry (make anxious)	узнемиравати (нг)	uznemirávati
to be worried	бринути се	brínuti se
worrying (n)	брига (ж)	bríga
anxiety	анксиозност (ж)	anksióznost
preoccupied (adj)	забринут, преокупиран	zábrinut, preokupiran
to be nervous	бити нервозан	bíti nérvozan
to panic (vi)	паничити (нг)	páničiti
hope	нада (ж)	náda
to hope (vi, vt)	надати се	nádati se
certainty	сигурност (ж)	sigúrnost
certain, sure (adj)	сигуран	síguran
uncertainty	несигурност (ж)	nesigúrnost
uncertain (adj)	несигуран	nésiguran
drunk (adj)	пијан	píjan
sober (adj)	трезан	trézan
weak (adj)	слаб	slab
happy (adj)	срећан	sréćan
to scare (vt)	уплашити (нг)	úplašiti

| fury (madness) | бес (м) | bes |
| rage (fury) | гнев, бес (м) | gnev, bes |

depression	депресија (ж)	deprésija
discomfort (unease)	нелагодност (ж)	nelágodnost
comfort	комфор (м)	kómfor
to regret (be sorry)	жалити (нг)	žáliti
regret	жаљење (с)	žáljenje
bad luck	несређа (ж)	nésreća
sadness	туга (ж)	túga

shame (remorse)	стид (м)	stid
gladness	весеље (с)	vesélje
enthusiasm, zeal	ентузијазам (м)	entuzijázam
enthusiast	ентузијаст (м)	entuzíjast
to show enthusiasm	показати ентузијазам	pokázati entuzijázam

62. Character. Personality

character	карактер (м)	karákter
character flaw	мана (ж)	mána
mind	ум (м)	um
reason	разум (м)	rázum

conscience	савест (ж)	sávest
habit (custom)	навика (ж)	návika
ability (talent)	способност (ж)	spósobnost
can (e.g., ~ swim)	умети (нг)	úmeti

patient (adj)	стрпљив	stŕpljiv
impatient (adj)	нестрпљив	nestŕpljiv
curious (inquisitive)	радознао	radóznao
curiosity	радозналост (ж)	radóznalost

modesty	скромност (ж)	skrómnost
modest (adj)	скроман	skróman
immodest (adj)	нескроман	néskroman

laziness	лењост (ж)	lénjost
lazy (adj)	лењ	lenj
lazy person (masc.)	ленчуга (м)	lénčuga

cunning (n)	лукавост (ж)	lúkavost
cunning (as adj)	лукав	lúkav
distrust	неповерење (с)	nepoverénje
distrustful (adj)	неповерљив	nepovérljiv

generosity	дарежљивост (ж)	daréžljivost
generous (adj)	дарежљив	daréžljiv
talented (adj)	талентован	tálentovan

talent	таленат (м)	tálenat
courageous (adj)	храбар	hrábar
courage	храброст (ж)	hrábrost
honest (adj)	искрен	ískren
honesty	искреност (ж)	ískrenost
careful (cautious)	опрезан	óprezan
brave (courageous)	одважан	ódvažan
serious (adj)	озбиљан	ózbiljan
strict (severe, stern)	строг	strog
decisive (adj)	одлучан	ódlučan
indecisive (adj)	неодлучан	néodlučan
shy, timid (adj)	стидљив	stídljiv
shyness, timidity	стидљивост (ж)	stídljivost
confidence (trust)	поверење (с)	poverénje
to believe (trust)	веровати (нг)	vérovati
trusting (credulous)	поверљив	povérljiv
sincerely (adv)	озбиљно	ózbiljno
sincere (adj)	озбиљан	ózbiljan
sincerity	искреност (ж)	ískrenost
open (person)	отворен	ótvoren
calm (adj)	тих	tih
frank (sincere)	искрен	ískren
naïve (adj)	наиван	náivan
absent-minded (adj)	расејан	rasejan
funny (odd)	смешан	sméšan
greed, stinginess	похлепа (ж)	póhlepa
greedy, stingy (adj)	похлепан	póhlepan
stingy (adj)	шкрт	škŕt
evil (adj)	зао	záo
stubborn (adj)	тврдоглав	tvrdóglav
unpleasant (adj)	непријатан	néprijatan
selfish person (masc.)	себичњак (м)	sébičnjak
selfish (adj)	себичан	sébičan
coward	кукавица (ж)	kúkavica
cowardly (adj)	кукавички	kúkavički

63. Sleep. Dreams

to sleep (vi)	спавати (нг)	spávati
sleep, sleeping	спавање (с)	spávanje
dream	сан (м)	san
to dream (in sleep)	сањати (нг)	sánjati
sleepy (adj)	сањив	sánjiv

bed	кревет (м)	krévet
mattress	душек (м)	dúšek
blanket (comforter)	јорган (м)	jórgan
pillow	јастук (м)	jástuk
sheet	чаршав (м)	čáršav

insomnia	несаница (ж)	nésanica
sleepless (adj)	бесан	bésan
sleeping pill	таблета (ж) за спавање	tabléta za spávanje
to take a sleeping pill	узети таблету (ж) за спавање	úzeti tablétu za spávanje

to feel sleepy	бити поспан	bíti póspan
to yawn (vi)	зевати (нг)	zévati
to go to bed	ићи на спавање	ići na spávanje
to make up the bed	намештати кревет	naméštati krévet
to fall asleep	заспати (нг)	záspati

nightmare	кошмар (м), мора (ж)	kóšmar, móra
snore, snoring	хркање (с)	hŕkanje
to snore (vi)	хркати (нг)	hŕkati

alarm clock	будилник (м)	búdilnik
to wake (vt)	пробудити (пг)	probúditi
to wake up	пробуђивати се	probuđívati se
to get up (vi)	устајати (нг)	ústajati
to wash up (wash face)	умивати се	umívati se

64. Humour. Laughter. Gladness

humor (wit, fun)	хумор (м)	húmor
sense of humor	смисао (м) за хумор	smísao za húmor
to enjoy oneself	уживати (нг)	užívati
cheerful (merry)	весео	véseo
merriment (gaiety)	весеље (с)	vesélje

smile	осмех (м)	ósmeh
to smile (vi)	осмехивати се	osmehívati se
to start laughing	засмејати се	zasméjati se
to laugh (vi)	смејати се	sméjati se
laugh, laughter	смех (м)	smeh
anecdote	виц (м)	vic
funny (anecdote, etc.)	смешан	sméšan
funny (odd)	смешан	sméšan

to joke (vi)	шалити се	šáliti se
joke (verbal)	шала (ж)	šála
joy (emotion)	радост (ж)	rádost
to rejoice (vi)	радовати се	rádovati se
joyful (adj)	радостан	rádostan

65. Discussion, conversation. Part 1

communication	општење (c)	ópštenje
to communicate	комуницирати (нг)	komunicírati
conversation	разговор (м)	rázgovor
dialog	дијалог (м)	dijálog
discussion (discourse)	дискусија (ж)	diskúsija
dispute (debate)	расправа (ж)	rásprava
to dispute, debate	расправљати се	ráspravljati se
interlocutor	саговорник (м)	ságovornik
topic (theme)	тема (ж)	téma
point of view	тачка (ж) гледишта	táčka glédišta
opinion (point of view)	мишљење (c)	míšljenje
speech (talk)	говор (м)	góvor
discussion (of report, etc.)	расправа, дискусија (ж)	rásprava, dískusija
to discuss (vt)	расправљати (пг)	ráspravljati
talk (conversation)	разговор (м)	rázgovor
to talk (to chat)	разговарати (нг)	razgovárati
meeting (encounter)	сусрет (м)	súsret
to meet (vi, vt)	сусрести се	súsresti se
proverb	пословица (ж)	póslovica
saying	пословица (ж)	póslovica
riddle (poser)	загонетка (ж)	zágonetka
to pose a riddle	загонетати (пг)	zagonétati
password	лозинка (ж)	lózinka
secret	тајна (ж)	tájna
oath (vow)	заклетва (ж)	zákletva
to swear (an oath)	клети се	kléti se
promise	обећање (c)	obećánje
to promise (vt)	обећати (пг)	obéćati
advice (counsel)	савет (м)	sávet
to advise (vt)	саветовати (пг)	sávetovati
to follow one's advice	слушати савет	slúšati sávet
to listen to … (obey)	слушати (пг)	slúšati
news	новост (ж)	nóvost
sensation (news)	сензација (ж)	senzácija
information (report)	информације (мн)	informácije
conclusion (decision)	закључак (м)	záključak
voice	глас (м)	glas
compliment	комплимент (м)	komplimént
kind (nice)	љубазан	ljúbazan
word	реч (ж)	reč
phrase	фраза (ж)	fráza

answer	одговор (м)	ódgovor
truth	истина (ж)	ístina
lie	лаж (ж)	laž

thought	мисао (ж)	mísao
idea (inspiration)	идеја (ж)	idéja
fantasy	фантазија (ж)	fantázija

66. Discussion, conversation. Part 2

respected (adj)	поштован	póštovan
to respect (vt)	поштовати (пг)	poštóvati
respect	поштовање (с)	poštovánje
Dear ... (letter)	Поштовани, ...	Póštovani, ...

to introduce (sb to sb)	упознати (пг)	upóznati
to make acquaintance	упознати се	upóznati se
intention	намера (ж)	námera
to intend (have in mind)	намеравати (нг)	namerávati
wish	жеља (ж)	žélja
to wish (~ good luck)	пожелети (пг)	požéleti

surprise (astonishment)	изненађење (с)	iznenađénje
to surprise (amaze)	чудити (пг)	čúditi
to be surprised	чудити се	čúditi se

to give (vt)	дати (пг)	dáti
to take (get hold of)	узети (пг)	úzeti
to give back	вратити (пг)	vrátiti
to return (give back)	вратити (пг)	vrátiti

to apologize (vi)	извињавати се	izvinjávati se
apology	извињење (с)	izvinjénje
to forgive (vt)	опраштати (пг)	opráštati

to talk (speak)	разговарати (нг)	razgovárati
to listen (vi)	слушати (пг)	slúšati
to hear out	саслушати (пг)	sáslušati
to understand (vt)	разумети (пг)	razúmeti

to show (to display)	показати (пг)	pokázati
to look at ...	гледати (пг)	glédati
to call (yell for sb)	позвати (пг)	pózvati
to distract (disturb)	сметати (пг)	smétati
to disturb (vt)	сметати (пг)	smétati
to pass (to hand sth)	предати (пг)	prédati

demand (request)	молба (ж)	mólba
to request (ask)	тражити, молити (пг)	trážiti, móliti
demand (firm request)	захтев (м)	záhtev

to demand (request firmly)	захтевати, тражити	zahtévati, trážiti
to tease (call names)	задиркивати (нг)	zadirkívati
to mock (make fun of)	подсмевати се	podsmévati se
mockery, derision	подсмех (м)	pódsmeh
nickname	надимак (м)	nádimak

insinuation	наговештај (м)	nágoveštaj
to insinuate (imply)	наговештавати (нг)	nagoveštávati
to mean (vt)	подразумевати (нг)	podrazumévati

description	опис (м)	ópis
to describe (vt)	описати (нг)	opísati
praise (compliments)	похвала (ж)	póhvala
to praise (vt)	похвалити (нг)	pohváliti

disappointment	разочарање (с)	razočaránje
to disappoint (vt)	разочарати (нг)	razočárati
to be disappointed	разочарати се	razočárati se

supposition	претпоставка (ж)	prétpostavka
to suppose (assume)	претпостављати (нг)	pretpóstavljati
warning (caution)	упозорење (с)	upozorénje
to warn (vt)	упозорити (нг)	upozóriti

67. Discussion, conversation. Part 3

| to talk into (convince) | наговорити (нг) | nagovóriti |
| to calm down (vt) | смиривати (нг) | smirívati |

silence (~ is golden)	ћутање (с)	ćútanje
to be silent (not speaking)	ћутати (нг)	ćútati
to whisper (vi, vt)	шапнути (нг)	šápnuti
whisper	шапат (м)	šápat

| frankly, sincerely (adv) | искрено | ískreno |
| in my opinion … | по мом мишљењу … | po mom míšljenju … |

detail (of the story)	детаљ (ж)	détalj
detailed (adj)	детаљан	détaljan
in detail (adv)	детаљно	détaljno

| hint, clue | наговештај (м) | nágoveštaj |
| to give a hint | дати миг | dáti mig |

look (glance)	поглед (м)	pógled
to have a look	погледати (нг)	pógledati
fixed (look)	непомичан	nepómičan
to blink (vi)	трептати (нг)	tréptati
to wink (vi)	намигнути (нг)	namígnuti
to nod (in assent)	климнути (нг)	klímnuti

sigh	уздах (м)	úzdah
to sigh (vi)	уздахнути (нг)	uzdáhnuti
to shudder (vi)	дрхтати (нг)	dŕhtati
gesture	гест (м)	gest
to touch (one's arm, etc.)	додирнути (пг)	dodírnuti
to seize	хватати (пг)	hvátati
(e.g., ~ by the arm)		
to tap (on the shoulder)	тапштати (нг)	tápštati
Look out!	Опрез!	Óprez!
Really?	Стварно?	Stvárno?
Are you sure?	Да ли си сигуран?	Da li si síguran?
Good luck!	Срећно!	Srécno!
I see!	Јасно!	Jásno!
What a pity!	Штета!	Štéta!

68. Agreement. Refusal

consent	пристанак (м)	prístanak
to consent (vi)	пристати (нг)	prístati
approval	одобрење (с)	odobrénje
to approve (vt)	одобрити (пг)	odóbriti
refusal	одбијање (с)	odbíjanje
to refuse (vi, vt)	одбијати се	odbíjati se
Great!	Одлично!	Ódlično!
All right!	Добро!	Dóbro!
Okay! (I agree)	Важи!	Váži!
forbidden (adj)	забрањен	zábranjen
it's forbidden	забрањено	zabránjeno
it's impossible	немогуће	némoguće
incorrect (adj)	погрешан	pógrešan
to reject (~ a demand)	одбити (пг)	ódbiti
to support (cause, idea)	подржати (пг)	podŕžati
to accept (~ an apology)	прихватити (пг)	príhvatiti
to confirm (vt)	потврдити (пг)	potvŕditi
confirmation	потврда (ж)	pótvrda
permission	дозвола (ж)	dózvola
to permit (vt)	дозволити (нг, пг)	dozvóliti
decision	одлука (ж)	ódluka
to say nothing	прећутати (нг)	precútati
(hold one's tongue)		
condition (term)	услов (м)	úslov
excuse (pretext)	изговор (м)	ízgovor
praise (compliments)	похвала (ж)	póhvala
to praise (vt)	похвалити (пг)	pohváliti

69. Success. Good luck. Failure

success	успех (м)	úspeh
successfully (adv)	успешно	úspešno
successful (adj)	успешан	úspešan
luck (good luck)	срећа (ж)	sréća
Good luck!	Сретно! Срећно!	Srétno! Srećno!
lucky (e.g., ~ day)	срећан	srećan
lucky (fortunate)	срећан	srećan
failure	неуспех (м)	néuspeh
misfortune	неуспех (м)	néuspeh
bad luck	несрећа (ж)	nésreća
unsuccessful (adj)	неуспешан	néuspešan
catastrophe	катастрофа (ж)	katastrófa
pride	понос (м)	pónos
proud (adj)	поносан	pónosan
to be proud	поносити се	ponósiti se
winner	победник (м)	póbednik
to win (vi)	победити (нг)	pobéditi
to lose (not win)	изгубити (нг, пг)	izgúbiti
try	покушај (м)	pókušaj
to try (vi)	покушавати (нг)	pokušávati
chance (opportunity)	шанса (ж)	šánsa

70. Quarrels. Negative emotions

shout (scream)	узвик (м)	úzvik
to shout (vi)	викати (нг)	víkati
to start to cry out	почети викати	póčeti víkati
quarrel	свађа (ж)	sváđa
to quarrel (vi)	свађати се	sváđati se
fight (squabble)	свађа (ж)	sváđa
to make a scene	свађати се	sváđati se
conflict	конфликт (м)	kónflikt
misunderstanding	неспоразум (м)	nésporazum
insult	увреда (ж)	úvreda
to insult (vt)	вређати (пг)	vréđati
insulted (adj)	увређен	úvređen
resentment	кивност (ж)	kívnost
to offend (vt)	увредити (пг)	uvréditi
to take offense	бити киван	biti kívan
indignation	негодовање (c)	négodovanje
to be indignant	индигнирати се	indignírati se

complaint	жалба (ж)	žálba
to complain (vi, vt)	жалити се	žáliti se
apology	извињење (с)	izvinjénje
to apologize (vi)	извињавати се	izvinjávati se
to beg pardon	извињавати се	izvinjávati se
criticism	критика (ж)	krítika
to criticize (vt)	критиковати (пг)	krítikovati
accusation (charge)	оптужба (ж)	óptužba
to accuse (vt)	окривљавати (пг)	okrivljávati
revenge	освета (ж)	ósveta
to avenge (get revenge)	освећивати се	osvećívati se
to pay back	отплатити (пг)	otplátiti
disdain	презир (м)	prézir
to despise (vt)	презирати (пг)	prézirati
hatred, hate	мржња (ж)	mȓžnja
to hate (vt)	мрзети (пг)	mȓzeti
nervous (adj)	нервозан	nérvozan
to be nervous	бити нервозан	bíti nérvozan
angry (mad)	љут	ljut
to make angry	разљутити (пг)	razljútiti
humiliation	понижење (с)	ponižénje
to humiliate (vt)	понижавати (пг)	ponižávati
to humiliate oneself	понижавати се	ponižávati se
shock	шок (м)	šok
to shock (vt)	шокирати (пг)	šokírati
trouble (e.g., serious ~)	неприлика (ж)	neprílika
unpleasant (adj)	непријатан	néprijatan
fear (dread)	страх (м)	strah
terrible (storm, heat)	страшан	strášan
scary (e.g., ~ story)	страшан	strášan
horror	ужас (м)	úžas
awful (crime, news)	ужасан	úžasan
to begin to tremble	почети дрхтати	póčeti dȓhtati
to cry (weep)	плакати (нг)	plákati
to start crying	заплакати (нг)	záplakati
tear	суза (ж)	súza
fault	грешка (ж)	gréška
guilt (feeling)	кривица (ж)	krivíca
dishonor (disgrace)	срамота (ж)	sramóta
protest	протест (м)	prótest
stress	стрес (м)	stres

to disturb (vt)	сметати (пг)	smétati
to be furious	љутити се	ljútiti se
mad, angry (adj)	љут	ljut
to end (~ a relationship)	прекидати (пг)	prekídati
to swear (at sb)	грдити (пг)	gŕditi
to scare (become afraid)	плашити се	plášiti se
to hit (strike with hand)	ударити (пг)	údariti
to fight (street fight, etc.)	тући се	túći se
to settle (a conflict)	решити (пг)	réšiti
discontented (adj)	незадовољан	nézadovoljan
furious (adj)	бесан	bésan
It's not good!	То није добро!	To níje dóbro!
It's bad!	То је лоше!	To je lóše!

Medicine

sickness	**болест** (ж)	bólest
to be sick	**боловати** (нг)	bolóvati
health	**здравље** (с)	zdrávlje
runny nose (coryza)	**кијавица** (ж)	kíjavica
tonsillitis	**ангина** (ж)	angína
cold (illness)	**прехлада** (ж)	préhlada
to catch a cold	**прехладити се**	prehláditi se
bronchitis	**бронхитис** (м)	bronhítis
pneumonia	**упала** (ж) **плућа**	úpala plúća
flu, influenza	**грип** (м)	grip
nearsighted (adj)	**кратковид**	kratkóvid
farsighted (adj)	**далековид**	dalekóvid
strabismus (crossed eyes)	**разрокост** (ж)	rázrokost
cross-eyed (adj)	**разрок**	rázrok
cataract	**катаракта** (ж)	katarákta
glaucoma	**глауком** (м)	gláukom
stroke	**мождани удар** (м)	móždani údar
heart attack	**инфаркт** (м)	ínfarkt
myocardial infarction	**инфаркт** (м) **миокарда**	ínfarkt míokarda
paralysis	**парализа** (ж)	paralíza
to paralyze (vt)	**парализовати** (пг)	parálizovati
allergy	**алергија** (ж)	alérgija
asthma	**астма** (ж)	ástma
diabetes	**дијабетес** (м)	dijabétes
toothache	**зубобоља** (ж)	zubóbolja
caries	**каријес** (м)	kárijes
diarrhea	**дијареја** (ж), **пролив** (м)	dijaréja, próliv
constipation	**затвор** (м)	zátvor
stomach upset	**лоша пробава** (ж)	lóša próbava
food poisoning	**тровање** (с)	tróvanje
to get food poisoning	**отровати се**	otróvati se
arthritis	**артритис** (м)	artrítis
rickets	**рахитис** (м)	rahítis
rheumatism	**реуматизам** (м)	reumatízam

atherosclerosis	атеросклероза (ж)	ateroskleróza
gastritis	гастритис (м)	gastrítis
appendicitis	апендицитис (м)	apendicítis
cholecystitis	холециститис (м)	holecístitis
ulcer	чир (м)	čir

measles	мале богиње (мн)	mále bóginje
rubella (German measles)	рубеола (ж)	rubéola
jaundice	жутица (ж)	žútica
hepatitis	хепатитис (м)	hepatítis

schizophrenia	шизофренија (ж)	šizofrénija
rabies (hydrophobia)	беснило (с)	bésnilo
neurosis	неуроза (ж)	neuróza
concussion	потрес (м) мозга	pótres mózga

cancer	рак (м)	rak
sclerosis	склероза (ж)	skleróza
multiple sclerosis	мултипла склероза (ж)	múltipla skleróza

alcoholism	алкохолизам (м)	alkoholízam
alcoholic (n)	алкохоличар (м)	alkohóličar
syphilis	сифилис (м)	sífilis
AIDS	Сида (ж)	Sída

tumor	тумор (м)	túmor
malignant (adj)	малигни, злоћудан	máligni, zlóćudan
benign (adj)	доброћудан	dóbroćudan

fever	грозница (ж)	gróznica
malaria	маларија (ж)	málarija
gangrene	гангрена (ж)	gangréna
seasickness	морска болест (ж)	mórska bólest
epilepsy	епилепсија (ж)	epilépsija

epidemic	епидемија (ж)	epidémija
typhus	тифус (м)	tífus
tuberculosis	туберкулоза (ж)	tuberkulóza
cholera	колера (ж)	koléra
plague (bubonic ~)	куга (ж)	kúga

72. Symptoms. Treatments. Part 1

symptom	симптом (м)	símptom
temperature	температура (ж)	temperatúra
high temperature (fever)	висока температура (ж)	vísoka temperatúra
pulse (heartbeat)	пулс (м)	puls

dizziness (vertigo)	вртоглавица (ж)	vrtóglavica
hot (adj)	врућ	vruć

shivering	**језа** (ж)	jéza
pale (e.g., ~ face)	**блед**	bled
cough	**кашаљ** (м)	kášalj
to cough (vi)	**кашљати** (нг)	kášljati
to sneeze (vi)	**кијати** (нг)	kíjati
faint	**несвестица** (ж)	nésvestica
to faint (vi)	**онесвестити се**	onesvéstiti se
bruise (hématome)	**модрица** (ж)	módrica
bump (lump)	**чворуга** (ж)	čvóruga
to bang (bump)	**ударити се**	údariti se
contusion (bruise)	**озледа** (ж)	ózleda
to get a bruise	**озледити се**	ozlédti se
to limp (vi)	**храмати** (нг)	hrámati
dislocation	**ишчашење** (с)	iščašénje
to dislocate (vt)	**ишчашити** (пг)	iščašiti
fracture	**прелом** (м)	prélom
to have a fracture	**задобити прелом**	zadóbiti prélom
cut (e.g., paper ~)	**посекотина** (ж)	posekótina
to cut oneself	**порезати се**	pórezati se
bleeding	**крварење** (с)	krvárenje
burn (injury)	**опекотина** (ж)	opekótina
to get burned	**опећи се**	ópeći se
to prick (vt)	**убости** (пг)	úbosti
to prick oneself	**убости се**	úbosti se
to injure (vt)	**повредити** (пг)	povréditi
injury	**повреда** (ж)	póvreda
wound	**рана** (ж)	rána
trauma	**траума** (ж)	tráuma
to be delirious	**бунцати** (нг)	búncati
to stutter (vi)	**муцати** (нг)	múcati
sunstroke	**сунчаница** (ж)	súnčanica

73. Symptoms. Treatments. Part 2

pain, ache	**бол** (ж)	bol
splinter (in foot, etc.)	**трн** (м)	trn
sweat (perspiration)	**зној** (м)	znoj
to sweat (perspire)	**знојити се**	znójiti se
vomiting	**повраћање** (с)	póvraćanje
convulsions	**грчеви** (мн)	gŕčevi
pregnant (adj)	**трудна**	trúdna
to be born	**родити се**	róditi se

delivery, labor	поро̄ђај (м)	pórođaj
to deliver (~ a baby)	ра̄ђати (пг)	ráđati
abortion	абортус, побачај (м)	abórtus, póbačaj

breathing, respiration	дисање (с)	dísanje
in-breath (inhalation)	удисај (м)	údisaj
out-breath (exhalation)	издах (м)	ízdah
to exhale (breathe out)	издахнути (нг)	izdáhnuti
to inhale (vi)	удисати (нг)	údisati

disabled person	инвалид (м)	inválid
cripple	богаљ (м)	bógalj
drug addict	наркоман (м)	nárkoman

deaf (adj)	глув	gluv
mute (adj)	нем	nem
deaf mute (adj)	глувонем	glúvonem

mad, insane (adj)	луд	lud
madman (demented person)	лудак (м)	lúdak
madwoman	луда (ж)	lúda
to go insane	полудети (нг)	polúdeti

gene	ген (м)	gen
immunity	имунитет (м)	imunítet
hereditary (adj)	наследни	následni
congenital (adj)	урођен	úrođen

virus	вирус (м)	vírus
microbe	микроб (м)	míkrob
bacterium	бактерија (ж)	baktérija
infection	инфекција (ж)	infékcija

74. Symptoms. Treatments. Part 3

| hospital | болница (ж) | bólnica |
| patient | пацијент (м) | pacíjent |

diagnosis	дијагноза (ж)	dijagnóza
cure	лечење (с)	léčenje
medical treatment	медицински третман (м)	médicinski trétman
to get treatment	лечити се	léčiti se
to treat (~ a patient)	лечити (пг)	léčiti
to nurse (look after)	неговати (нг)	négovati
care (nursing ~)	нега (ж)	néga

operation, surgery	операција (ж)	operácija
to bandage (head, limb)	превити (пг)	préviti
bandaging	превијање (с)	prevíjanje

vaccination	вакцинација (ж)	vakcinácija
to vaccinate (vt)	вакцинисати (пг)	vakcinísati
injection, shot	ињекција (ж)	injékcija
to give an injection	давати ињекцију	dávati injékciju

attack	напад (м)	nápad
amputation	ампутација (ж)	amputácija
to amputate (vt)	ампутирати (пг)	amputírati
coma	кома (ж)	kóma
to be in a coma	бити у коми	bíti u kómi
intensive care	реанимација (ж)	reanimácija

to recover (~ from flu)	оздрављати (нг)	ódzdravljati
condition (patient's ~)	стање (с)	stánje
consciousness	свест (ж)	svest
memory (faculty)	памћење (с)	pámćenje

to pull out (tooth)	вадити (пг)	váditi
filling	пломба (ж)	plómba
to fill (a tooth)	пломбирати (пг)	plombírati

| hypnosis | хипноза (ж) | hipnóza |
| to hypnotize (vt) | хипнотизирати (пг) | hipnotizírati |

75. Doctors

doctor	лекар (м)	lékar
nurse	медицинска сестра (ж)	médicinska séstra
personal doctor	лични лекар (м)	líčni lékar

dentist	зубар (м)	zúbar
eye doctor	окулиста (м)	okulísta
internist	терапеут (м)	terapéut
surgeon	хирург (м)	hírurg

psychiatrist	психијатар (м)	psihijátar
pediatrician	педијатар (м)	pedíjatar
psychologist	психолог (м)	psihólog
gynecologist	гинеколог (м)	ginekólog
cardiologist	кардиолог (м)	kardiólog

76. Medicine. Drugs. Accessories

medicine, drug	лек (м)	lek
remedy	средство (с)	srédstvo
to prescribe (vt)	преписивати (пг)	prepisívati
prescription	рецепт (м)	récept
tablet, pill	таблета (ж)	tabléta

ointment	маст (ж)	mast
ampule	ампула (ж)	ámpula
mixture, solution	микстура (ж)	mikstúra
syrup	сируп (м)	sírup
capsule	пилула (ж)	pílula
powder	прашак (м)	prášak

gauze bandage	завој (м)	závoj
cotton wool	вата (ж)	váta
iodine	јод (м)	jod

Band-Aid	фластер (м)	fláster
eyedropper	пипета (ж)	pipéta
thermometer	термометар (м)	térmometar
syringe	шприц (м)	špric

| wheelchair | инвалидска колица (мн) | inválidska kolíca |
| crutches | штаке (мн) | štáke |

painkiller	аналгетик (м)	analgétik
laxative	лаксатив (м)	láksativ
spirits (ethanol)	алкохол (м)	álkohol
medicinal herbs	лековито биље (с)	lékovito bílje
herbal (~ tea)	биљни	bíljni

77. Smoking. Tobacco products

tobacco	дуван (м)	dúvan
cigarette	цигарета (ж)	cigaréta
cigar	цигара (ж)	cigára
pipe	лула (ж)	lúla
pack (of cigarettes)	пакло (с)	páklo

matches	шибице (мн)	šíbice
matchbox	кутија (ж) шибица	kútija šíbica
lighter	упаљач (м)	upáljač
ashtray	пепељара (ж)	pepéljara
cigarette case	табакера (ж)	tabakéra

| cigarette holder | муштикла (ж) | múštikla |
| filter (cigarette tip) | филтар (м) | fíltar |

to smoke (vi, vt)	пушити (нг, пг)	púšiti
to light a cigarette	запалити цигарету	zapáliti cigarétu
smoking	пушење (с)	púšenje
smoker	пушач (м)	púšač

stub, butt (of cigarette)	опушак (м)	ópušak
smoke, fumes	дим (м)	dim
ash	пепео (м)	pépeo

HUMAN HABITAT

City

78. City. Life in the city

city, town	град (м)	grad
capital city	главни град (м), престоница (ж)	glávni grad, préstonica
village	село (с)	sélo
city map	план (м) града	plan gráda
downtown	центар (м) града	céntar gráda
suburb	предграђе (с)	prédgrađe
suburban (adj)	приградски	prígradski
outskirts	предграђе (с)	prédgrađe
environs (suburbs)	околина (ж)	ókolina
city block	четврт (ж)	čétvrt
residential block (area)	стамбена четврт (ж)	stámbena čétvrt
traffic	саобраћај (м)	sáobraćaj
traffic lights	семафор (м)	sémafor
public transportation	градски превоз (м)	grádski prévoz
intersection	раскрсница (ж)	ráskrsnica
crosswalk	пешачки прелаз (м)	péšački prélaz
pedestrian underpass	подземни пролаз (м)	pódzemni prólaz
to cross (~ the street)	прелазити (пг)	prélaziti
pedestrian	пешак (м)	péšak
sidewalk	тротоар (м)	trotóar
bridge	мост (м)	most
embankment (river walk)	кеј (м)	kej
fountain	чесма (ж)	čésma
allée (garden walkway)	алеја (ж)	aléja
park	парк (м)	park
boulevard	булевар (м)	bulévar
square	трг (м)	tŕg
avenue (wide street)	авенија (ж)	avénija
street	улица (ж)	úlica
side street	споредна улица (ж)	spóredna úlica
dead end	ћорсокак (м)	ćorsókak
house	кућа (ж)	kúća

| building | зграда (ж) | zgráda |
| skyscraper | небодер (м) | néboder |

facade	фасада (ж)	fasáda
roof	кров (м)	krov
window	прозор (м)	prózor
arch	лук (м)	luk
column	колона (ж)	kolóna
corner	угао, ћошак (м)	úgao, ćóšak

store window	излог (м)	ízlog
signboard (store sign, etc.)	натпис (м)	nátpis
poster (e.g., playbill)	плакат (м)	plákat
advertising poster	рекламни постер (м)	réklamni póster
billboard	билборд (м)	bílbord

garbage, trash	смеће, ђубре (с)	smeće, đúbre
trash can (public ~)	корпа (ж) за смеће	kórpa za sméće
to litter (vi)	бацати ђубре	bácati đúbre
garbage dump	депонија (ж)	depónija

phone booth	говорница (ж)	góvornica
lamppost	стуб (м)	stub
bench (park ~)	клупа (ж)	klúpa

police officer	полицајац (м)	policájac
police	полиција (ж)	polícija
beggar	просјак (м)	prósjak
homeless (n)	бескућник (м)	béskućnik

79. Urban institutions

store	продавница (ж)	pródavnica
drugstore, pharmacy	апотека (ж)	apotéka
eyeglass store	оптика (ж)	óptika
shopping mall	тржни центар (м)	tržni céntar
supermarket	супермаркет (м)	supermárket

bakery	пекара (ж)	pékara
baker	пекар (м)	pékar
pastry shop	посластичарница (ж)	poslastičárnica
grocery store	бакалница (ж)	bakálnica
butcher shop	месара (ж)	mésara

| produce store | пиљарница (ж) | píljarnica |
| market | пијаца (ж) | píjaca |

coffee house	кафић (м), кафана (ж)	káfić, kafána
restaurant	ресторан (м)	restóran
pub, bar	пивница (ж)	pívnica

pizzeria	пицерија (ж)	picérija
hair salon	фризерски салон (м)	frízerski sálon
post office	пошта (ж)	póšta
dry cleaners	хемијско чишћење (с)	hémijsko číšćenje
photo studio	фото атеље (м)	fóto atélje
shoe store	продавница (ж) обуће	pródavnica óbuće
bookstore	књижара (ж)	knjížara
sporting goods store	спортска радња (ж)	spórtska rádnja
clothes repair shop	поправка (ж) одеће	pópravka ódeće
formal wear rental	изнајмљивање (с) одеће	iznajmljívanje ódeće
video rental store	изнајмљивање (с) филмова	iznajmljívanje fílmova
circus	циркус (м)	církus
zoo	зоолошки врт (м)	zoóloški vŕt
movie theater	биоскоп (м)	bíoskop
museum	музеј (м)	múzej
library	библиотека (ж)	bibliotéka
theater	позориште (с)	pózorište
opera (opera house)	опера (ж)	ópera
nightclub	ноћни клуб (м)	nóćni klub
casino	коцкарница (ж)	kóckarnica
mosque	џамија (ж)	džámija
synagogue	синагога (ж)	sinagóga
cathedral	катедрала (ж)	katedrála
temple	храм (м)	hram
church	црква (ж)	cŕkva
college	институт (м)	instítut
university	универзитет (м)	univerzitét
school	школа (ж)	škóla
prefecture	управа (ж)	úprava
city hall	градска кућа (ж)	grádska kúća
hotel	хотел (м)	hótel
bank	банка (ж)	bánka
embassy	амбасада (ж)	ambasáda
travel agency	туристичка агенција (ж)	turística agéncija
information office	биро (с) за информације	bíro za informácije
currency exchange	мењачница (ж)	menjáčnica
subway	метро (м)	métro
hospital	болница (ж)	bólnica
gas station	бензинска станица (ж)	bénzinska stánica
parking lot	паркиралиште (с)	parkíralište

80. Signs

signboard (store sign, etc.)	натпис (м)	nátpis
notice (door sign, etc.)	натпис (м)	nátpis
poster	плакат (м)	plákat
direction sign	путоказ (м)	pútokaz
arrow (sign)	стрелица (ж)	strélica
caution	упозорење (с)	upozorénje
warning sign	знак (м) упозорења	znak upozorénja
to warn (vt)	упозорити (пг)	upozóriti
rest day (weekly ~)	слободан дан (м)	slóbodan dan
timetable (schedule)	распоред (м)	ráspored
opening hours	радно време (с)	rádno vréme
WELCOME!	ДОБРО ДОШЛИ!	DOBRO DOŠLI!
ENTRANCE	УЛАЗ	ULAZ
EXIT	ИЗЛАЗ	IZLAZ
PUSH	ГУРАЈ	GURAJ
PULL	ВУЦИ	VUCI
OPEN	ОТВОРЕНО	OTVORENO
CLOSED	ЗАТВОРЕНО	ZATVORENO
WOMEN	ЖЕНЕ	ŽENE
MEN	МУШКАРЦИ	MUŠKARCI
DISCOUNTS	ПОПУСТИ	POPUSTI
SALE	РАСПРОДАЈА	RASPRODAJA
NEW!	НОВО!	NOVO!
FREE	БЕСПЛАТНО	BESPLATNO
ATTENTION!	ПАЖЊА!	PAŽNJA!
NO VACANCIES	НЕМА СЛОБОДНИХ СОБА	NEMA SLOBODNIH SOBA
RESERVED	РЕЗЕРВИСАНО	REZERVISANO
ADMINISTRATION	УПРАВА	UPRAVA
STAFF ONLY	САМО ЗА ОСОБЉЕ	SAMO ZA OSOBLJE
BEWARE OF THE DOG!	ЧУВАЈ СЕ ПСА	ČUVAJ SE PSA
NO SMOKING	ЗАБРАЊЕНО ПУШЕЊЕ	ZABRANJENO PUŠENJE
DO NOT TOUCH!	НЕ ДИРАТИ	NE DIRATI
DANGEROUS	ОПАСНО	OPASNO
DANGER	ОПАСНОСТ	OPASNOST
HIGH VOLTAGE	ВИСОКИ НАПОН	VISOKI NAPON
NO SWIMMING!	ЗАБРАЊЕНО КУПАЊЕ	ZABRANJENO KUPANJE
OUT OF ORDER	НЕ РАДИ	NE RADI
FLAMMABLE	ЗАПАЉИВО	ZAPALJIVO

FORBIDDEN	ЗАБРАЊЕНО	ZABRANJENO
NO TRESPASSING!	ЗАБРАЊЕН ПРОЛАЗ	ZABRANJEN PROLAZ
WET PAINT	СВЕЖЕ ОФАРБАНО	SVEŽE OFARBANO

81. Urban transportation

bus	аутобус (м)	autóbus
streetcar	трамвај (м)	trámvaj
trolley bus	тролејбус (м)	troléjbus
route (of bus, etc.)	маршрута (ж)	maršrúta
number (e.g., bus ~)	број (м)	broj
to go by ...	ићи ...	ići ...
to get on (~ the bus)	ући у ...	úći u ...
to get off ...	сићи (нг), изаћи из ...	síći, ízaći iz ...
stop (e.g., bus ~)	станица (ж)	stánica
next stop	следећа станица (ж)	slédeća stánica
terminus	последња станица (ж)	póslednja stánica
schedule	ред (м) вожње	red vóžnje
to wait (vt)	чекати (нг, пг)	čékati
ticket	карта (ж)	kárta
fare	цена (ж) карте	céna kárte
cashier (ticket seller)	благајник (м)	blágajnik
ticket inspection	контрола (ж)	kontróla
ticket inspector	контролер (м)	kontróler
to be late (for ...)	каснити (нг)	kásniti
to miss (~ the train, etc.)	пропустити (пг)	propústiti
to be in a hurry	журити (нг)	žúriti
taxi, cab	такси (м)	táksi
taxi driver	таксиста (м)	táksista
by taxi	таксијем	táksijem
taxi stand	такси станица (ж)	táksi stánica
to call a taxi	позвати такси	pózvati táksi
to take a taxi	узети такси	úzeti taksi
traffic	саобраћај (м)	sáobraćaj
traffic jam	гужва (ж)	gúžva
rush hour	шпиц (м)	špic
to park (vi)	паркирати се	parkírati se
to park (vt)	паркирати (пг)	parkírati
parking lot	паркиралиште (с)	parkíralište
subway	метро (м)	métro
station	станица (ж)	stánica
to take the subway	ићи метроом	ići metróom

| train | воз (м) | voz |
| train station | железничка станица (ж) | žéleznička stánica |

82. Sightseeing

monument	споменик (м)	spómenik
fortress	тврђава (ж)	tvŕđava
palace	палата (ж)	paláta
castle	замак (м)	zámak
tower	кула (ж)	kúla
mausoleum	маузолеј (м)	mauzólej

architecture	архитектура (ж)	arhitektúra
medieval (adj)	средњовековни	srednjovékovni
ancient (adj)	старински	starínski
national (adj)	национални	nacionálni
famous (monument, etc.)	чувен	čúven

tourist	туриста (м)	turísta
guide (person)	водич (м)	vódič
excursion, sightseeing tour	екскурзија (ж)	ekskúrzija
to show (vt)	показивати (пr)	pokazívati
to tell (vt)	причати (пr)	príčati

to find (vt)	наћи (пr)	náći
to get lost (lose one's way)	изгубити се	izgúbiti se
map (e.g., subway ~)	мапа (ж)	mápa
map (e.g., city ~)	план (м)	plan

souvenir, gift	сувенир (м)	suvénir
gift shop	продавница (ж) сувенира	pródavnica suveníra
to take pictures	сликати (пr)	slíkati
to have one's picture taken	сликати се	slíkati se

83. Shopping

to buy (purchase)	куповати (пr)	kupóvati
purchase	куповина (ж)	kupóvina
to go shopping	ићи у шопинг	ići u šóping
shopping	куповина (ж)	kupóvina

| to be open (ab. store) | бити отворен | bíti ótvoren |
| to be closed | бити затворен | bíti zátvoren |

footwear, shoes	обућа (ж)	óbuća
clothes, clothing	одећа (ж)	ódeća
cosmetics	козметика (ж)	kozmétika

food products	намирнице (мн)	námirnice
gift, present	поклон (м)	póklon
salesman	продавач (м)	prodávač
saleswoman	продавачица (ж)	prodaváčica
check out, cash desk	благајна (ж)	blágajna
mirror	огледало (с)	oglédalo
counter (store ~)	тезга (ж)	tézga
fitting room	кабина (ж)	kabína
to try on	пробати (пг)	próbati
to fit (ab. dress, etc.)	пристајати (нг)	prístajati
to like (I like ...)	свиђати се	svíđati se
price	цена (ж)	céna
price tag	ценовник (м)	cénovnik
to cost (vt)	коштати (нг)	kôštati
How much?	Колико?	Kolíko?
discount	попуст (м)	pópust
inexpensive (adj)	није скуп	níje skup
cheap (adj)	јефтин	jéftin
expensive (adj)	скуп	skup
It's expensive	То је скупо	To je skúpo
rental (n)	изнајмљивање (с)	iznajmljívanje
to rent (~ a tuxedo)	изнајмити (пг)	iznájmiti
credit (trade credit)	кредит (м)	krédit
on credit (adv)	на кредит	na krédit

84. Money

money	новац (м)	nóvac
currency exchange	размена (ж)	rázmena
exchange rate	курс (м)	kurs
ATM	банкомат (м)	bánkomat
coin	новчић (м)	nóvčić
dollar	долар (м)	dólar
euro	евро (м)	évro
lira	италијанска лира (ж)	itálijanska líra
Deutschmark	немачка марка (ж)	némačka márka
franc	франак (м)	frának
pound sterling	фунта (ж)	fúnta
yen	јен (м)	jen
debt	дуг (м)	dug
debtor	дужник (м)	dúžnik

| to lend (money) | посудити | posúditi |
| to borrow (vi, vt) | позајмити (пг) | pozájmiti |

bank	банка (ж)	bánka
account	рачун (м)	ráčun
to deposit (vt)	положити (пг)	polóžiti
to deposit into the account	положити на рачун	polóžiti na ráčun
to withdraw (vt)	подићи са рачуна	pódići sa račúna

credit card	кредитна картица (ж)	kréditna kártica
cash	готовина (ж)	gótovina
check	чек (м)	ček
to write a check	написати чек	napísati ček
checkbook	чековна књижица (ж)	čékovna knjížica

wallet	новчаник (м)	novčánik
change purse	новчаник (м)	novčánik
safe	сеф (м)	sef

heir	наследник (м)	následnik
inheritance	наследство (с)	následstvo
fortune (wealth)	богатство (с)	bogátstvo

lease	закуп, најам (м)	zákup, nájam
rent (money)	станарина (ж)	stánarina
to rent (sth from sb)	изнајмити (пг)	iznájmiti

price	цена (ж)	céna
cost	вредност (ж)	vrédnost
sum	износ (м)	íznos

to spend (vt)	трошити (пг)	tróšiti
expenses	трошкови (мн)	tróškovi
to economize (vi, vt)	штедети (нг, пг)	štédeti
economical	штедљив	štédljiv

to pay (vi, vt)	платити (нг, пг)	plátiti
payment	плаћање (с)	pláćanje
change (give the ~)	кусур (м)	kúsur

tax	порез (м)	pórez
fine	новчана казна (ж)	nóvčana kázna
to fine (vt)	кажњавати (пг)	kažnjávati

85. Post. Postal service

post office	пошта (ж)	póšta
mail (letters, etc.)	пошта (ж)	póšta
mailman	поштар (м)	póštar
opening hours	радно време (с)	rádno vréme

letter	писмо (c)	písmo
registered letter	препоручено писмо (c)	préporučeno písmo
postcard	разгледница (ж)	rázglednica
telegram	телеграм (м)	télegram
package (parcel)	пакет (м)	páket
money transfer	пренос (м) новца	prénos nóvca
to receive (vt)	примити (пг)	prímiti
to send (vt)	послати (пг)	póslati
sending	слање (c)	slánje
address	адреса (ж)	adrésa
ZIP code	поштански број (м)	póštanski broj
sender	пошиљалац (м)	póšiljalac
receiver	прималац (м)	prímalac
name (first name)	име (c)	íme
surname (last name)	презиме (c)	prézime
postage rate	тарифа (ж)	tarífa
standard (adj)	обичан	óbičan
economical (adj)	економичан	ekónomičan
weight	тежина (ж)	težína
to weigh (~ letters)	вагати (пг)	vágati
envelope	коверат (м)	kovérat
postage stamp	поштанска марка (ж)	poštanska márka
to stamp an envelope	лепити марку	lépiti márku

Dwelling. House. Home

86. House. Dwelling

house	кућа (ж)	kúća
at home (adv)	код куће	kod kúće
yard	двориште (с)	dvórište
fence (iron ~)	ограда (ж)	ógrada
brick (n)	опека, цигла (ж)	ópeka, cígla
brick (as adj)	циглени	cígleni
stone (n)	камен (м)	kámen
stone (as adj)	камени	kámeni
concrete (n)	бетон (м)	béton
concrete (as adj)	бетонски	bétonski
new (new-built)	нов	nov
old (adj)	стар	star
ramshackle	трошан	tróšan
modern (adj)	савремен	sávremen
multistory (adj)	вишеспратни	višesprátni
tall (~ building)	висок	vísok
floor, story	спрат (м)	sprat
single-story (adj)	једноспратан	jédnospratan
1st floor	приземље (с)	prízemlje
top floor	горњи спрат (м)	górnji sprat
roof	кров (м)	krov
chimney	димњак (м)	dímnjak
roof tiles	цреп (м)	crep
tiled (adj)	поплочан, од црепа	pópločan, od crépa
attic (storage place)	поткровље (с), таван (м)	pótkrovlje, távan
window	прозор (м)	prózor
glass	стакло (с)	stáklo
window ledge	прозорска даска (ж)	prózorska dáska
shutters	прозорски капци (мн)	prózorski kápci
wall	зид (м)	zid
balcony	балкон (м)	bálkon
downspout	олучна цев (ж)	ólučna cev
upstairs (to be ~)	на горњем спрату	na górnjem sprátu
to go upstairs	пењати се	pénjati se
to come down (the stairs)	спуштати се	spúštati se
to move (to new premises)	преселити се	preséliti se

87. House. Entrance. Lift

entrance	улаз (м)	úlaz
stairs (stairway)	степениште (с)	stépenište
steps	степенице (мн)	stépenice
banister	ограда (ж) за степенице	ógrada za stépenice
lobby (hotel ~)	хол (м)	hol
mailbox	поштанско сандуче (с)	póštansko sánduče
garbage can	канта (ж) за ђубре	kánta za đúbre
trash chute	одводна цев (ж) за ђубре	ódvodna cev za đúbre
elevator	лифт (м)	lift
freight elevator	теретни лифт (м)	téretni lift
elevator cage	кабина (ж)	kabína
to take the elevator	возити се лифтом	vóziti se líftom
apartment	стан (м)	stan
residents (~ of a building)	станари (мн)	stánari
neighbor (masc.)	комшија (м)	kómšija
neighbor (fem.)	комшиница (ж)	kómšinica
neighbors	комшије (мн)	kómšije

88. House. Electricity

electricity	струја (ж)	strúja
light bulb	сијалица (ж)	síjalica
switch	прекидач (м)	prekídač
fuse (plug fuse)	осигурач (м)	osigúrač
cable, wire (electric ~)	жица (ж), кабл (м)	žíca, kabl
wiring	електрична инсталација (ж)	eléktrična instalácija
electricity meter	струјомер (м)	strújomer
readings	стање (с)	stánje

89. House. Doors. Locks

door	врата (мн)	vráta
gate (vehicle ~)	капија (ж)	kápija
handle, doorknob	квака (ж)	kváka
to unlock (unbolt)	откључати (пг)	otkljúčati
to open (vt)	отварати (пг)	otvárati
to close (vt)	затварати (пг)	zatvárati
key	кључ (м)	ključ
bunch (of keys)	свежањ (м)	svéžanj

to creak (door, etc.)	шкрипати (нг)	škrípati
creak	шкрипа (ж)	škrípa
hinge (door ~)	шарка (ж)	šárka
doormat	отирач (м)	otírač

door lock	брава (ж)	bráva
keyhole	кључаоница (ж)	ključaónica
crossbar (sliding bar)	засун (м)	zásun
door latch	реза (ж)	réza
padlock	катанац (м)	kátanac

to ring (~ the door bell)	звонити (нг)	zvóniti
ringing (sound)	звоно (с)	zvóno
doorbell	звонце (с)	zvónce
doorbell button	дугме (с)	dúgme
knock (at the door)	куцање (с)	kúcanje
to knock (vi)	куцати (нг)	kúcati

code	код (м)	kod
combination lock	брава (ж) са шифром	bráva sa šífrom
intercom	интерфон (м)	ínterfon
number (on the door)	број (м)	broj
doorplate	плочица (ж) на вратима	plóčica na vrátima
peephole	шпијунка (ж)	špíjunka

90. Country house

village	село (с)	sélo
vegetable garden	повртњак (м)	póvrtnjak
fence	ограда (ж)	ógrada

| picket fence | дрвена ограда (ж) | dŕvena ógrada |
| wicket gate | капија (ж), капиџик (м) | kápija, kapídžik |

| granary | амбар (м) | ámbar |
| root cellar | подрум (м) | pódrum |

| shed (garden ~) | шупа (ж) | šúpa |
| water well | бунар (м) | búnar |

| stove (wood-fired ~) | пећ (ж) | peć |
| to stoke the stove | ложити пећ | lóžiti peć |

| firewood | дрва (мн) | dŕva |
| log (firewood) | цепаница (ж) | cépanica |

veranda	веранда (ж)	veránda
deck (terrace)	тераса (ж)	terása
stoop (front steps)	трем (м)	trem
swing (hanging seat)	љуљашка (ж)	ljúljaška

91. Villa. Mansion

country house	сеоска кућа (ж)	séoska kúća
villa (seaside ~)	вила (ж)	víla
wing (~ of a building)	крило (с)	krílo
garden	врт (м)	vŕt
park	парк (м)	park
conservatory (greenhouse)	стакленик (м)	stáklenik
to look after (garden, etc.)	припазити на ...	pripaziti na ...
swimming pool	базен (м)	bázen
gym (home gym)	теретана (ж)	teretána
tennis court	тениски терен (м)	téniski téren
home theater (room)	кућни биоскоп (м)	kúćni bíoskop
garage	гаража (ж)	garáža
private property	приватна својина (ж)	prívatna svójina
private land	приватни посед (м)	prívatni pósed
warning (caution)	упозорење (с)	upozorénje
warning sign	знак (м) упозорења	znak upozorénja
security	обезбеђење (с)	obezbeđénje
security guard	чувар (м)	čúvar
burglar alarm	аларм (м)	alárm

92. Castle. Palace

castle	замак (м)	zámak
palace	палата (ж)	paláta
fortress	тврђава (ж)	tvŕđava
wall (round castle)	зид (м)	zid
tower	кула (ж)	kúla
keep, donjon	главна кула (ж)	glávna kúla
portcullis	подизна решетка (ж)	pódizna réšetka
underground passage	подземни пролаз (м)	pódzemni prólaz
moat	шанац (м)	šánac
chain	ланац (м)	lánac
arrow loop	пушкарница (ж)	púškarnica
magnificent (adj)	велелепан	velelépan
majestic (adj)	величанствен	veličánstven
impregnable (adj)	неосвојив	neosvójiv
medieval (adj)	средњовековни	srednjovékovni

93. Apartment

apartment	стан (м)	stan
room	соба (ж)	sóba
bedroom	спаваћа соба (ж)	spávaća sóba
dining room	трпезарија (ж)	trpezárija
living room	дневна соба (ж)	dnévna sóba
study (home office)	кабинет (м)	kabínet
entry room	ходник (м)	hódnik
bathroom (room with a bath or shower)	купатило (с)	kupátilo
half bath	тоалет (м)	toálet
ceiling	плафон (м)	pláfon
floor	под (м)	pod
corner	угао, ћошак (м)	úgao, ćóšak

94. Apartment. Cleaning

to clean (vi, vt)	поспремати (нг)	posprémati
to put away (to stow)	склонити (нг)	sklóniti
dust	прашина (ж)	prášina
dusty (adj)	прашњав	prášnjav
to dust (vt)	брисати прашину	brísati prášinu
vacuum cleaner	усисивач (м)	usisívač
to vacuum (vt)	усисавати (нг, нг)	usisávati
to sweep (vi, vt)	мести (нг, нг)	mésti
sweepings	прљавштина (ж)	prljávština
order	ред (м)	red
disorder, mess	неред (м)	néred
mop	џогер (м)	džóger
dust cloth	крпа (ж)	kŕpa
short broom	метла (ж)	métla
dustpan	ђубровник (м)	đúbrovnik

95. Furniture. Interior

furniture	намештај (м)	námeštaj
table	сто (м)	sto
chair	столица (ж)	stólica
bed	кревет (м)	krévet
couch, sofa	диван (м)	dívan
armchair	фотеља (ж)	fotélja
bookcase	орман (м) за књиге	órman za knjíge

shelf	полица (ж)	pólica
wardrobe	орман (м)	órman
coat rack (wall-mounted ~)	вешалица (ж)	véšalica
coat stand	чивилук (м)	číviluk

| bureau, dresser | комода (ж) | komóda |
| coffee table | столиц́ (м) за кафу | stólic za kafu |

mirror	огледало (с)	oglédalo
carpet	тепих (м)	tépih
rug, small carpet	ћилимче (с)	ćilímče

fireplace	камин (м)	kámin
candle	свећа (ж)	svéća
candlestick	свећњак (м)	svéćnjak

drapes	завесе (мн)	závese
wallpaper	тапете (мн)	tapéte
blinds (jalousie)	ролетна (ж)	róletna

table lamp	стона лампа (ж)	stóna lámpa
wall lamp (sconce)	зидна светиљка (ж)	zídna svétiljka
floor lamp	подна лампа (ж)	pódna lámpa
chandelier	лустер (м)	lúster

leg (of chair, table)	нога (ж)	nóga
armrest	наслон (м) за руку	náslon za rúku
back (backrest)	наслон (м)	náslon
drawer	фиока (ж)	fióka

96. Bedding

bedclothes	постељина (ж)	posteljína
pillow	јастук (м)	jástuk
pillowcase	јастучница (ж)	jástučnica
duvet, comforter	јорган (м)	jórgan
sheet	чаршав (м)	čáršav
bedspread	покривач (м)	pokrívač

97. Kitchen

kitchen	кухиња (ж)	kúhinja
gas	гас (м)	gas
gas stove (range)	плински шпорет (м)	plínski špóret
electric stove	електрични шпорет (м)	eléktrični šporet
oven	рерна (ж)	rérna
microwave oven	микроталасна рерна (ж)	mikrotálasna rérna
refrigerator	фрижидер (м)	frížider

freezer	замрзивач (м)	zamrzívač
dishwasher	машина (ж) за прање судова	mašína za pránje súdova
meat grinder	млин (м) за месо	mlin za méso
juicer	соковник (м)	sókovnik
toaster	тостер (м)	tóster
mixer	миксер (м)	míkser
coffee machine	апарат (м) за кафу	apárat za káfu
coffee pot	лонче (с) за кафу	lónče za káfu
coffee grinder	млин (м) за кафу	mlin za káfu
kettle	кувало, чајник (м)	kúvalo, čájnik
teapot	чајник (м)	čájnik
lid	поклопац (м)	póklopac
tea strainer	цедиљка (ж)	cédiljka
spoon	кашика (ж)	kášika
teaspoon	кашичица (ж)	kášičica
soup spoon	супена кашика (ж)	súpena kášika
fork	виљушка (ж)	víljuška
knife	нож (м)	nož
tableware (dishes)	посуђе (с)	pósuđe
plate (dinner ~)	тањир (м)	tánjir
saucer	тацна (ж)	tácna
shot glass	чашица (ж)	čášica
glass (tumbler)	чаша (ж)	čáša
cup	шоља (ж)	šólja
sugar bowl	шећерница (ж)	šéćernica
salt shaker	сланик (м)	slánik
pepper shaker	биберница (ж)	bíbernica
butter dish	посуда (ж) за маслац	pósuda za máslac
stock pot (soup pot)	шерпа (ж), лонац (м)	šerpa, lónac
frying pan (skillet)	тигањ (м)	tíganj
ladle	кутлача (ж)	kútlača
colander	цедиљка (ж)	cédiljka
tray (serving ~)	послужавник (м)	poslúžavnik
bottle	боца, флаша (ж)	bóca, fláša
jar (glass)	тегла (ж)	tégla
can	лименка (ж)	límenka
bottle opener	отварач (м)	otvárač
can opener	отварач (м)	otvárač
corkscrew	вадичеп (м)	vádičep
filter	филтар (м)	fíltar
to filter (vt)	филтрирати (пг)	filtrírati

trash, garbage (food waste, etc.)	смеће, ђубре (c)	smeće, đúbre
trash can (kitchen ~)	канта (ж) за ђубре	kánta za đúbre

98. Bathroom

bathroom	купатило (c)	kupátilo
water	вода (ж)	vóda
faucet	славина (ж)	slávina
hot water	топла вода (ж)	tópla vóda
cold water	хладна вода (ж)	hládna vóda
toothpaste	паста (ж) за зубе	pásta za zúbe
to brush one's teeth	прати зубе	práti zúbe
toothbrush	четкица (ж) за зубе	čétkica za zúbe
to shave (vi)	бријати се	bríjati se
shaving foam	пена (ж) за бријање	péna za bríjanje
razor	бријач (м)	bríjač
to wash (one's hands, etc.)	прати (пг)	práti
to take a bath	купати се	kúpati se
shower	туш (м)	tuš
to take a shower	туширати се	tušírati se
bathtub	када (ж)	káda
toilet (toilet bowl)	ВЦ шоља (ж)	VC šólja
sink (washbasin)	лавабо (м)	lavábo
soap	сапун (м)	sápun
soap dish	кутија (ж) за сапун	kútija za sápun
sponge	сунђер (м)	súnđer
shampoo	шампон (м)	šámpon
towel	пешкир (м)	péškir
bathrobe	баде мантил (м)	báde mántil
laundry (laundering)	прање (c)	pránje
washing machine	веш машина (ж)	veš mašína
to do the laundry	прати веш	práti veš
laundry detergent	прашак (м) за веш	prášak za veš

99. Household appliances

TV set	телевизор (м)	televízor
tape recorder	касетофон (м)	kasetofon
VCR (video recorder)	видео рекордер (м)	vídeo rekórder
radio	радио (м)	rádio

player (CD, MP3, etc.)	плејер (м)	pléjer
video projector	видео пројектор (м)	vídeo projéktor
home movie theater	кућни биоскоп (м)	kúćni bíoskop
DVD player	ДВД плејер (м)	DVD plejer
amplifier	појачало (с)	pojáčalo
video game console	играћа конзола (ж)	ígraća konzóla
video camera	видеокамера (ж)	vídeokámera
camera (photo)	фотоапарат (м)	fotoapárat
digital camera	дигитални фотоапарат (м)	dígitalni fotoapárat
vacuum cleaner	усисивач (м)	usisívač
iron (e.g., steam ~)	пегла (ж)	pégla
ironing board	даска (ж) за пеглање	dáska za péglanje
telephone	телефон (м)	teléfon
cell phone	мобилни телефон (м)	móbilni teléfon
typewriter	писаћа машина (ж)	písaća mašína
sewing machine	шиваћа машина (ж)	šívaća mašína
microphone	микрофон (м)	míkrofon
headphones	слушалице (мн)	slúšalice
remote control (TV)	даљински управљач (м)	daljínski uprávljač
CD, compact disc	ЦД диск (м)	CD disk
cassette, tape	касета (ж)	kaséta
vinyl record	плоча (ж)	plóča

100. Repairs. Renovation

renovations	реновирање (с)	renovíranje
to renovate (vt)	реновирати (пг)	renovírati
to repair, to fix (vt)	поправљати (пг)	pópravljati
to put in order	доводити у ред	dovóditi u red
to redo (do again)	поново урадити	pónovo uráditi
paint	фарба (ж)	fárba
to paint (~ a wall)	бојити (пг)	bójiti
house painter	молер (м)	móler
paintbrush	четка (ж)	čétka
whitewash	белило (с), креч (м)	bélilo, kreč
to whitewash (vt)	белити (нг)	béliti
wallpaper	тапете (мн)	tapéte
to wallpaper (vt)	налепити тапете	nálepiti tapéte
varnish	лак (м)	lak
to varnish (vt)	лакирати	lakírati

101. Plumbing

water	вода (ж)	vóda
hot water	топла вода (ж)	tópla vóda
cold water	хладна вода (ж)	hládna vóda
faucet	славина (ж)	slávina
drop (of water)	кап (ж)	kap
to drip (vi)	капати (нг)	kápati
to leak (ab. pipe)	цурити (нг)	cúriti
leak (pipe ~)	цурење (с)	cúrenje
puddle	бара (ж)	bára
pipe	цев (ж)	cev
valve (e.g., ball ~)	вентил (м)	véntil
to be clogged up	зачепити се	začépiti se
tools	алати (мн)	álati
adjustable wrench	подешавајући кључ (м)	podešávajući ključ
to unscrew (lid, filter, etc.)	одврнути (пг)	odvŕnuti
to screw (tighten)	заврнути, стегнути (пг)	závrnuti, stégnuti
to unclog (vt)	отпушити (пг)	otpúšiti
plumber	водоинсталатер (м)	vodoinstaláter
basement	подрум (м)	pódrum
sewerage (system)	канализација (ж)	kanalizácija

102. Fire. Conflagration

fire (accident)	пожар (м)	póžar
flame	пламен (м)	plámen
spark	искра (ж)	ískra
smoke (from fire)	дим (м)	dim
torch (flaming stick)	бакља (ж)	báklja
campfire	логорска ватра (ж)	lógorska vátra
gas, gasoline	бензин (м)	bénzin
kerosene (type of fuel)	керозин (м)	kerózin
flammable (adj)	запаљив	zápaljiv
explosive (adj)	експлозиван	éksplozivan
NO SMOKING	ЗАБРАЊЕНО ПУШЕЊЕ	ZABRANJENO PUŠENJE
safety	безбедност (ж)	bezbédnost
danger	опасност (ж)	opásnost
dangerous (adj)	опасан	ópasan
to catch fire	запалити се	zapáliti se
explosion	експлозија (ж)	eksplózija
to set fire	запалити (пг)	zapáliti

arsonist	потпаљивач (м)	potpaljívač
arson	палеж (м), паљевина (ж)	pálež, páljevina
to blaze (vi)	пламтети (нг)	plámteti
to burn (be on fire)	горети (нг)	góreti
to burn down	изгорети (нг)	izgóreti
to call the fire department	позвати ватрогасце	pózvati vátrogasce
firefighter, fireman	ватрогасац (м)	vatrogásac
fire truck	ватрогасно возило (с)	vátrogasno vózilo
fire department	ватрогасна бригада (ж)	vátrogasna brigáda
fire truck ladder	ватрогасне мердевине (мн)	vátrogasne mérdevine
fire hose	црево (с)	crévo
fire extinguisher	противпожарни апарат (м)	protivpóžarni apárat
helmet	шлем (м)	šlem
siren	сирена (ж)	siréna
to cry (for help)	викати (нг)	víkati
to call for help	звати у помоћ	zváti u pómoć
rescuer	спасилац (м)	spásilac
to rescue (vt)	спасавати (пг)	spasávati
to arrive (vi)	пристићи (нг)	prístići
to extinguish (vt)	гасити (пг)	gásiti
water	вода (ж)	vóda
sand	песак (м)	pésak
ruins (destruction)	рушевине (мн)	rúševine
to collapse (building, etc.)	срушити се	srúšiti se
to fall down (vi)	срушити се	srúšiti se
to cave in (ceiling, floor)	срушити се	srúšiti se
piece of debris	крхотина (ж)	krhótina
ash	пепео (м)	pépeo
to suffocate (die)	загушити се	zagušiti se
to be killed (perish)	погинути (нг)	póginuti

HUMAN ACTIVITIES

Job. Business. Part 1

103. Office. Working in the office

office (company ~)	биро (c)	bíro
office (of director, etc.)	кабинет (м)	kabínet
reception desk	рецепција (ж)	recépcija
secretary	секретар (м)	sekrétar
secretary (fem.)	секретарица (ж)	sekretárica
director	директор (м)	dírektor
manager	менаџер (м)	ménadžer
accountant	књиговођа (м)	knjígovođa
employee	радник (м)	rádnik
furniture	намештај (м)	námeštaj
desk	сто (м)	sto
desk chair	столица (ж)	stólica
drawer unit	мобилна касета (ж)	móbilna kaseta
coat stand	чивилук (м)	číviluk
computer	рачунар (м)	račúnar
printer	штампач (м)	štámpač
fax machine	факс (м)	faks
photocopier	фотокопир (м)	fotokópir
paper	папир (м)	pápir
office supplies	канцеларијски прибор (м)	kancelárijski príbor
mouse pad	подлога (ж) за миша	pódloga za miša
sheet (of paper)	лист (м)	list
binder	фасцикла (ж)	fáscikla
catalog	каталог (м)	katálog
phone directory	телефонски именик (м)	teléfonski ímenik
documentation	документација (ж)	dokumentácija
brochure (e.g., 12 pages ~)	брошура (ж)	brošúra
leaflet (promotional ~)	летак (м)	létak
sample	узорак (м)	úzorak
training meeting	тренинг (м)	tréning
meeting (of managers)	састанак (м)	sástanak

lunch time	пауза (ж) за ручак	páuza za rúčak
to make a copy	направити копију	nápraviti kópiju
to make multiple copies	направити копије	nápraviti kópije
to receive a fax	примати факс	prímati faks
to send a fax	послати факс	póslati faks

to call (by phone)	позвати (пг)	pózvati
to answer (vt)	јавити се	jáviti se
to put through	повезати (пг)	povézati

to arrange, to set up	наместити (пг)	námestiti
to demonstrate (vt)	показати (пг)	pokázati
to be absent	одсуствовати (нг)	ódsustvovati
absence	пропуштање (с)	propúštanje

104. Business processes. Part 1

business	посао (м)	pósao
occupation	занимање (с)	zanímanje
firm	фирма (ж)	fírma
company	компанија (ж)	kompánija
corporation	корпорација (ж)	korporácija
enterprise	предузеће (с)	preduzéće
agency	агенција (ж)	agéncija

agreement (contract)	споразум (м)	spórazum
contract	уговор (м)	úgovor
deal	погодба (ж)	pógodba
order (to place an ~)	наруџбина (ж)	nárudžbina
terms (of the contract)	услов (м)	úslov

wholesale (adv)	на велико	na véliko
wholesale (adj)	на велико	na véliko
wholesale (n)	велепродаја (ж)	velepródaja
retail (adj)	малопродајни	malopródajni
retail (n)	малопродаја (ж)	malopródaja

competitor	конкурент (м)	konkúrent
competition	конкуренција (ж)	konkuréncija
to compete (vi)	конкурисати (пг)	konkúrisati

| partner (associate) | партнер (м) | pártner |
| partnership | партнерство (с) | pártnerstvo |

crisis	криза (ж)	kríza
bankruptcy	банкротство (с)	bankrótstvo
to go bankrupt	банкротирати (нг)	bankrotírati
difficulty	потешкоћа (ж)	poteškóća
problem	проблем (м)	próblem
catastrophe	катастрофа (ж)	katastrófa

economy	економика (ж)	ekonómika
economic (~ growth)	економски	ekónomski
economic recession	економски пад (м)	ekónomski pad

| goal (aim) | циљ (м) | cilj |
| task | задатак (м) | zadátak |

to trade (vi)	трговати (нг)	trgóvati
network (distribution ~)	мрежа (ж)	mréža
inventory (stock)	залихе (мн)	zálihe
range (assortment)	асортиман (м)	asortíman

leader (leading company)	вођа (м)	vóđa
large (~ company)	велик	vélik
monopoly	монопол (м)	mónopol

theory	теорија (ж)	téorija
practice	пракса (ж)	práksa
experience (in my ~)	искуство (с)	iskústvo
trend (tendency)	тенденција (ж)	tendéncija
development	развој (м)	rázvoj

105. Business processes. Part 2

| profit (foregone ~) | профит (м), добит (ж) | prófit, dóbit |
| profitable (~ deal) | пробитачан | próbitačan |

delegation (group)	делегација (ж)	delegácija
salary	плата, зарада (ж)	pláta, zárada
to correct (an error)	исправљати (нг)	íspravljati
business trip	службено путовање (с)	slúžbeno putovánje
commission	комисија (ж)	komísija

to control (vt)	контролисати (нг)	kontrólisati
conference	конференција (ж)	konferéncija
license	лиценца (ж)	licénca
reliable (~ partner)	поуздан	póuzdan

initiative (undertaking)	иницијатива (ж)	inicijatíva
norm (standard)	норма (ж)	nórma
circumstance	околност (ж)	okólnost
duty (of employee)	дужност (ж)	dúžnost

organization (company)	организација (ж)	organizácija
organization (process)	организација (ж)	organizácija
organized (adj)	организован	orgánizovan
cancellation	отказивање (с)	otkazívanje
to cancel (call off)	отказати (нг)	otkázati
report (official ~)	извештај (м)	ízveštaj
patent	патент (м)	pátent

| to patent (obtain patent) | патентирати (пг) | patentírati |
| to plan (vt) | планирати (пг) | planírati |

bonus (money)	бонус (м)	bónus
professional (adj)	професионалан	prófesionalan
procedure	поступак (м)	póstupak

to examine (contract, etc.)	размотрити (пг)	razmótriti
calculation	обрачун (м)	óbračun
reputation	репутација (ж)	reputácija
risk	ризик (м)	rízik

to manage, to run	руководити (пг)	rukovóditi
information (report)	информације (мн)	informácije
property	својина (ж)	svojína
union	савез (м)	sávez

life insurance	животно осигурање (с)	žívotno osiguránje
to insure (vt)	осигурати (пг)	osigúrati
insurance	осигурање (с)	osiguránje

auction (~ sale)	лицитација (ж)	licitácija
to notify (inform)	обавестити (пг)	obavéstiti
management (process)	управљање (с)	úpravljanje
service (~ industry)	услуга (ж)	úsluga

forum	форум (м)	fórum
to function (vi)	функционисати (нг)	funkcionísati
stage (phase)	етапа (ж)	etápa
legal (~ services)	правни	právni
lawyer (legal advisor)	правник (м)	právnik

106. Production. Works

plant	фабрика (ж)	fábrika
factory	фабрика (ж)	fábrika
workshop	радионица (ж)	radiónica
works, production site	производња (ж)	próizvodnja

industry (manufacturing)	индустрија (ж)	indústrija
industrial (adj)	индустријски	indústrijski
heavy industry	тешка индустрија (ж)	téška indústrija
light industry	лака индустрија (ж)	láka indústrija

| products | производ (м) | proízvod |
| to produce (vt) | производити (пг) | proizvóditi |

| raw materials | сировине (мн) | sírovine |
| foreman (construction ~) | бригадир, предрадник (м) | brigádir, prédradnik |

workers team (crew)	екипа (ж)	ekípa
worker	радник (м)	rádnik
working day	радни дан (м)	rádni dan
pause (rest break)	станка (ж)	stánka
meeting	састанак (м)	sástanak
to discuss (vt)	расправљати (пг)	ráspravljati
plan	план (м)	plan
to fulfill the plan	испунити план	íspuniti plan
rate of output	норма (ж) производње	nórma próizvodnje
quality	квалитет (м)	kvalítet
control (checking)	контрола (ж)	kontróla
quality control	контрола (ж) квалитета	kontróla kvalitéta
workplace safety	безбедност (ж) на раду	bezbédnost na rádu
discipline	дисциплина (ж)	disciplína
violation	кршење (с)	kŕšenje
(of safety rules, etc.)		
to violate (rules)	кршити (пг)	kŕšiti
strike	штрајк (м)	štrajk
striker	штрајкач (м)	štrájkač
to be on strike	штрајковати (нг)	štrájkovati
labor union	синдикат (м)	sindíkat
to invent (machine, etc.)	проналазити (пг)	pronálaziti
invention	проналазак, изум (м)	pronálazak, ízum
research	истраживање (с)	istražívanje
to improve (make better)	побољшати (пг)	pobóljšati
technology	технологија (ж)	tehnológija
technical drawing	цртеж (м)	cŕtež
load, cargo	терет (м)	téret
loader (person)	утоваривач (м)	utovarívač
to load (vehicle, etc.)	товарити (пг)	tóvariti
loading (process)	утовар (м)	útovar
to unload (vi, vt)	истоваривати (пг)	istovarívati
unloading	истовар (м)	ístovar
transportation	превоз (м)	prévoz
transportation company	транспортно предузеће (с)	tránsportno preduzéće
to transport (vt)	превозити (пг)	prevóziti
freight car	теретни вагон (м)	téretni vágon
tank (e.g., oil ~)	цистерна (ж)	cistérna
truck	камион (м)	kamíon
machine tool	строј (м), машина (ж) токарски	stroj, mašina токарски
mechanism	механизам (м)	mehanízam

industrial waste	отпад (м)	ótpad
packing (process)	паковање (с)	pákovanje
to pack (vt)	упаковати (пг)	upakóvati

107. Contract. Agreement

contract	уговор (м)	úgovor
agreement	споразум (м)	spórazum
addendum	прилог (м)	prílog

to sign a contract	склопити уговор	sklópiti úgovor
signature	потпис (м)	pótpis
to sign (vt)	потписати (пг)	potpísati
seal (stamp)	печат (м)	péčat

subject of the contract	предмет (м) уговора	prédmet úgovora
clause	тачка (ж)	táčka
parties (in contract)	стране (мн)	stráne
legal address	легална адреса (ж)	légalna adrésa

to violate the contract	прекршити уговор	prékršiti úgovor
commitment (obligation)	обавеза (ж)	óbaveza
responsibility	одговорност (ж)	odgovórnost
force majeure	виша сила (ж)	viša sila
dispute	спор (м)	spor
penalties	казне (мн)	kázne

108. Import & Export

import	увоз (м)	úvoz
importer	увозник (м)	úvoznik
to import (vt)	импортирати, увозити	importírati, uvóziti
import (as adj.)	увозни	úvozni

export (exportation)	извоз (м)	ízvoz
exporter	извозник (м)	ízvoznik
to export (vi, vt)	извозити (пг)	izvóziti
export (as adj.)	извозни	ízvozni

| goods (merchandise) | роба (ж) | róba |
| consignment, lot | партија (ж) | pártija |

weight	тежина (ж)	težína
volume	запремина (ж)	zápremina
cubic meter	кубни метар (м)	kúbni métar

| manufacturer | произвођач (м) | proizvóđač |
| transportation company | превозник (м) | prévoznik |

container	контејнер (м)	kontéjner
border	граница (ж)	gránica
customs	царина (ж)	cárina
customs duty	царинска дажбина (ж)	cárinska dážbina
customs officer	цариник (м)	cárinik
smuggling	шверц (м)	šverc
contraband (smuggled goods)	шверцована роба (ж)	švércovana róba

109. Finances

stock (share)	акција (ж)	ákcija
bond (certificate)	обвезница (ж)	óbveznica
promissory note	меница (ж)	ménica

| stock exchange | берза (ж) | bérza |
| stock price | цена (ж) акција | céna ákcija |

| to go down (become cheaper) | појефтинити (нг) | pojeftíniti |
| to go up (become more expensive) | поскупјети (нг) | poskúpjeti |

share	удео (м)	údeo
controlling interest	контролни пакет (м)	kóntrolni páket
investment	инвестиција (ж)	investícija
to invest (vt)	инвестирати (нг, пг)	investírati
percent	проценат, постотак (м)	prócenat, póstotak
interest (on investment)	камата (ж)	kámata

profit	профит (м)	prófit
profitable (adj)	профитабилан	prófitabilan
tax	порез (м)	pórez

currency (foreign ~)	валута (ж)	valúta
national (adj)	национални	nacionálni
exchange (currency ~)	размена (ж)	rázmena

| accountant | књиговођа (м) | knjígovođa |
| accounting | књиговодство (с) | knjigovódstvo |

bankruptcy	банкротство (с)	bankrótstvo
collapse, crash	крах (м)	krah
ruin	пропаст (ж)	própast
to be ruined (financially)	пропасти (нг)	própasti
inflation	инфлација (ж)	inflácija
devaluation	девалвација (ж)	devalvácija

| capital | капитал (м) | kapítal |
| income | приход (м) | príhod |

turnover	промет (м)	prómet
resources	ресурси (мн)	resúrsi
monetary resources	новац (м)	nóvac
overhead	режијски трошкови (мн)	réžijski tróškovi
to reduce (expenses)	смањити (пг)	smánjiti

110. Marketing

marketing	маркетинг (м)	márketing
market	тржиште (с)	tŕžište
market segment	тржишни сегмент (м)	tŕžišni ségment
product	производ (м)	proízvod
goods (merchandise)	роба (ж)	róba

brand	марка (ж), бренд (м)	márka, brend
trademark	заштитни знак (м)	záštitni znak
logotype	логотип, лого (м)	lógotip, lógo
logo	лого (м)	lógo

demand	потражња (ж)	pótražnja
supply	понуда (ж)	pónuda
need	потреба (ж)	pótreba
consumer	потрошач (м)	potróšač

analysis	анализа (ж)	analíza
to analyze (vt)	анализирати (пг)	analizírati
positioning	позиционирање (с)	pozicioníranje
to position (vt)	позиционирати (пг)	pozicionírati

price	цена (ж)	céna
pricing policy	политика (ж) цена	polítika céna
price formation	формирање (с) цена	formíranje céna

111. Advertising

advertising	реклама (ж)	rekláma
to advertise (vt)	рекламирати (пг)	reklamírati
budget	буџет (м)	búdžet

ad, advertisement	реклама (ж)	rekláma
TV advertising	телевизијска реклама (ж)	televízijska rekláma
radio advertising	радио оглашавање (с)	rádio oglašávanje
outdoor advertising	спољна реклама (ж)	spóljna rékláma

mass media	масовни медији (мн)	másovni médiji
periodical (n)	периодично издање (с)	períódično izdánje
image (public appearance)	имиц (м)	ímidž

| slogan | слоган (м) | slógan |
| motto (maxim) | девиза (ж) | devíza |

campaign	кампања (ж)	kampánja
advertising campaign	рекламна кампања (ж)	réklamna kampánja
target group	циљна група (ж)	cíljna grúpa

business card	визиткарта (ж)	vízitkarta
leaflet (promotional ~)	летак (м)	létak
brochure (e.g., 12 pages ~)	брошура (ж)	brošúra
pamphlet	брошура (ж)	brošúra
newsletter	билтен (м)	bílten

signboard (store sign, etc.)	натпис (м)	nátpis
poster	плакат (м)	plákat
billboard	билборд (м)	bílbord

112. Banking

| bank | банка (ж) | bánka |
| branch (of bank, etc.) | експозитура (ж) | ekspozitúra |

| bank clerk, consultant | банкарски службеник (м) | bánkarski slúžbenik |
| manager (director) | менаџер (м) | ménadžer |

bank account	рачун (м)	ráčun
account number	број (м) рачуна	broj račúna
checking account	текући рачун (м)	tékući ráčun
savings account	штедни рачун (м)	štédni ráčun

to open an account	отворити рачун	ótvoriti ráčun
to close the account	затворити рачун	zatvóriti ráčun
to deposit into the account	поставити на рачун	póstaviti na ráčun
to withdraw (vt)	подићи са рачуна	pódići sa račúna

deposit	депозит (м)	depózit
to make a deposit	ставити новац на рачун	stáviti nóvac na ráčun
wire transfer	трансфер (м) новца	tránsfer nóvca
to wire, to transfer	послати новац	póslati nóvac

| sum | износ (м) | íznos |
| How much? | Колико? | Kolíko? |

signature	потпис (м)	pótpis
to sign (vt)	потписати (nr)	potpísati
credit card	кредитна картица (ж)	kréditna kártica
code (PIN code)	код (м)	kod
credit card number	број (м) кредитне картице	broj kréditne kártice

ATM	банкомат (м)	bánkomat
check	чек (м)	ček
to write a check	написати чек	napísati ček
checkbook	чековна књижица (ж)	čékovna knjížica

loan (bank ~)	кредит (м)	krédit
to apply for a loan	затражити кредит	zátražiti krédit
to get a loan	узимати кредит	uzímati krédit
to give a loan	давати кредит	dávati krédit
guarantee	гаранција (ж)	garáncija

113. Telephone. Phone conversation

telephone	телефон (м)	teléfon
cell phone	мобилни телефон (м)	móbilni teléfon
answering machine	секретарица (ж)	sekretárica

| to call (by phone) | звати (нг) | zváti |
| phone call | позив (м) | póziv |

to dial a number	позвати број	pózvati broj
Hello!	Хало!	Hálo!
to ask (vt)	упитати (нг)	upítati
to answer (vi, vt)	јавити се	jáviti se

to hear (vt)	чути (нг, пг)	čúti
well (adv)	добро	dóbro
not well (adv)	лоше	loše
noises (interference)	сметње (мн)	smétnje
receiver	слушалица (ж)	slúšalica
to pick up (~ the phone)	подићи слушалицу	pódići slúšalicu
to hang up (~ the phone)	спустити слушалицу	spústiti slúšalicu

busy (engaged)	заузето	záuzeto
to ring (ab. phone)	звонити (нг)	zvóniti
telephone book	телефонски именик (м)	teléfonski ímenik

local (adj)	локалан	lókalan
local call	локални позив (м)	lókalni póziv
long distance (~ call)	међуградски	međugrádski
long-distance call	међуградски позив (м)	međugrádski póziv
international (adj)	међународни	međunárodni
international call	међународни позив (м)	međunárodni póziv

114. Cell phone

| cell phone | мобилни телефон (м) | móbilni teléfon |
| display | дисплеј (м) | displéj |

| button | дугме (c) | dúgme |
| SIM card | СИМ картица (ж) | SIM kártica |

battery	батерија (ж)	báterija
to be dead (battery)	испразнити се	isprázniti se
charger	пуњач (м)	púnjač

menu	мени (м)	méni
settings	подешавања (мн)	podešávanja
tune (melody)	мелодија (ж)	mélodija
to select (vt)	изабрати (пг)	izábrati

calculator	калкулатор (м)	kalkulátor
voice mail	говорна пошта (ж)	góvorna póšta
alarm clock	будилник (м)	búdilnik
contacts	контакти (мн)	kóntakti

| SMS (text message) | СМС порука (ж) | SMS póruka |
| subscriber | претплатник (м) | prétplatnik |

115. Stationery

| ballpoint pen | хемијска оловка (ж) | hémijska ólovka |
| fountain pen | наливперо (c) | nálivpero |

pencil	оловка (ж)	ólovka
highlighter	маркер (м)	márker
felt-tip pen	фломастер (м)	flómaster

| notepad | нотес (м) | nótes |
| agenda (diary) | роковник (м) | rokóvnik |

ruler	лењир (м)	lénjir
calculator	калкулатор (м)	kalkulátor
eraser	гумица (ж)	gúmica
thumbtack	пајснадла (ж)	pájsnadla
paper clip	спајалица (ж)	spájalica

glue	лепак (м)	lépak
stapler	хефталица (ж)	héftalica
hole punch	бушилица (ж) за папир	búšilica za pápir
pencil sharpener	резач (м)	rézač

116. Various kinds of documents

account (report)	извештај (м)	ízveštaj
agreement	споразум (м)	spórazum
application form	пријава (ж)	príjava

authentic (adj)	оригиналан	óriginalan
badge (identity tag)	беџ (м), ИД картица (ж)	bédž, ID kartica
business card	визиткарта (ж)	vízitkarta
certificate (~ of quality)	сертификат (м)	sertífikat
check (e.g., draw a ~)	чек (м)	ček
check (in restaurant)	рачун (м)	ráčun
constitution	устав (м)	ústav
contract (agreement)	уговор (м)	úgovor
copy	копија (ж)	kópija
copy (of contract, etc.)	примерак (м)	prímerak
customs declaration	царинска декларација (ж)	cárinska deklarácija
document	докуменат (м)	dokúmenat
driver's license	возачка дозвола (ж)	vózačka dózvola
addendum	прилог (м)	prílog
form	анкета (ж)	ankéta
ID card (e.g., FBI ~)	легитимација (ж)	legitimácija
inquiry (request)	упит (м)	úpit
invitation card	позивница (ж)	pózivnica
invoice	рачун (м), фактура (ж)	ráčun, faktúra
law	закон (м)	zákon
letter (mail)	писмо (с)	písmo
letterhead	меморандум (м)	memorándum
list (of names, etc.)	списак (м)	spísak
manuscript	рукопис (м)	rúkopis
newsletter	билтен (м)	bílten
note (short letter)	порука, белешка (ж)	póruka, béleška
pass (for worker, visitor)	пропусница (ж)	própusnica
passport	пасош (м)	pásoš
permit	дозвола (ж)	dózvola
résumé	резиме (м)	rezíme
debt note, IOU	признаница (ж)	príznanica
receipt (for purchase)	признаница (ж)	príznanica
sales slip, receipt	фискални рачун (м)	fískalni ráčun
report (mil.)	рапорт, извештај (м)	ráport, ízveštaj
to show (ID, etc.)	показивати (пг)	pokazívati
to sign (vt)	потписати (пг)	potpísati
signature	потпис (м)	pótpis
seal (stamp)	печат (м)	péčat
text	текст (м)	tekst
ticket (for entry)	улазница (ж)	úlaznica
to cross out	прецртати (пг)	précrtati
to fill out (~ a form)	попунити (пг)	pópuniti
waybill (shipping invoice)	товарни лист (м)	tóvarni list
will (testament)	тестамент (м)	téstament

117. Kinds of business

accounting services	рачуноводствене услуге (мн)	računovódstvene úsluge
advertising	реклама (ж)	rekláma
advertising agency	рекламна агенција (ж)	réklamna agéncija
air-conditioners	клима уређаји (мн)	klíma úređaji
airline	авио-компанија (ж)	ávio-kompánija
alcoholic beverages	алкохолна пића (мн)	álkoholna píća
antiques (antique dealers)	антиквитет (м)	antikvitét
art gallery (contemporary ~)	уметничка галерија (ж)	umétnička gálerija
audit services	ревизорске услуге (мн)	revízorske úsluge
banking industry	банкарство (с)	bankárstvo
bar	бар (м)	bar
beauty parlor	козметички салон (м)	kozmétički sálon
bookstore	књижара (ж)	knjížara
brewery	пивара (ж)	pívara
business center	пословни центар (м)	póslovni céntar
business school	пословна школа (ж)	póslovna škóla
casino	коцкарница (ж)	kóckarnica
construction	грађевинарство (с)	građevinárstvo
consulting	консалтинг (м)	konsálting
dental clinic	стоматологија (ж)	stomatológija
design	дизајн (м)	dízajn
drugstore, pharmacy	апотека (ж)	apotéka
dry cleaners	хемијско чишћење (с)	hémijsko číšćenje
employment agency	регрутна агенција (ж)	régrutna agéncija
financial services	финансијске услуге (мн)	finánsijske úsluge
food products	намирнице (мн)	námirnice
funeral home	погребно предузеће (с)	pógrebno preduzéće
furniture (e.g., house ~)	намештај (м)	námeštaj
clothing, garment	одећа (ж)	ódeća
hotel	хотел (м)	hótel
ice-cream	сладолед (м)	sládoled
industry (manufacturing)	индустрија (ж)	indústrija
insurance	осигурање (с)	osiguránje
Internet	интернет (м)	ínternet
investments (finance)	инвестиције (мн)	investícije
jeweler	златар (м)	zlátar
jewelry	накит (м)	nákit
laundry (shop)	перионица (ж)	periónica
legal advisor	правне услуге (мн)	právne úsluge

light industry	лака индустрија (ж)	láka indústrija
magazine	часопис (м)	čásopis
mail order selling	каталошка продаја (ж)	katáloška pródaja
medicine	медицина (ж)	medicína
movie theater	биоскоп (м)	bíoskop
museum	музеј (м)	múzej

news agency	новинска агенција (ж)	nóvinska agéncija
newspaper	новине (мн)	nóvine
nightclub	ноћни клуб (м)	nóćni klub

oil (petroleum)	нафта (ж)	náfta
courier services	курирска служба (ж)	kúrirska slúžba
pharmaceutics	фармацеутика (ж)	farmacéutika
printing (industry)	полиграфија (ж)	poligráfija
publishing house	издавачка кућа (ж)	izdávačka kúća

radio (~ station)	радио (м)	rádio
real estate	некретнина (ж)	nekretnína
restaurant	ресторан (м)	restóran

security company	агенција (ж) за обезбеђење	agéncija za obezbeđénje
sports	спорт (м)	sport
stock exchange	берза (ж)	bérza
store	продавница (ж)	pródavnica
supermarket	супермаркет (м)	supermárket
swimming pool (public ~)	базен (м)	bázen

tailor shop	кројачка радња (ж)	krójačka rádnja
television	телевизија (ж)	televízija
theater	позориште (с)	pózorište
trade (commerce)	трговина (ж)	trgóvina
transportation	превоз (м)	prévoz
travel	туризам (м)	turízam

veterinarian	ветеринар (м)	veterínar
warehouse	складиште (с)	skládište
waste collection	одношење (с) смећа	ódnošenje sméća

Job. Business. Part 2

exhibition, show	изложба (ж)	ízložba
trade show	трговински сајам (м)	trgóvinski sájam
participation	учешће (с)	účešće
to participate (vi)	учествовати (нг)	účestvovati
participant (exhibitor)	учесник (м)	účesnik
director	директор (м)	dírektor
organizers' office	дирекција (ж)	dirékcija
organizer	организатор (м)	organízator
to organize (vt)	организовати (нг)	orgánizovati
participation form	пријава (ж) за излагаче	príjava za izlagače
to fill out (vt)	попунити (нг)	pópuniti
details	детаљи (мн)	détalji
information	информација (ж)	informácija
price (cost, rate)	цена (ж)	céna
including	укључујући	uključujući
to include (vt)	укључивати (нг)	uključívati
to pay (vi, vt)	платити (нг, пг)	plátiti
registration fee	уписнина (ж)	upisnína
entrance	улаз (м)	úlaz
pavilion, hall	павиљон (м)	pavíljon
to register (vt)	регистровати (нг)	régistrovati
badge (identity tag)	беџ (м), ИД картица (ж)	bédž, ID kartica
booth, stand	штанд (м)	štand
to reserve, to book	резервисати (нг)	rezervísati
display case	витрина (ж)	vitrína
spotlight	рефлектор (м)	réflektor
design	дизајн (м)	dízajn
to place (put, set)	смештати (нг)	sméštati
to be placed	бити постављен	bíti póstavljen
distributor	дистрибутер (м)	distribúter
supplier	добављач (м)	dobávljač
to supply (vt)	снабдевати (нг)	snabdévati
country	земља (ж)	zémlja
foreign (adj)	стран	stran

product	производ (м)	proízvod
association	удружење (с)	udružénje
conference hall	сала (ж)	sála
	за конференције	za konferéncije
congress	конгрес (м)	kóngres
contest (competition)	конкурс (м)	kónkurs
visitor (attendee)	посетилац (м)	posétilac
to visit (attend)	посећивати (пг)	posećívati
customer	муштерија (м)	muštérija

119. Mass Media

newspaper	новине (мн)	nóvine
magazine	часопис (м)	čásopis
press (printed media)	штампа (ж)	štámpa
radio	радио (м)	rádio
radio station	радио станица (ж)	rádio stánica
television	телевизија (ж)	televízija
presenter, host	водитељ (м)	vóditelj
newscaster	спикер (м)	spíker
commentator	коментатор (м)	koméntator
journalist	новинар (м)	nóvinar
correspondent (reporter)	дописник (м)	dópisnik
press photographer	фоторепортер (м)	fotorepórter
reporter	репортер (м)	repórter
editor	уредник (м)	úrednik
editor-in-chief	главни уредник (м)	glávni úrednik
to subscribe (to …)	претплатити се	pretplátiti se
subscription	претплата (ж)	prétplata
subscriber	претплатник (м)	prétplatnik
to read (vi, vt)	читати (нг, пг)	čítati
reader	читалац (м)	čítalac
circulation (of newspaper)	тираж (м)	tíraž
monthly (adj)	месечни	mésečni
weekly (adj)	недељни	nédeljni
issue (edition)	број (м)	broj
new (~ issue)	нов	nov
headline	наслов (м)	náslov
short article	чланак (м)	člának
column (regular article)	рубрика (ж)	rúbrika
article	чланак (м)	člának
page	страна (ж)	strána
reportage, report	репортажа (ж)	reportáža

event (happening)	догађај (м)	dógađaj
sensation (news)	сензација (ж)	senzácija
scandal	скандал (м)	skándal
scandalous (adj)	скандалозан	skándalozan
great (~ scandal)	велики	véliki

show (e.g., cooking ~)	емисија (ж)	emísija
interview	интервју (м)	intérvju
live broadcast	директан пренос (м)	diréktan prénos
channel	канал (м)	kánal

120. Agriculture

agriculture	пољопривреда (ж)	poljoprívreda
peasant (masc.)	сељак (м)	séljak
peasant (fem.)	сељанка (ж)	séljanka
farmer	фармер (м)	fármer

| tractor (farm ~) | трактор (м) | tráktor |
| combine, harvester | комбајн (м) | kómbajn |

plow	плуг (м)	plug
to plow (vi, vt)	орати (пг)	órati
plowland	ораница (ж)	óranica
furrow (in field)	бразда (ж)	brázda

to sow (vi, vt)	сејати (нг, пг)	séjati
seeder	сејалица (ж)	séjalica
sowing (process)	сетва (ж)	sétva

| scythe | коса (ж) | kósa |
| to mow, to scythe | косити (пг) | kósiti |

| spade (tool) | лопата (ж) | lópata |
| to till (vt) | орати (пг) | órati |

hoe	мотика (ж)	mótika
to hoe, to weed	плевити (пг)	pléviti
weed (plant)	коров (м)	kórov

watering can	канта (ж) за заливање	kánta za zalívanje
to water (plants)	заливати (пг)	zalívati
watering (act)	заливање (с)	zalívanje

| pitchfork | виле (ж) | víle |
| rake | грабуље (мн) | grábulje |

fertilizer	ђубриво (с)	đúbrivo
to fertilize (vt)	ђубрити (пг)	đúbriti
manure (fertilizer)	балега (ж)	bálega

field	поље (с)	pólje
meadow	ливада (ж)	lívada
vegetable garden	повртњак (м)	póvrtnjak
orchard (e.g., apple ~)	воћњак (м)	vóćnjak

to graze (vt)	пасти (пг)	pásti
herder (herdsman)	пастир, чобан (м)	pástir, čóban
pasture	пашњак (м)	pášnjak

| cattle breeding | сточарство (с) | stočárstvo |
| sheep farming | овчарство (с) | ovčárstvo |

plantation	плантажа (ж)	plantáža
row (garden bed ~s)	гредица (ж)	grédica
hothouse	стакленик (м)	stáklenik

| drought (lack of rain) | суша (ж) | súša |
| dry (~ summer) | сушан | súšan |

grain	зрно (с)	zŕno
cereal crops	житарице (мн)	žitárice
to harvest, to gather	брати (пг)	bráti

miller (person)	млинар (м)	mlínar
mill (e.g., gristmill)	млин (м)	mlin
to grind (grain)	мљети (пг)	mljéti
flour	брашно (с)	brášno
straw	слама (ж)	sláma

121. Building. Building process

construction site	градилиште (с)	grádilište
to build (vt)	градити (пг)	gráditi
construction worker	грађевинар (м)	građevínar

project	пројекат (м)	projékat
architect	архитекта (м)	arhitékta
worker	радник (м)	rádnik

foundation (of a building)	темељ (м)	témelj
roof	кров (м)	krov
foundation pile	шип (м)	šip
wall	зид (м)	zid

| reinforcing bars | арматура (ж) | armatúra |
| scaffolding | скеле (мн) | skéle |

concrete	бетон (м)	béton
granite	гранит (м)	gránit
stone	камен (м)	kámen

brick	опека, цигла (ж)	ópeka, cígla
sand	песак (м)	pésak
cement	цемент (м)	cément
plaster (for walls)	малтер (м)	málter
to plaster (vt)	малтерисати (пг)	maltérisati
paint	фарба (ж)	fárba
to paint (~ a wall)	бојити (пг)	bójiti
barrel	буре (с)	búre

crane	дизалица (ж)	dízalica
to lift, to hoist (vt)	дизати (пг)	dízati
to lower (vt)	спуштати (пг)	spúštati

bulldozer	булдожер (м)	búldožer
excavator	багер (м)	báger
scoop, bucket	кашика (ж)	kášika
to dig (excavate)	копати (пг)	kópati
hard hat	шлем (м)	šlem

122. Science. Research. Scientists

science	наука (ж)	náuka
scientific (adj)	научни	náučni
scientist	научник (м)	náučnik
theory	теорија (ж)	téorija

axiom	аксиом (м)	aksíom
analysis	анализа (ж)	analíza
to analyze (vt)	анализирати (пг)	analizírati
argument (strong ~)	аргумент (м)	argúment
substance (matter)	материја, супстанца (ж)	máterija, supstánca

hypothesis	хипотеза (ж)	hipotéza
dilemma	дилема (ж)	diléma
dissertation	дисертација (ж)	disertácija
dogma	догма (ж)	dógma

doctrine	доктрина (ж)	doktrína
research	истраживање (с)	istraživanje
to research (vt)	истраживати (пг)	istraživati
tests (laboratory ~)	контрола (ж)	kontróla
laboratory	лабораторија (ж)	laboratórija

method	метода (ж)	metóda
molecule	молекул (м)	molékul
monitoring	мониторинг, надзор (м)	monitóring, nádzor
discovery (act, event)	откриће (с)	otkríće

| postulate | постулат (м) | postúlat |
| principle | принцип (м) | príncip |

forecast	прогноза (ж)	prognóza
to forecast (vt)	прогнозирати (пг)	prognozírati
synthesis	синтеза (ж)	sintéza
trend (tendency)	тенденција (ж)	tendéncija
theorem	теорема (ж)	teoréma
teachings	учење (с)	účenje
fact	чињеница (ж)	čínjenica
expedition	експедиција (ж)	ekspedícija
experiment	експеримент (м)	eksperíment
academician	академик (м)	akadémik
bachelor (e.g., ~ of Arts)	бакалавр (м)	bákalavr
doctor (PhD)	доктор (м)	dóktor
Associate Professor	доцент (м)	dócent
Master (e.g., ~ of Arts)	магистар (м)	magístar
professor	професор (м)	prófesor

Professions and occupations

job	посао (м)	pósao
staff (work force)	особље (с)	ósoblje
personnel	особље (с)	ósoblje
career	каријера (ж)	karijéra
prospects (chances)	изгледи (мн)	ízgledi
skills (mastery)	мајсторство (с)	májstorstvo
selection (screening)	одабирање (с)	odábiranje
employment agency	регрутна агенција (ж)	régrutna agéncija
résumé	резиме (м)	rezíme
job interview	разговор (м) за посао	rázgovor za pósao
vacancy, opening	слободно место (с)	slóbodno mésto
salary, pay	плата, зарада (ж)	pláta, zárada
fixed salary	фиксна зарада (ж)	fíksna zárada
pay, compensation	плата (ж)	pláta
position (job)	положај (м)	póložaj
duty (of employee)	дужност (ж)	dúžnost
range of duties	радни задаци (мн)	rádni zadáci
busy (I'm ~)	заузет	záuzet
to fire (dismiss)	отпустити (пг)	otpústiti
dismissal	отпуст (м)	ótpust
unemployment	незапосленост (ж)	nezáposlenost
unemployed (n)	незапослен (м)	nezáposlen
retirement	пензија (ж)	pénzija
to retire (from job)	отићи у пензију	ótići u pénziju

director	директор (м)	dírektor
manager (director)	менаџер (м)	ménadžer
boss	шеф (м)	šef
superior	шеф, начелник (м)	šef, náčelnik
superiors	руководство (с)	rúkovodstvo
president	председник (м)	prédsednik
chairman	председник (м)	prédsednik

deputy (substitute)	заменик (м)	zámenik
assistant	помоћник (м)	pomóćnik
secretary	секретар (м), секретарица (ж)	sekrétar, sekretárica
personal assistant	лични секретар (м)	líčni sekrétar

businessman	бизнисмен (м)	bíznismen
entrepreneur	предузетник (м)	preduzétnik
founder	оснивач (м)	osnívač
to found (vt)	основати (пг)	osnóvati

incorporator	оснивач (м)	osnívač
partner	партнер (м)	pártner
stockholder	акционар (м)	akciónar

millionaire	милионер (м)	milióner
billionaire	милијардер (м)	milijárder
owner, proprietor	власник (м)	vlásnik
landowner	земљопоседник (м)	zemljopósednik

client	клијент (м)	klíjent
regular client	стална муштерија (м)	stálna múšterija
buyer (customer)	купац (м)	kúpac
visitor	посетилац (м)	posétilac
professional (n)	професионалац (м)	profesionálac
expert	експерт (м)	ékspert
specialist	стручњак (м)	strúčnjak

| banker | банкар (м) | bánkar |
| broker | брокер (м) | bróker |

cashier, teller	благајник (м)	blágajnik
accountant	књиговођа (м)	knjígovođa
security guard	чувар (м)	čúvar

investor	инвеститор (м)	invéstitor
debtor	дужник (м)	dúžnik
creditor	зајмодавац, поверилац (м)	zajmodávac, povérilac
borrower	зајмопримац (м)	zajmoprímac

| importer | увозник (м) | úvoznik |
| exporter | извозник (м) | ízvoznik |

manufacturer	произвођач (м)	proizvóđač
distributor	дистрибутер (м)	distribúter
middleman	посредник (м)	pósrednik

consultant	саветодавац (м)	savetodávac
sales representative	представник (м)	prédstavnik
agent	агент (м)	ágent
insurance agent	агент (м) осигурања	ágent osiguránja

125. Service professions

cook	кувар (м)	kúvar
chef (kitchen chef)	главни кувар (м)	glávni kúvar
baker	пекар (м)	pékar
bartender	бармен (м)	bármen
waiter	конобар (м)	kónobar
waitress	конобарица (ж)	konobárica
lawyer, attorney	адвокат (м)	advókat
lawyer (legal expert)	правник (м)	právnik
notary public	јавни бележник (м)	jávni béležnik
electrician	електричар (м)	eléktričar
plumber	водоинсталатер (м)	vodoinstaláter
carpenter	столар (м)	stólar
masseur	масер (м)	máser
masseuse	масерка (ж)	máserka
doctor	лекар (м)	lékar
taxi driver	таксиста (м)	táksista
driver	возач (м)	vózač
delivery man	курир (м)	kúrir
chambermaid	собарица (ж)	sóbarica
security guard	чувар (м)	čúvar
flight attendant (fem.)	стјуардеса (ж)	stjuardésa
schoolteacher	учитељ (м)	účitelj
librarian	библиотекар (м)	bibliotékar
translator	преводилац (м)	prevódilac
interpreter	преводилац (м)	prevódilac
guide	водич (м)	vódič
hairdresser	фризер (м)	frízer
mailman	поштар (м)	póštar
salesman (store staff)	продавач (м)	prodávač
gardener	баштован (м)	báštovan
domestic servant	слуга (м)	slúga
maid (female servant)	слушкиња (ж)	slúškinja
cleaner (cleaning lady)	чистачица (ж)	čistáčica

126. Military professions and ranks

private	редов (м)	rédov
sergeant	наредник (м)	nárednik

| lieutenant | поручник (м) | póručnik |
| captain | капетан (м) | kapétan |

major	мајор (м)	májor
colonel	пуковник (м)	púkovnik
general	генерал (м)	генерал
marshal	маршал (м)	máršal
admiral	адмирал (м)	admíral

military (n)	војно лице (с)	vójno líce
soldier	војник (м)	vójnik
officer	официр (м)	ofícir
commander	командант (м)	komándant

border guard	граничар (м)	gráničar
radio operator	радио оператер (м)	rádio operáter
scout (searcher)	извиђач (м)	izvíđač
pioneer (sapper)	деминер (м)	demíner
marksman	стрелац (м)	strélac
navigator	навигатор (м)	navígator

127. Officials. Priests

| king | краљ (м) | kralj |
| queen | краљица (ж) | králjica |

| prince | принц (м) | princ |
| princess | принцеза (ж) | princéza |

| czar | цар (м) | car |
| czarina | царица (ж) | cárica |

president	председник (м)	prédsednik
Secretary (minister)	министар (м)	mínistar
prime minister	премијер (м)	prémijer
senator	сенатор (м)	sénator

diplomat	дипломат (м)	diplómat
consul	конзул (м)	kónzul
ambassador	амбасадор (м)	ambásador
counselor (diplomatic officer)	саветник (м)	sávetnik

official, functionary (civil servant)	чиновник (м)	činóvnik
prefect	префект (м)	préfekt
mayor	градоначелник (м)	gradonáčelnik
judge	судија (м)	súdija
prosecutor (e.g., district attorney)	тужилац (м)	túžilac

missionary	мисионар (м)	misiónar
monk	монах (м)	mónah
abbot	опат (м)	ópat
rabbi	рабин (м)	rábin
vizier	везир (м)	vézir
shah	шах (м)	šah
sheikh	шеик (м)	šéik

128. Agricultural professions

beekeeper	пчелар (м)	pčélar
herder, shepherd	пастир, чобан (м)	pástir, čóban
agronomist	агроном (м)	agrónom
cattle breeder	сточар (м)	stóčar
veterinarian	ветеринар (м)	veterínar
farmer	фармер (м)	fármer
winemaker	винар (м)	vínar
zoologist	зоолог (м)	zoólog
cowboy	каубој (м)	káuboj

129. Art professions

actor	глумац (м)	glúmac
actress	глумица (ж)	glúmica
singer (masc.)	певач (м)	pévač
singer (fem.)	певачица (ж)	peváčica
dancer (masc.)	плесач (м)	plésač
dancer (fem.)	плесачица (ж)	plesáčica
performer (masc.)	Уметник (м)	Úmetnik
performer (fem.)	Уметница (ж)	Úmetnica
musician	музичар (м)	múzičar
pianist	пијаниста (м)	pijanísta
guitar player	гитариста (м)	gitárista
conductor (orchestra ~)	диригент (м)	dírigent
composer	композитор (м)	kompózitor
impresario	импресарио (м)	impresário
film director	редитељ (м)	réditelj
producer	продуцент (м)	prodúcent
scriptwriter	сценариста (м)	scenárista
critic	критичар (м)	krítičar

writer	писац (м)	písac
poet	песник (м)	pésnik
sculptor	вајар (м)	vájar
artist (painter)	сликар (м)	slíkar

juggler	жонглер (м)	žóngler
clown	кловн (м)	klovn
acrobat	акробата (м)	akróbata
magician	мађионичар (м)	mađióničar

130. Various professions

doctor	лекар (м)	lékar
nurse	медицинска сестра (ж)	médicinska séstra
psychiatrist	психијатар (м)	psihijátar
dentist	стоматолог (м)	stomatólog
surgeon	хирург (м)	hírurg

astronaut	астронаут (м)	astronáut
astronomer	астроном (м)	astrónom
pilot	пилот (м)	pílot

driver (of taxi, etc.)	возач (м)	vózač
engineer (train driver)	машиновођа (м)	mašinóvođa
mechanic	механичар (м)	meháničar

miner	рудар (м)	rúdar
worker	радник (м)	rádnik
locksmith	бравар (м)	brávar
joiner (carpenter)	столар (м)	stólar
turner (lathe operator)	стругар (м)	strúgar
construction worker	грађевинар (м)	građevínar
welder	варилац (м)	várilac

professor (title)	професор (м)	prófesor
architect	архитекта (м)	arhitékta
historian	историчар (м)	istóričar
scientist	научник (м)	náučnik
physicist	физичар (м)	fízičar
chemist (scientist)	хемичар (м)	hémičar

archeologist	археолог (м)	arheólog
geologist	геолог (м)	geólog
researcher (scientist)	истраживач (м)	istražívač

babysitter	дадиља (ж)	dádilja
teacher, educator	учитељ, наставник (м)	účitelj, nástavnik

editor	уредник (м)	úrednik
editor-in-chief	главни уредник (м)	glávni úrednik

| correspondent | дописник (м) | dópisnik |
| typist (fem.) | дактилографкиња (ж) | daktilógrafkinja |

designer	дизајнер (м)	dizájner
computer expert	компјутерски стручњак (м)	kompjúterski strúčnjak
programmer	програмер (м)	prográmer
engineer (designer)	инжењер (м)	inžénjer

sailor	поморац, морнар (м)	pómorac, mórnar
seaman	морнар (м)	mórnar
rescuer	спасилац (м)	spásilac

fireman	ватрогасац (м)	vatrogásac
police officer	полицајац (м)	policájac
watchman	чувар (м)	čúvar
detective	детектив (м)	detéktiv

customs officer	цариник (м)	cárinik
bodyguard	телохранитељ (м)	telohránitelj
prison guard	чувар (м)	čúvar
inspector	инспектор (м)	ínspektor

sportsman	спортиста (м)	sportísta
trainer, coach	тренер (м)	tréner
butcher	касапин (м)	kásapin
cobbler (shoe repairer)	обућар (м)	óbućar
merchant	трговац (м)	tŕgovac
loader (person)	утоваривач (м)	utovarívač

| fashion designer | модни креатор (м) | módni kreátor |
| model (fem.) | манекенка (ж) | manékenka |

131. Occupations. Social status

| schoolboy | ђак (м) | đak |
| student (college ~) | студент (м) | stúdent |

philosopher	филозоф (м)	filózof
economist	економиста (м)	ekonómista
inventor	проналазач (м)	pronalázač

unemployed (n)	незапослен (м)	nezáposlen
retiree	пензионер (м)	penzióner
spy, secret agent	шпијун (м)	špíjun

prisoner	затвореник (м)	zatvorénik
striker	штрајкач (м)	štrájkač
bureaucrat	бирократа (м)	birókrata
traveler (globetrotter)	путник (м)	pútnik

gay, homosexual (n)	хомосексуалац (м)	homoseksuálac
hacker	хакер (м)	háker
hippie	хипији (мн)	hípiji

bandit	бандит (м)	bándit
hit man, killer	плаћени убица (м)	pláćeni úbica
drug addict	наркоман (м)	nárkoman
drug dealer	продавац (м) дроге	prodávac dróge
prostitute (fem.)	проститутка (ж)	próstitutka
pimp	макро (м)	mákro

sorcerer	чаробњак (м)	čaróbnjak
sorceress (evil ~)	чаробница (ж)	čárobnica
pirate	гусар (м)	gúsar
slave	роб (м)	rob
samurai	самурај (м)	samúraj
savage (primitive)	дивљак (м)	dívljak

Sports

sportsman	спортиста (м)	sportísta
kind of sports	врста (ж) спорта	vŕsta spórta
basketball	кошарка (ж)	kóšarka
basketball player	кошаркаш (м)	košárkaš
baseball	бејзбол (м)	béjzbol
baseball player	играч бејзбола (м)	ígrač béjzbola
soccer	фудбал (м)	fúdbal
soccer player	фудбалер (м)	fudbáler
goalkeeper	голман (м)	gólman
hockey	хокеј (м)	hókej
hockey player	хокејаш (м)	hokéjaš
volleyball	одбојка (ж)	ódbojka
volleyball player	одбојкаш (м)	odbójkaš
boxing	бокс (м)	boks
boxer	боксер (м)	bókser
wrestling	рвање (с), борба (ж)	rvánje, bórba
wrestler	рвач (м)	ŕvač
karate	карате (м)	karáte
karate fighter	каратиста (м)	karátista
judo	џудо (с)	džúdo
judo athlete	џудиста (м)	džudísta
tennis	тенис (м)	ténis
tennis player	тенисер (м)	téniser
swimming	пливање (с)	plívanje
swimmer	пливач (м)	plívač
fencing	мачевање (с)	mačévanje
fencer	мачевалац (м)	mačévalac
chess	шах (м)	šah
chess player	шахиста (м)	šahísta

| alpinism | планинарење (с) | planinárenje |
| alpinist | планинар (м) | planínar |

| running | трчање (с) | tŕčanje |
| runner | тркач (м) | tŕkač |

| athletics | лака атлетика (ж) | láka atlétika |
| athlete | атлетичар (м) | atlétičar |

| horseback riding | јахање (с) | jáhanje |
| horse rider | јахач (м) | jáhač |

figure skating	уметничко клизање (с)	umétničko klízanje
figure skater (masc.)	Клизач (м)	Klízač
figure skater (fem.)	клизачица (ж)	klizáčica

powerlifting	дизање (с) тегова	dízanje tégova
powerlifter	дизач (м) тегова	dízač tégova
car racing	аутомобилске трке (мн)	automóbilske tŕke
racer (driver)	возач (м)	vózač

| cycling | бициклизам (м) | biciklízam |
| cyclist | бициклиста (м) | bicíklista |

broad jump	скок (м) у даљ	skok u dalj
pole vault	скок (м) с мотком	skok s mótkom
jumper	скакач (м)	skákač

133. Kinds of sports. Miscellaneous

football	амерички фудбал (м)	américki fúdbal
badminton	бадминтон (м)	bádminton
biathlon	биатлон (м)	bíatlon
billiards	билијар (м)	bilíjar

bobsled	боб (м)	bob
bodybuilding	бодибилдинг (м)	bódibilding
water polo	ватерполо (м)	váterpolo
handball	рукомет (м)	rúkomet
golf	голф (м)	golf
rowing, crew	веслање (с)	véslanje
scuba diving	роњење (с)	rónjenje
cross-country skiing	скијашко трчање (с)	skíjaško tŕčanje
table tennis (ping-pong)	стони тенис (м)	stóni ténis

sailing	једрење (с)	jédrenje
rally racing	рели (м)	réli
rugby	рагби (м)	rágbi
snowboarding	сноуборд (м)	snóubord
archery	стреличарство (с)	stréličarstvo

134. Gym

barbell	шипка (ж) за тегове	šípka za tégove
dumbbells	бучице (мн)	búčice
training machine	справа (ж) за везбање	správa za vézbanje
exercise bicycle	собни бицикл (м)	sóbni bicíkl
treadmill	тркачка стаза (ж)	tŕkačka stáza
horizontal bar	вратило (с)	vrátilo
parallel bars	разбој (м)	rázboj
vault (vaulting horse)	коњ (м)	konj
mat (exercise ~)	струњача (ж)	strúnjača
jump rope	вијача (ж), уже (с)	víjača, úže
aerobics	аеробик (м)	aeróbik
yoga	јога (ж)	jóga

135. Hockey

hockey	хокеј (м)	hókej
hockey player	хокејаш (м)	hokéjaš
to play hockey	играти хокеј	ígrati hókej
ice	лед (м)	led
puck	пак (м)	pak
hockey stick	палица (ж)	pálica
ice skates	клизаљке (мн)	klízaljke
board (ice hockey rink ~)	ограда (ж)	ógrada
shot	хитац (м)	hítac
goaltender	голман (м)	gólman
goal (score)	гол (м)	gol
to score a goal	постићи гол	póstići gol
period	трећина (ж)	trećína
second period	друга трећина	drúga trećína
substitutes bench	резервна клупа (ж)	rézervna klúpa

136. Soccer

soccer	фудбал (м)	fúdbal
soccer player	фудбалер (м)	fudbáler
to play soccer	играти фудбал	ígrati fúdbal
major league	виша лига (ж)	víša líga
soccer club	фудбалски клуб (м)	fúdbalski klub

| coach | тренер (м) | tréner |
| owner, proprietor | власник (м) | vlásnik |

team	екипа (ж)	ekípa
team captain	капитен (м) екипе	kapíten ekípe
player	играч (м)	ígrač
substitute	резервни играч (м)	rézervni ígrač

forward	нападач (м)	napádač
center forward	центарфор (м)	céntarfor
scorer	стрелац (м)	strélac
defender, back	играч (м) одбране	ígrač odbrane
midfielder, halfback	везни играч (м)	vézni ígrač

match	меч (м)	meč
to meet (vi, vt)	сусрести се	súsresti se
final	финале (с)	finále
semi-final	полуфинале (м)	polufinále
championship	првенство (с)	prvénstvo

period, half	полувреме (с)	póluvreme
first period	прво полувреме (с)	pŕvo póluvreme
half-time	одмор (м)	ódmor

goal	гол (м)	gol
goalkeeper	голман (м)	gólman
goalpost	статива (ж)	statíva
crossbar	пречка (ж)	préčka
net	мрежа (ж)	mréža
to concede a goal	примити гол	prímiti gol

ball	лопта (ж)	lópta
pass	пас (м)	pas
kick	ударац (м)	údarac
to kick (~ the ball)	шутнути (пг)	šútnuti
free kick (direct ~)	казнени ударац (м)	kázneni údarac
corner kick	корнер (м)	kórner

attack	напад (м)	nápad
counterattack	контранапад (м)	kontranápad
combination	комбинација (ж)	kombinácija

referee	судија (м)	súdija
to blow the whistle	звиждати (нг)	zvíždati
whistle (sound)	звиждаљка (ж)	zvíždaljka
foul, misconduct	прекршај (м)	prékršaj
to commit a foul	прекршити (пг)	prekršiti
to send off	одстранити с терена	ódstraniti s teréna

yellow card	жути картон (м)	žúti kárton
red card	црвени картон (м)	crvéni kárton
disqualification	дисквалификација (ж)	diskvalifikácija

to disqualify (vt)	дисквалификовати (пг)	diskvalifikóvati
penalty kick	пенал (м)	pénal
wall	живи зид (м)	žívi zid
to score (vi, vt)	забити (пг)	zábiti
goal (score)	гол (м)	gol
to score a goal	постићи гол	póstići gol
substitution	измена (ж)	ízmena
to replace (a player)	заменити (пг)	zaméniti
rules	правила (мн)	právila
tactics	тактика (ж)	táktika
stadium	стадион (м)	stádion
stand (bleachers)	трибина (ж)	tríbina
fan, supporter	навијач (м)	navíjač
to shout (vi)	викати (нг)	víkati
scoreboard	семафор (м)	sémafor
score	резултат (м)	rezúltat
defeat	пораз (м)	póraz
to lose (not win)	изгубити (нг, пг)	izgúbiti
tie	нерешена игра (ж)	neréšena ígra
to tie (vi)	одиграти нерешено	ódigrati nérešeno
victory	победа (ж)	póbeda
to win (vi, vt)	победити (нг)	pobéditi
champion	шампион (м)	šampíon
best (adj)	најбољи	najbólji
to congratulate (vt)	честитати (пг)	čestítati
commentator	коментатор (м)	koméntator
to commentate (vt)	коментарисати (пг)	komentárisati
broadcast	емисија (ж)	emísija

137. Alpine skiing

skis	скије (мн)	skíje
to ski (vi)	скијати (нг)	skíjati
mountain-ski resort	скијалиште (с)	skíjalište
ski lift	ски лифт (м)	ski lift
ski poles	штапови (мн)	štápovi
slope	нагиб (м)	nágib
slalom	слалом (м)	slálom

138. Tennis. Golf

golf	голф (м)	golf
golf club	голф клуб (м)	golf klub

golfer	играч (м) голфа	ígrač gólfa
hole	рупа (ж)	rúpa
club	палица (ж)	pálica
golf trolley	колица (мн) за палице	kolíca za pálice

tennis	тенис (м)	ténis
tennis court	тениски терен (м)	téniski téren
serve	сервис (м)	sérvis
to serve (vt)	сервирати (пг)	servírati
racket	рекет (м)	réket
net	мрежа (ж)	mréža
ball	лоптица (ж)	lóptica

139. Chess

chess	шах (м)	šah
chessmen	шаховске фигуре (мн)	šáhovske figúre
chess player	шахиста (м)	šahísta
chessboard	шаховска табла (ж)	šáhovska tábla
chessman	фигура (ж)	figúra

| White (white pieces) | беле фигуре (мн) | béle figúre |
| Black (black pieces) | црне (мн) | cŕne |

pawn	пешак, пион (м)	péšak, píon
bishop	ловац (м)	lóvac
knight	коњ (м)	konj
rook	топ (м)	top
queen	краљица (ж)	králjica
king	краљ (м)	kralj

move	потез (м)	pótez
to move (vi, vt)	повлачити потез	povláčiti pótez
to sacrifice (vt)	жртвовати (пг)	žŕtvovati
castling	рокада (ж)	rokáda
check	шах (м)	šah
checkmate	мат (м)	mat

chess tournament	шаховски турнир (м)	šáhovski túrnir
Grand Master	велемајстор (м)	velemájstor
combination	комбинација (ж)	kombinácija
game (in chess)	партија (ж)	pártija
checkers	даме (мн)	dáme

140. Boxing

| boxing | бокс (м) | boks |
| fight (bout) | бокс-меч (м) | boks-meč |

| boxing match | двобој (м) | dvóboj |
| round (in boxing) | рунда (ж) | rúnda |

| ring | ринг (м) | ring |
| gong | гонг (м) | gong |

punch	ударац (м)	údarac
knockdown	нокдаун (м)	nokdáun
knockout	нокаут (м)	nokáut
to knock out	нокаутирати (пг)	nokautírati

| boxing glove | боксерска рукавица (ж) | bókserska rukávica |
| referee | судија (м) | súdija |

lightweight	лака категорија (ж)	láka kategórija
middleweight	средња категорија (ж)	srédnja kategórija
heavyweight	тешка категорија (ж)	téška kategórija

141. Sports. Miscellaneous

Olympic Games	Олимпијске игре (мн)	Olímpijske ígre
winner	победник (м)	póbednik
to be winning	побеђивати (нг)	pobeđívati
to win (vi)	победити (нг), добити (пг)	pobédити, dóbiti

| leader | лидер (м) | líder |
| to lead (vi) | бити у вођству | bíti u vóđstvu |

first place	прво место (с)	pŕvo mésto
second place	друго место (с)	drúgo mésto
third place	треће место (с)	tréće mésto

medal	медаља (ж)	médalja
trophy	трофеј (м)	trófej
prize cup (trophy)	куп (м)	kup
prize (in game)	награда (ж)	nágrada
main prize	главна награда (ж)	glávna nágrada

| record | рекорд (м) | rékord |
| to set a record | поставити рекорд | póstaviti rékord |

| final | финале (с) | finále |
| final (adj) | финални | fínalni |

| champion | шампион (м) | šampíon |
| championship | првенство (с) | prvénstvo |

stadium	стадион (м)	stádion
stand (bleachers)	трибина (ж)	tríbina
fan, supporter	навијач (м)	navíjač

opponent, rival	противник (м)	prótivnik
start (start line)	старт (м)	start
finish line	циљ (м)	cilj
defeat	пораз (м)	póraz
to lose (not win)	изгубити (нг, пг)	izgúbiti
referee	судија (м)	súdija
jury (judges)	жири (м)	žíri
score	резултат (м)	rezúltat
tie	нерешена игра (ж)	neréšena ígra
to tie (vi)	одиграти нерешено	ódigrati nérešeno
point	бод (м)	bod
result (final score)	резултат (м)	rezúltat
period	период (м)	períod
half-time	одмор (м)	ódmor
doping	допинг (м)	dóping
to penalize (vt)	кажњавати (пг)	kažnjávati
to disqualify (vt)	дисквалификовати (пг)	diskvalifikóvati
apparatus	справа (ж)	správa
javelin	копље (с)	kóplje
shot (metal ball)	кугла (ж)	kúgla
ball (snooker, etc.)	кугла (ж)	kúgla
aim (target)	циљ (м)	cilj
target	мета (ж)	méta
to shoot (vi)	пуцати (нг)	púcati
accurate (~ shot)	тачан	táčan
trainer, coach	тренер (м)	tréner
to train (sb)	тренирати (пг)	trenírati
to train (vi)	тренирати (нг)	trenírati
training	тренинг (м),	tréning,
	вежбање (с)	véžbanje
gym	теретана (ж)	teretána
exercise (physical)	вежба (ж)	véžba
warm-up (athlete ~)	загревање (с)	zágrevanje

Education

school	школа (ж)	škóla
principal (headmaster)	директор (м)	dírektor
pupil (boy)	ученик (м)	účenik
pupil (girl)	ученица (ж)	účenica
schoolboy	школарац, ђак (м)	škólarac, đak
schoolgirl	школарка, ђак (ж)	škólarka, đak
to teach (sb)	учити (пг)	účiti
to learn (language, etc.)	учити (пг)	účiti
to learn by heart	учити напамет	účiti nápamet
to learn (~ to count, etc.)	учити (нг)	účiti
to be in school	ходати у школу	hódati u škólu
to go to school	ићи у школу	íći u škólu
alphabet	азбука, абецеда (ж)	ázbuka, abecéda
subject (at school)	предмет (м)	prédmet
classroom	учионица (ж)	učiónica
lesson	час (м)	čas
recess	одмор (м)	ódmor
school bell	звоно (с)	zvóno
school desk	клупа (ж)	klúpa
chalkboard	школска табла (ж)	škólska tábla
grade	оцена (ж)	ócena
good grade	добра оцена (ж)	dóbra ócena
bad grade	лоша оцена (ж)	lóša ócena
to give a grade	давати оцену	dávati ócenu
mistake, error	грешка (ж)	gréška
to make mistakes	правити грешке	práviti gréške
to correct (an error)	исправљати (пг)	íspravljati
cheat sheet	пушкица (ж)	púškica
homework	домаћи задатак (м)	dómaći zadátak
exercise (in education)	вежба (ж)	véžba
to be present	присуствовати (нг)	prísustvovati
to be absent	одсуствовати (нг)	ódsustvovati
to miss school	пропуштати школу	propúštati škólu

to punish (vt)	кажњавати (пг)	kažnjávati
punishment	казна (ж)	kázna
conduct (behavior)	понашање (с)	ponášanje

report card	ђачка књижица (ж)	đáčka knjížica
pencil	оловка (ж)	ólovka
eraser	гумица (ж)	gúmica
chalk	креда (ж)	kréda
pencil case	перница (ж)	pérnica

schoolbag	торба (ж)	tórba
pen	оловка (ж)	ólovka
school notebook	свеска (ж)	svéska
textbook	уџбеник (м)	údžbenik
drafting compass	шестар (м)	šéstar

to make technical drawings	цртати (нг, пг)	cŕtati
technical drawing	цртеж (м)	cŕtež

poem	песма (ж)	pésma
by heart (adv)	напамет	nápamet
to learn by heart	учити напамет	účiti nápamet

school vacation	распуст (м)	ráspust
to be on vacation	бити на распусту	bíti na ráspustu
to spend one's vacation	провести распуст	próvesti ráspust

test (written math ~)	контролни рад (м)	kóntrolni rad
essay (composition)	састав (м)	sástav
dictation	диктат (м)	díktat
exam (examination)	испит (м)	íspit
to take an exam	полагати испит	polágati íspit
experiment (e.g., chemistry ~)	експеримент (м)	eksperíment

143. College. University

academy	академија (ж)	akadémija
university	универзитет (м)	univerzitét
faculty (e.g., ~ of Medicine)	факултет (м)	fakúltet

student (masc.)	студент (м)	stúdent
student (fem.)	студенткиња (ж)	stúdentkinja
lecturer (teacher)	предавач (м)	predávač

lecture hall, room	слушаоница (ж)	slušaónica
graduate	дипломац (м)	diplómac
diploma	диплома (ж)	diplóma

dissertation	дисертација (ж)	disertácija
study (report)	истраживање (с)	istražívanje
laboratory	лабораторија (ж)	laboratórija

lecture	предавање (с)	predávanje
coursemate	факултетски друг (м)	fakúltetski drug
scholarship	стипендија (ж)	stipéndija
academic degree	академски степен (м)	ákademski stépen

144. Sciences. Disciplines

mathematics	математика (ж)	matemátika
algebra	алгебра (ж)	álgebra
geometry	геометрија (ж)	geométrija

astronomy	астрономија (ж)	astronómija
biology	биологија (ж)	biológija
geography	географија (ж)	geográfija
geology	геологија (ж)	geológija
history	историја (ж)	istórija

medicine	медицина (ж)	medicína
pedagogy	педагогија (ж)	pedagógija
law	право (с)	právo

physics	физика (ж)	fízika
chemistry	хемија (ж)	hémija
philosophy	филозофија (ж)	filozófija
psychology	психологија (ж)	psihológija

145. Writing system. Orthography

grammar	граматика (ж)	gramátika
vocabulary	лексикон (м)	léksikon
phonetics	фонетика (ж)	fonétika

noun	именица (ж)	ímenica
adjective	придев (м)	prídev
verb	глагол (м)	glágol
adverb	прилог (м)	prílog

pronoun	заменица (ж)	zámenica
interjection	узвик (м)	úzvik
preposition	предлог (м)	prédlog

root	корен (м) речи	koŕen réči
ending	наставак (м)	nástavak
prefix	префикс (м)	préfiks

syllable	слог (м)	slog
suffix	суфикс (м)	súfiks
stress mark	акцент (м)	ákcent
apostrophe	апостроф (м)	ápostrof
period, dot	тачка (ж)	táčka
comma	зарез (м)	zárez
semicolon	тачка (ж) и зарез	táčka i zárez
colon	две тачке (мн)	dve táčke
ellipsis	три тачке (мн)	tri táčke
question mark	упитник (м)	úpitnik
exclamation point	ускличник, узвичник (м)	úskličnik, úzvičnik
quotation marks	наводници (мн)	návodnici
in quotation marks	под наводницима	pod návodnicima
parenthesis	заграда (ж)	zágrada
in parenthesis	у загради	u zágradi
hyphen	цртица (ж)	cŕtica
dash	повлака (ж)	póvlaka
space (between words)	размак (м)	rázmak
letter	слово (с)	slóvo
capital letter	велико слово (с)	véliko slóvo
vowel (n)	самогласник (м)	sámoglasnik
consonant (n)	сугласник (м)	súglasnik
sentence	реченица (ж)	rečénica
subject	субјект (м)	súbjekt
predicate	предикат (м)	prédikat
line	ред (м)	red
on a new line	у новом реду	u nóvom rédu
paragraph	пасус (м)	pásus
word	реч (ж)	reč
group of words	група (ж) речи	grúpa réči
expression	израз (м)	ízraz
synonym	синоним (м)	sinónim
antonym	антоним (м)	antónim
rule	правило (с)	právilo
exception	изузетак (м)	izuzétak
correct (adj)	исправан	íspravan
conjugation	коњугација (ж)	konjugácija
declension	деклинација (ж)	deklinácija
nominal case	падеж (м)	pádež
question	питање (с)	pítanje

to underline (vt)	подвући (пг)	pódvući
dotted line	испрекидана линија (ж)	isprékidana línija

146. Foreign languages

language	језик (м)	jézik
foreign (adj)	стран	stran
foreign language	страни језик (м)	stráni jézik
to study (vt)	студирати (пг)	studírati
to learn (language, etc.)	учити (пг)	účiti
to read (vi, vt)	читати (нг, пг)	čítati
to speak (vi, vt)	говорити (нг)	govóriti
to understand (vt)	разумевати (пг)	razumévati
to write (vt)	писати (пг)	písati
fast (adv)	брзо	bŕzo
slowly (adv)	споро, полако	spóro, poláko
fluently (adv)	течно	téčno
rules	правила (мн)	právila
grammar	граматика (ж)	gramátika
vocabulary	лексикон (м)	léksikon
phonetics	фонетика (ж)	fonétika
textbook	уџбеник (м)	údžbenik
dictionary	речник (м)	réčnik
teach-yourself book	приручник (м)	príručnik
phrasebook	приручник (м) за конверзацију	príručnik za konverzáciju
cassette, tape	касета (ж)	kaséta
videotape	видео касета (ж)	vídeo kaséta
CD, compact disc	ЦД диск (м)	CD disk
DVD	ДВД (м)	DVD
alphabet	азбука, абецеда (ж)	ázbuka, abecéda
to spell (vt)	спеловати (пг)	spélovati
pronunciation	изговор (м)	ízgovor
accent	нагласак (м)	náglasak
with an accent	са нагласком	sa náglaskom
without an accent	без нагласка	bez náglaska
word	реч (ж)	reč
meaning	смисао (м)	smísao
course (e.g., a French ~)	течај (м)	téčaj
to sign up	уписати се	upísati se
teacher	професор (м)	prófesor

translation (process)	превођење (c)	prevóđenje
translation (text, etc.)	превод (м)	prévod
translator	преводилац (м)	prevódilac
interpreter	преводилац (м)	prevódilac
polyglot	полиглота (м)	poliglóta
memory	памћење (c)	pámćenje

147. Fairy tale characters

Santa Claus	Деда Мраз (м)	Déda Mraz
Cinderella	Пепељуга (ж)	Pepéljuga
mermaid	сирена (ж)	siréna
Neptune	Нептун (м)	Néptun
magician, wizard	чаробњак (м)	čaróbnjak
fairy	чаробница (ж)	čárobnica
magic (adj)	чаробан	čároban
magic wand	чаробни штап (м)	čárobni štap
fairy tale	бајка (ж)	bájka
miracle	чудо (c)	čúdo
dwarf	патуљак (м)	patúljak
to turn into ...	претворити се у ...	pretvóriti se u ...
ghost	дух (м)	duh
phantom	сабласт (ж)	sáblast
monster	чудовиште (c)	čúdovište
dragon	змај (м)	zmaj
giant	див (м)	div

148. Zodiac Signs

Aries	Ован (м)	Óvan
Taurus	Бик (м)	Bik
Gemini	Близанци (мн)	Blizánci
Cancer	Рак (м)	Rak
Leo	Лав (м)	Lav
Virgo	Девица (ж)	Dévica
Libra	Вага (ж)	Vága
Scorpio	Шкорпија (ж)	Škórpija
Sagittarius	Стрелац (м)	Strélac
Capricorn	Јарац (м)	Járac
Aquarius	Водолија (м)	Vodólija
Pisces	Рибе (мн)	Ríbe
character	карактер (м)	karákter
character traits	црте (мн) карактера	cŕte káraktera

behavior	понашање (с)	ponášanje
to tell fortunes	гатати (нг)	gátati
fortune-teller	гатара (ж)	gátara
horoscope	хороскоп (м)	hóroskop

Arts

theater	позориште (с)	pózorište
opera	опера (ж)	ópera
operetta	оперета (ж)	operéta
ballet	балет (м)	bálet

theater poster	плакат (м)	plákat
troupe (theatrical company)	трупа (ж)	trúpa

tour	гостовање (с)	góstovanje
to be on tour	гостовати (нг)	gostóvati
to rehearse (vi, vt)	пробати (пг)	próbati
rehearsal	проба (ж)	próba
repertoire	репертоар (м)	repertóar

performance	представа (ж)	prédstava
theatrical show	представа (ж)	prédstava
play	драма (ж)	dráma

ticket	улазница (ж)	úlaznica
box office (ticket booth)	благајна (ж)	blágajna
lobby, foyer	фоаје (м)	foáje
coat check (cloakroom)	гардероба (ж)	garderóba
coat check tag	број (м)	broj
binoculars	двоглед (м)	dvógled
usher	разводник (м)	rázvodnik

orchestra seats	партер (м)	párter
balcony	балкон (м)	bálkon
dress circle	прва галерија (ж)	pŕva galérija
box	ложа (ж)	lóža
row	ред (м)	red
seat	седиште (с)	sédište

audience	публика (ж)	públika
spectator	гледалац (м)	glédalac
to clap (vi, vt)	тапшати (нг)	tápšati
applause	аплауз (м)	áplauz
ovation	овација (ж)	ovácija

stage	бина (ж)	bína
curtain	завеса (ж)	závesa
scenery	декорација (ж)	dekorácija

backstage	кулиса (ж)	kulísa
scene (e.g., the last ~)	сцена (ж)	scéna
act	акт, чин (м)	akt, čin
intermission	пауза (ж)	páuza

150. Cinema

| actor | глумац (м) | glúmac |
| actress | глумица (ж) | glúmica |

movies (industry)	кино (с)	kino
movie	филм (м)	film
episode	епизода (ж)	epizóda

detective movie	детектив (м)	detéktiv
action movie	акциони филм (м)	ákcioni film
adventure movie	авантуристички филм (м)	avantúristički film
sci-fi movie	научнофантастични филм (м)	náučnofantástični film
horror movie	хорор филм (м)	hóror film

comedy movie	комедија (ж)	kómedija
melodrama	мелодрама (ж)	mélodrama
drama	драма (ж)	dráma

fictional movie	играни филм (м)	ígrani fílm
documentary	документарни филм (м)	dókumentarni film
cartoon	цртани филм (м)	cȑtani film
silent movies	неми филм (м)	némi film

role (part)	улога (ж)	úloga
leading role	главна улога (ж)	glávna úloga
to play (vi, vt)	играти (пг)	ígrati

movie star	филмска звезда (ж)	fílmska zvézda
well-known (adj)	чувен	čúven
famous (adj)	познат	póznat
popular (adj)	популаран	pópularan

script (screenplay)	сценарио (м)	scenário
scriptwriter	сценариста (м)	scenárista
movie director	режисер (м)	režíser
producer	продуцент (м)	prodúcent
assistant	асистент (м)	asístent
cameraman	сниматељ (м)	snímatelj
stuntman	каскадер (м)	kaskáder
double (stand-in)	двојник (м)	dvójnik
to shoot a movie	снимати филм	snímati film
audition, screen test	аудиција (ж)	audícija

shooting	снимање (с)	snímanje
movie crew	филмска екипа (ж)	fílmska ekípa
movie set	терен (м)	téren
camera	филмска камера (ж)	fílmska kámera

movie theater	биоскоп (м)	bíoskop
screen (e.g., big ~)	екран (м)	ékran
to show a movie	приказивати филм	prikazívati film

soundtrack	звучни запис (м)	zvúčni zápis
special effects	специјални ефекти (мн)	spécijalni efékti
subtitles	титлови (мн)	títlovi
credits	имена (мн) глумаца	iména glúmaca
translation	превод (м)	prévod

151. Painting

art	уметност (ж)	úmetnost
fine arts	ликовна уметност (ж)	líkovna úmetnost
art gallery	уметничка галерија (ж)	umétnička gálerija
art exhibition	изложба (ж) слика	ízložba slíka

painting (art)	сликарство (с)	slikárstvo
graphic art	графика (ж)	gráfika
abstract art	апстракционизам (м)	apstrakcionízam
impressionism	импресионизам (м)	impresionízam

picture (painting)	слика (ж)	slíka
drawing	цртеж (м)	cŕtež
poster	постер (м)	póster

illustration (picture)	илустрација (ж)	ilustrácija
miniature	минијатура (ж)	minijatúra
copy (of painting, etc.)	копија (ж)	kópija
reproduction	репродукција (ж)	reprodúkcija

mosaic	мозаик (м)	mozáik
stained glass window	витраж (м)	vítraž
fresco	фреска (ж)	fréska
engraving	гравура (ж)	gravúra

bust (sculpture)	попрсје (с)	póprsje
sculpture	скулптура (ж)	skulptúra
statue	кип (м)	kip
plaster of Paris	гипс (м)	gips
plaster (as adj)	од гипса	od gípsa

portrait	портрет (м)	pórtret
self-portrait	аутопортрет (м)	autopórtret
landscape painting	пејзаж (м)	péjzaž

still life	мртва природа (ж)	mŕtva príroda
caricature	карикатура (ж)	karikatúra
sketch	нацрт (м)	nacrt

paint	боја (ж)	bója
watercolor paint	акварел (м)	akvárel
oil (paint)	уљана боја (ж)	úljana bója
pencil	оловка (ж)	ólovka
India ink	туш (м)	tuš
charcoal	угаљ (м)	úgalj

to draw (vi, vt)	цртати (нг, пг)	cŕtati
to paint (vi, vt)	сликати (пг)	slíkati

to pose (vi)	позирати (нг)	pozírati
artist's model (masc.)	сликарски модел (м)	slíkarski módel
artist's model (fem.)	сликарски модел (м)	slíkarski módel

artist (painter)	сликар (м)	slíkar
work of art	уметничко дело (с)	umétničko délo
masterpiece	ремек-дело (с)	rémek-délo
studio (artist's workroom)	радионица (ж)	radiónica

canvas (cloth)	платно (м)	plátno
easel	штафелај (м)	štafélaj
palette	палета (ж)	paléta

frame (picture ~, etc.)	оквир (м)	ókvir
restoration	рестаурација (ж)	restaurácija
to restore (vt)	рестаурирати (пг)	restaurírati

152. Literature & Poetry

literature	књижевност (ж)	knjíževnost
author (writer)	аутор (м)	áutor
pseudonym	псеудоним (м)	pseudónim

book	књига (ж)	knjíga
volume	том (м)	tom
table of contents	садржај (м)	sádržaj
page	страна (ж)	strána
main character	главни јунак (м)	glávni júnak
autograph	аутограм (м)	autógram

short story	кратка прича (ж)	krátka príča
story (novella)	прича (ж)	príča
novel	роман (м)	róman
work (writing)	дело (с)	délo
fable	басна (ж)	básna
detective novel	детектив (м)	detéktiv

poem (verse)	песма (ж)	pésma
poetry	поезија (ж)	póezija
poem (epic, ballad)	поема (ж)	póema
poet	песник (м)	pésnik

fiction	белетристика (ж)	beletrístika
science fiction	научна фантастика (ж)	náučna fantástika
adventures	доживљаји (мн)	dóživljaji
educational literature	образовна литература (ж)	óbrazovna literatúra
children's literature	књижевност (ж) за децу	knižévnost za décu

153. Circus

circus	циркус (м)	církus
traveling circus	путујући циркус (м)	pútujući církus
program	програм (м)	prógram
performance	представа (ж)	prédstava

| act (circus ~) | тачка (ж) | táčka |
| circus ring | арена (ж) | aréna |

pantomime (act)	пантомима (ж)	pantomíma
clown	кловн (м)	klovn
acrobat	акробата (м)	akróbata
acrobatics	акробатика (ж)	akrobátika
gymnast	гимнастичар (м)	gimnástičar
acrobatic gymnastics	гимнастика (ж)	gimnástika
somersault	салто (м)	sálto

athlete (strongman)	атлета (м)	atleta
tamer (e.g., lion ~)	укротитељ (м)	ukrótitelj
rider (circus horse ~)	јахач (м)	jáhač
assistant	асистент (м)	asístent
stunt	трик (м)	trik
magic trick	трик (м)	trik
conjurer, magician	мађионичар (м)	mađióničar

juggler	жонглер (м)	žóngler
to juggle (vi, vt)	жонглирати (нг)	žonglírati
animal trainer	дресер (м)	dréser
animal training	дресура (ж)	dresúra
to train (animals)	дресирати (пг)	dresírati

154. Music. Pop music

| music | музика (ж) | múzika |
| musician | музичар (м) | múzičar |

musical instrument	музички инструмент (м)	múzički instrúment
to play …	свирати …	svírati …
guitar	гитара (ж)	gitára
violin	виолина (ж)	violína
cello	виолончело (с)	violónčelo
double bass	контрабас (м)	kóntrabas
harp	харфа (ж)	hárfa
piano	клавир (м)	klávir
grand piano	велики клавир (м)	véliki klávir
organ	оргуље (мн)	órgulje
wind instruments	дувачки инструменти (мн)	dúvački instruménti
oboe	обоа (ж)	obóa
saxophone	саксофон (м)	sáksofon
clarinet	кларинет (м)	klarínet
flute	флаута (ж)	fláuta
trumpet	труба (ж)	trúba
accordion	хармоника (ж)	harmónika
drum	бубањ (м)	búbanj
duo	дует (м)	dúet
trio	трио (м)	trío
quartet	квартет (м)	kvártet
choir	хор (м)	hor
orchestra	оркестар (м)	órkestar
pop music	поп музика (ж)	pop múzika
rock music	рок музика (ж)	rok múzika
rock group	рок група (ж)	rok grúpa
jazz	џез (м)	džez
idol	идол (м)	ídol
admirer, fan	поштовалац (м)	poštóvalac
concert	концерт (м)	kóncert
symphony	симфонија (ж)	símfonija
composition	дело (с)	délo
to compose (write)	компоновати (пг)	komponóvati
singing (n)	певање (с)	pévanje
song	песма (ж)	pésma
tune (melody)	мелодија (ж)	mélodija
rhythm	ритам (м)	rítam
blues	блуз (м)	blúz
sheet music	ноте (мн)	nóte
baton	палица (ж)	pálica
bow	гудало (с)	gúdalo

string	**жица** (ж)	žíca
case (e.g., guitar ~)	**футрола** (ж)	futróla

Rest. Entertainment. Travel

tourism, travel	туризам (м)	turízam
tourist	туриста (м)	turísta
trip, voyage	путовање (с)	putovánje
adventure	авантура (ж)	avantúra
trip, journey	путовање (с)	putovánje
vacation	одмор (м)	ódmor
to be on vacation	бити на годишњем одмору	bíti na gódišnjem ódmoru
rest	одмор (м)	ódmor
train	воз (м)	voz
by train	возом	vózom
airplane	авион (м)	avíon
by airplane	авионом	aviónom
by car	колима, аутом	kólima, áutom
by ship	бродом	bródom
luggage	пртљаг (м)	pŕtljag
suitcase	кофер (м)	kófer
luggage cart	колица (мн) за пртљаг	kolíca za pŕtljag
passport	пасош (м)	pásoš
visa	виза (ж)	víza
ticket	карта (ж)	kárta
air ticket	авионска карта (ж)	aviónska kárta
guidebook	водич (м)	vódič
map (tourist ~)	мапа (ж)	mápa
area (rural ~)	подручје (с)	pódručje
place, site	место (с)	mésto
exotica (n)	егзотика (ж)	egzótika
exotic (adj)	егзотичан	egzótičan
amazing (adj)	диван	dívan
group	група (ж)	grúpa
excursion, sightseeing tour	екскурзија (ж)	ekskúrzija
guide (person)	водич (м)	vódič

156. Hotel

hotel	хотел (м)	hótel
motel	мотел (м)	mótel
three-star (~ hotel)	три звездице	tri zvézdice
five-star	пет звездица	pet zvézdica
to stay (in a hotel, etc.)	одсести (нг)	ódsesti
room	соба (ж)	sóba
single room	једнокреветна соба (ж)	jédnokrevetna sóba
double room	двокреветна соба (ж)	dvókrevetna sóba
to book a room	резервисати собу	rezervísati sóbu
half board	полупансион (м)	polupansíon
full board	пун пансион (м)	pun pansíon
with bath	са кадом	sa kádom
with shower	са тушем	sa túšem
satellite television	сателитска телевизија (ж)	satelítska televízija
air-conditioner	клима (ж)	klíma
towel	пешкир (м)	péškir
key	кључ (м)	ključ
administrator	администратор (м)	administrátor
chambermaid	собарица (ж)	sóbarica
porter, bellboy	носач (м)	nósač
doorman	вратар (м)	vrátar
restaurant	ресторан (м)	restóran
pub, bar	бар (м)	bar
breakfast	доручак (м)	dóručak
dinner	вечера (ж)	véčera
buffet	шведски сто (м)	švédski sto
lobby	фоаје (м)	foáje
elevator	лифт (м)	lift
DO NOT DISTURB	НЕ УЗНЕМИРАВАТИ	NE UZNEMIRAVATI
NO SMOKING	ЗАБРАЊЕНО ПУШЕЊЕ	ZABRANJENO PUŠENJE

157. Books. Reading

book	књига (ж)	knjíga
author	аутор (м)	áutor
writer	писац (м)	písac
to write (~ a book)	написати (пг)	napísati
reader	читалац (м)	čítalac

to read (vi, vt)	**читати** (нг, пг)	čítati
reading (activity)	**читање** (с)	čítanje
silently (to oneself)	**у себи**	u sébi
aloud (adv)	**наглас**	náglas
to publish (vt)	**издавати** (пг)	izdávati
publishing (process)	**издање** (с)	izdánje
publisher	**издавач** (м)	izdávač
publishing house	**издавачка кућа** (ж)	izdávačka kúća
to come out (be released)	**изаћи** (нг)	ízaći
release (of a book)	**излазак** (м)	ízlazak
print run	**тираж** (м)	tíraž
bookstore	**књижара** (ж)	knjížara
library	**библиотека** (ж)	bibliotéka
story (novella)	**прича** (ж)	príča
short story	**кратка прича** (ж)	krátka príča
novel	**роман** (м)	róman
detective novel	**детектив** (м)	detéktiv
memoirs	**мемоари** (мн)	memoári
legend	**легенда** (ж)	légenda
myth	**мит** (м)	mit
poetry, poems	**песме** (мн)	pésme
autobiography	**аутобиографија** (ж)	autobiográfija
selected works	**изабрана дела** (мн)	ízabrana déla
science fiction	**научна фантастика** (ж)	náučna fantástika
title	**назив** (м)	náziv
introduction	**увод** (м)	úvod
title page	**насловна страна** (ж)	náslovna strána
chapter	**поглавље** (с)	póglavlje
extract	**одломак** (м)	ódlomak
episode	**епизода** (ж)	epizóda
plot (storyline)	**сиже** (м)	síže
contents	**садржина** (ж)	sádržina
table of contents	**садржај** (м)	sádržaj
main character	**главни јунак** (м)	glávni júnak
volume	**том** (м)	tom
cover	**корица** (ж)	kórica
binding	**корице** (мн)	kórice
bookmark	**ознака** (ж)	óznaka
page	**страна** (ж)	strána
to page through	**листати** (пг)	lístati

margins	маргине (мн)	márgine
annotation (marginal note, etc.)	забелешка (ж)	zábeleška
footnote	фуснота (ж)	fúsnota

text	текст (м)	tekst
type, font	фонт (м)	font
misprint, typo	штампарска грешка (ж)	štámparska gréška

translation	превод (м)	prévod
to translate (vt)	преводити (нг)	prevóditi
original (n)	оригинал (м)	orígínal

famous (adj)	познат	póznat
unknown (not famous)	непознат	népoznat
interesting (adj)	интересантан	interesántan
bestseller	бестселер (м)	bestséler

dictionary	речник (м)	réčnik
textbook	уџбеник (м)	údžbenik
encyclopedia	енциклопедија (ж)	enciklopédija

158. Hunting. Fishing

hunting	лов (м)	lov
to hunt (vi, vt)	ловити (нг)	lóviti
hunter	ловац (м)	lóvac

to shoot (vi)	пуцати (нг)	púcati
rifle	пушка (ж)	púška
bullet (shell)	метак (м)	métak
shot (lead balls)	сачма (ж)	sáčma

steel trap	замка (ж)	zámka
snare (for birds, etc.)	клопка (ж)	klópka
to fall into the steel trap	упасти у замку	úpasti u zámku
to lay a steel trap	поставити замку	póstaviti zámku

poacher	ловокрадица (м)	lovokrádica
game (in hunting)	дивљач (ж)	dívljač
hound dog	ловачки пас (м)	lóvački pas
safari	сафари (м)	safári
mounted animal	препарирана животиња (ж)	preparírana živótinja

fisherman, angler	риболовац, пецарош (м)	ríbolovac, pécaroš
fishing (angling)	пецање (с), риболов (м)	pecanje, ríbolov
to fish (vi)	пецати (нг)	pécati
fishing rod	пецаљка (ж)	pécaljka
fishing line	струна (ж)	strúna

hook	удица (ж)	údica
float, bobber	пловак (м)	plóvak
bait	мамац (м)	mámac

to cast a line	бацити удицу	báciti údicu
to bite (ab. fish)	гристи (нг)	grísti
catch (of fish)	улов (м)	úlov
ice-hole	рупа (ж) у леду	rúpa u lédu

fishing net	мрежа (ж)	mréža
boat	чамац (м)	čámac
to net (to fish with a net)	ловити мрежом	lóviti mréžom
to cast[throw] the net	бацати мрежу	bácati mréžu
to haul the net in	извлачити мрежу	izvláčiti mréžu
to fall into the net	упасти у мрежу	úpasti u mréžu

whaler (person)	китоловац (м)	kitolóvac
whaleboat	китоловац (м)	kitolóvac
harpoon	харпун (м)	hárpun

159. Games. Billiards

billiards	билијар (м)	bilíjar
billiard room, hall	билијарска сала (ж)	bilíjarska sála
ball (snooker, etc.)	билијарска кугла (ж)	bilíjarska kugla

to pocket a ball	убацити (пг) куглу	úbaciti kúglu
cue	так (м)	tak
pocket	рупа (ж)	rúpa

160. Games. Playing cards

diamonds	каро (м)	káro
spades	пик (м)	pik
hearts	херц (м)	herc
clubs	треф (м)	tref

ace	кец (м)	kec
king	краљ (м)	kralj
queen	дама (ж)	dáma
jack, knave	жандар (м)	žándar

playing card	карта (ж) за играње	kárta za ígranje
cards	карте (мн)	kárte
trump	адут (м)	ádut
deck of cards	шпил (м)	špil
point	бод (м)	bod
to deal (vi, vt)	делити (пг)	déliti

to shuffle (cards)	мешати (пг)	méšati
lead, turn (n)	потез (м)	pótez
cardsharp	варалица (м)	váralica

161. Casino. Roulette

casino	коцкарница (ж)	kóckarnica
roulette (game)	рулет (м)	rulét
bet	улог (м)	úlog
to place bets	кладити се (нг)	kláditi se

red	црвено (с)	cŕveno
black	црно (с)	cŕno
to bet on red	ставити на црвено	stáviti na crvéno
to bet on black	ставити на црно	stáviti na cŕno

croupier (dealer)	крупје (м)	krúpje
to spin the wheel	вртети рулет	vŕteti rúlet
rules (of game)	правила (мн) игре	právila ígre
chip	жетон (м)	žéton

| to win (vi, vt) | добити (пг) | dóbiti |
| win (winnings) | добитак (м) | dobítak |

| to lose (~ 100 dollars) | изгубити (нг, пг) | izgúbiti |
| loss (losses) | губитак (м) | gubítak |

player	играч (м)	ígrač
blackjack (card game)	блек џек (м)	blek džek
craps (dice game)	игра (ж) са коцкицама	ígra sa kóckicama
dice (a pair of ~)	коцкице (мн)	kóckice
slot machine	слот машина (ж)	slot mašína

162. Rest. Games. Miscellaneous

to stroll (vi, vt)	шетати се	šétati se
stroll (leisurely walk)	шетња (ж)	šétnja
car ride	излет (м)	ízlet
adventure	авантура (ж)	avantúra
picnic	пикник (м)	píknik

game (chess, etc.)	игра (ж)	ígra
player	играч (м)	ígrač
game (one ~ of chess)	партија (ж)	pártija

collector (e.g., philatelist)	колекционар (м)	kolékcionar
to collect (stamps, etc.)	колектирати (пг)	kolektírati
collection	колекција (ж)	kolékcija

crossword puzzle	укрштеница (ж)	úkrštenica
racetrack	хиподром (м)	hípodrom
(horse racing venue)		
disco (discotheque)	дискотека (ж)	diskotéka

| sauna | сауна (ж) | sáuna |
| lottery | лутрија (ж) | lútrija |

camping trip	камповање (с)	kampovanje
camp	камп (м)	kamp
tent (for camping)	шатор (м)	šátor
compass	компас (м)	kómpas
camper	кампер (м)	kámper

to watch (movie, etc.)	гледати (пг)	glédati
viewer	гледалац (м)	glédalac
TV show (TV program)	телевизијска емисија (ж)	televízijska emísija

163. Photography

| camera (photo) | фотоапарат (м) | fotoapárat |
| photo, picture | фотографија (ж) | fotográfija |

photographer	фотограф (м)	fotógraf
photo studio	фото студио (м)	fóto stúdio
photo album	фото албум (м)	fóto álbum

camera lens	објектив (м)	óbjektiv
telephoto lens	телеобјектив (м)	teleobjéktiv
filter	филтар (м)	fíltar
lens	сочиво (с)	sóčivo

optics (high-quality ~)	оптика (ж)	óptika
diaphragm (aperture)	дијафрагма (ж)	dijafrágma
exposure time	експозиција (ж)	ekspozícija
(shutter speed)		
viewfinder	тражило (с)	trážilo

digital camera	дигитална камера (ж)	dígitalna kámera
tripod	троножац (м)	trónožac
flash	блиц (м)	blic

to photograph (vt)	сликати (пг)	slíkati
to take pictures	сликати (пг)	slíkati
to have one's picture taken	сликати се	slíkati se

focus	фокус (м)	fókus
to focus	фокусирати (пг)	fokusírati
sharp, in focus (adj)	оштар	óštar
sharpness	оштрина (ж)	oštrína

| contrast | контраст (м) | kóntrast |
| contrast (as adj) | контрастан | kóntrastan |

picture (photo)	слика (ж)	slíka
negative (n)	негатив (м)	négativ
film (a roll of ~)	филм (м)	film
frame (still)	кадар (м)	kádar
to print (photos)	штампати (пг)	štámpati

164. Beach. Swimming

beach	плажа (ж)	pláža
sand	песак (м)	pésak
deserted (beach)	пуст	pust

suntan	преплануост (ж)	preplánulost
to get a tan	сунчати се	súnčati se
tan (adj)	преплануо	preplánuo
sunscreen	крема (ж) за сунчање	kréma za súnčanje

bikini	бикини (м)	bikíni
bathing suit	купаћи костим (м)	kúpaći kóstim
swim trunks	купаће гаће (мн)	kúpaće gáće

swimming pool	базен (м)	bázen
to swim (vi)	пливати (нг)	plívati
shower	туш (м)	tuš
to change (one's clothes)	пресвлачити се	presvláčiti se
towel	пешкир (м)	péškir

| boat | чамац (м) | čámac |
| motorboat | моторни брод (м) | mótorni brod |

water ski	водене скије (мн)	vódene skije
paddle boat	педалина (ж)	pedalína
surfing	сурфовање (с)	súrfovanje
surfer	сурфер (м)	súrfer

scuba set	ронилачка опрема (ж)	rónilačka óprema
flippers (swim fins)	пераја (мн)	péraja
mask (diving ~)	маска (ж)	máska
diver	ронилац (м)	rónilac
to dive (vi)	ронити (нг)	róniti
underwater (adv)	под водом	pod vódom

beach umbrella	сунцобран (м)	súncobran
sunbed (lounger)	лежаљка (ж)	léžaljka
sunglasses	наочаре (мн)	náočare
air mattress	душек (м) за пливање	dúšek za plívanje
to play (amuse oneself)	играти се	ígrati se

to go for a swim	купати се	kúpati se
beach ball	лопта (ж)	lópta
to inflate (vt)	пумпати (пг)	púmpati
inflatable, air (adj)	на надувавање	na naduvavanje
wave	талас (м)	tálas
buoy (line of ~s)	бова (ж)	bóva
to drown (ab. person)	давити се	dáviti se
to save, to rescue	спасавати (пг)	spasávati
life vest	прслук (м) за спасавање	pŕsluk za spásavanje
to observe, to watch	посматрати (нг)	posmátrati
lifeguard	спасилац (м)	spásilac

TECHNICAL EQUIPMENT. TRANSPORTATION

Technical equipment

165. Computer

computer	рачунар (м)	račúnar
notebook, laptop	лаптоп (м)	láptop
to turn on	укључити (пг)	uključiti
to turn off	искључити (пг)	isključiti
keyboard	тастатура (ж)	tastatúra
key	тастер (м)	táster
mouse	миш (ж)	miš
mouse pad	подлога (ж) за миша	pódloga za miša
button	дугме (с)	dúgme
cursor	курсор (м)	kúrsor
monitor	монитор (м)	mónitor
screen	екран (м)	ékran
hard disk	хард диск (м)	hard disk
hard disk capacity	капацитет (м) хард диска	kapacítet hard díska
memory	меморија (ж)	mémorija
random access memory	РАМ меморија (ж)	RAM mémorija
file	фајл (м)	fajl
folder	фолдер (м)	fólder
to open (vt)	отворити (пг)	ótvoriti
to close (vt)	затворити (пг)	zatvóriti
to save (vt)	снимити, сачувати (пг)	snímiti, sačúvati
to delete (vt)	избрисати (пг)	ízbrisati
to copy (vt)	копирати (пг)	kopírati
to sort (vt)	сортирати (пг)	sortírati
to transfer (copy)	пребацити (пг)	prebáciti
program	програм (м)	prógram
software	софтвер (м)	sóftver
programmer	програмер (м)	prográmer
to program (vt)	програмирати (пг)	programírati
hacker	хакер (м)	háker
password	лозинка (ж)	lózinka

virus	вирус (м)	vírus
to find, to detect	пронаћи (пг)	prónaći
byte	бајт (м)	bajt
megabyte	мегабајт (м)	mégabajt
data	подаци (мн)	pódaci
database	база (ж) података	báza pódataka
cable (USB, etc.)	кабл (м)	kabl
to disconnect (vt)	искључити (пг)	isključiti
to connect (sth to sth)	спојити (пг)	spójiti

166. Internet. E-mail

Internet	интернет (м)	ínternet
browser	прегледач (м)	prégledač
search engine	претраживач (м)	pretražívač
provider	провајдер (м)	provájder
webmaster	вебмастер (м)	vebmáster
website	веб-сајт (м)	veb-sajt
webpage	веб-страница (ж)	veb-stránica
address (e-mail ~)	адреса (ж)	adrésa
address book	адресар (м)	adrésar
mailbox	поштанско сандуче (с)	póštansko sánduče
mail	пошта (ж)	póšta
full (adj)	пун	pun
message	порука (ж)	póruka
incoming messages	долазне поруке (мн)	dólazne póruke
outgoing messages	одлазне поруке (мн)	ódlazne póruke
sender	пошиљалац (м)	póšiljalac
to send (vt)	послати (пг)	póslati
sending (of mail)	слање (с)	slánje
receiver	прималац (м)	prímalac
to receive (vt)	примити (пг)	prímiti
correspondence	дописивање (с)	dopisívanje
to correspond (vi)	водити преписку	vóditi prépisku
file	фајл (м)	fajl
to download (vt)	преузети (пг)	preúzeti
to create (vt)	створити (пг)	stvóriti
to delete (vt)	избрисати (пг)	ízbrisati
deleted (adj)	избрисан	ízbrisan
connection (ADSL, etc.)	веза (ж)	véza

speed	брзина (ж)	brzína
modem	модем (м)	módem
access	приступ (м)	prístup
port (e.g., input ~)	порт (м)	port

| connection (make a ~) | повезивање (с) | povezívanje |
| to connect to ... (vi) | повезати се | povézati se |

| to select (vt) | изабрати (пг) | izábrati |
| to search (for ...) | тражити (пг) | trážiti |

167. Electricity

electricity	струја (ж)	strúja
electric, electrical (adj)	електрични	eléktrični
electric power plant	електрана (ж)	elektrána
energy	енергија (ж)	enérgija
electric power	електрична енергија (ж)	eléktrična enérgija

light bulb	сијалица (ж)	síjalica
flashlight	батеријска лампа (ж)	batérijska lámpa
street light	улична расвета (ж)	úlična rásveta

light	светло (с)	svétlo
to turn on	укључивати (пг)	uključívati
to turn off	угасити (пг)	ugásiti
to turn off the light	угасити светло	ugásiti svétlo

to burn out (vi)	прегорети (нг)	pregóreti
short circuit	кратак спој (м)	krátak spoj
broken wire	прекид (м)	prékid
contact (electrical ~)	контакт (м)	kóntakt

light switch	прекидач (м)	prekídač
wall socket	утичница (ж)	útičnica
plug	утикач (м)	utíkač
extension cord	продужни кабл (м)	pródužni kabl

fuse	осигурач (м)	osigúrač
cable, wire	жица (ж), кабл (м)	žíca, kabl
wiring	електрична инсталација (ж)	eléktrična instalácija

ampere	ампер (м)	ámper
amperage	јачина (ж) струје	jačína strúje
volt	волт (м)	volt
voltage	напон (м)	nápon

| electrical device | електрични апарат (м) | eléktrični apárat |
| indicator | индикатор (м) | indikátor |

electrician	електричар (м)	eléktričar
to solder (vt)	лемити (пг)	lémiti
soldering iron	лемилица (с)	lémilica
electric current	струја (ж)	strúja

168. Tools

tool, instrument	алат (м)	álat
tools	алати (мн)	álati
equipment (factory ~)	опрема (ж)	óprema

hammer	чекић (м)	čékić
screwdriver	шрафцигер (м)	šráfciger
ax	секира (ж)	sekíra

saw	тестера (ж)	téstera
to saw (vt)	тестерисати (пг)	testérisati
plane (tool)	блања (ж)	blánja
to plane (vt)	стругати (пг)	strúgati
soldering iron	лемилица (с)	lémilica
to solder (vt)	лемити (пг)	lémiti

file (tool)	турпија (ж)	túrpija
carpenter pincers	клешта (ж)	kléšta
lineman's pliers	пљосната клешта (ж)	pljósnata kléšta
chisel	длето (с)	dléto

drill bit	бургија (ж)	búrgija
electric drill	бушилица (ж)	búšilica
to drill (vi, vt)	бушити (пг)	búšiti

| knife | нож (м) | nož |
| blade | сечиво (с) | séčivo |

sharp (blade, etc.)	оштар	óštar
dull, blunt (adj)	тупи	túpi
to get blunt (dull)	затупити се	zatúpiti se
to sharpen (vt)	оштрити (пг)	óštriti

bolt	завртањ (м)	závrtanj
nut	навртка (ж)	návrtka
thread (of a screw)	навој (м)	návoj
wood screw	шраф (м)	šraf

| nail | ексер (м) | ékser |
| nailhead | глава (ж) | gláva |

ruler (for measuring)	лењир (м)	lénjir
tape measure	метар (м)	métar
spirit level	либела (ж)	libéla

magnifying glass	лупа (ж)	lúpa
measuring instrument	апарат (м) за мерење	apárat za mérenje
to measure (vt)	измерити (пг)	ízmeriti
scale (of thermometer, etc.)	скала (ж)	skála
readings	стање (с)	stánje

compressor	компресор (м)	kómprésor
microscope	микроскоп (м)	míkroskop

pump (e.g., water ~)	пумпа (ж)	púmpa
robot	робот (м)	róbot
laser	ласер (м)	láser

wrench	матични кључ (м)	mátični ključ
adhesive tape	лепљива трака (ж)	lépljiva tráka
glue	лепак (м)	lépak

sandpaper	шмиргла (ж)	šmírgla
spring	опруга (ж)	ópruga
magnet	магнет (м)	mágnet
gloves	рукавице (мн)	rukávice

rope	уже (с)	úže
cord	врпца (ж)	vŕpca
wire (e.g., telephone ~)	жица (ж), кабл (м)	žíca, kabl
cable	кабл (м)	kabl

sledgehammer	маљ (м)	malj
prybar	ћускија (ж)	ćúskija
ladder	мердевине (мн)	mérdevine
stepladder	мердевине (мн) на расклапање	mérdevine na rásklapanje

to screw (tighten)	завртати (пг)	závrtati
to unscrew (lid, filter, etc.)	одвртати (пг)	ódvrtati
to tighten (e.g., with a clamp)	стезати (пг)	stézati
to glue, to stick	прилепити (пг)	prilépiti
to cut (vt)	сећи (пг)	séći

malfunction (fault)	неисправност (ж)	neisprávnost
repair (mending)	поправка (ж)	pópravka
to repair, to fix (vt)	поправљати (пг)	pópravljati
to adjust (machine, etc.)	регулисати (пг)	regulísati

to check (to examine)	проверавати (пг)	proverávati
checking	провера (ж)	próvera
readings	стање (с)	stánje

reliable, solid (machine)	поуздан	póuzdan
complex (adj)	сложен	slóžen

to rust (get rusted)	**рђати** (нг)	rđati
rusty, rusted (adj)	**рђав**	rđav
rust	**рђа** (ж)	rđa

Transportation

airplane	авион (м)	avíon
air ticket	авионска карта (ж)	aviónska kárta
airline	авио-компанија (ж)	ávio-kompánija
airport	аеродром (м)	aeródrom
supersonic (adj)	суперсоничан	supersóničan

captain	капетан (м) авиона	kapétan avíona
crew	посада (ж)	pósada
pilot	пилот (м)	pílot
flight attendant (fem.)	стјуардеса (ж)	stjuardésa
navigator	навигатор (м)	navígator

wings	крила (мн)	kríla
tail	реп (м)	rep
cockpit	кабина (ж)	kabína
engine	мотор (м)	mótor
undercarriage (landing gear)	шасија (ж)	šásija
turbine	турбина (ж)	turbína

propeller	пропелер (м)	propéler
black box	црна кутија (ж)	cŕna kútija
yoke (control column)	управљач (м)	uprávljač
fuel	гориво (м)	górivo

safety card	упутство (с) за ванредне ситуације	úputstvo za vanredne situácije
oxygen mask	маска (ж) за кисеоник	máska za kiseónik
uniform	униформа (ж)	úniforma
life vest	прслук (м) за спасавање	pŕsluk za spásavanje
parachute	падобран (м)	pádobran

takeoff	полетање, узлетање (с)	polétanje, uzlétanje
to take off (vi)	полетати (нг)	polétati
runway	писта (ж)	písta

visibility	видљивост (ж)	vídljivost
flight (act of flying)	лет (м)	let
altitude	висина (ж)	visína
air pocket	ваздушни џеп (м)	vázduši džep
seat	седиште (с)	sédište
headphones	слушалице (мн)	slúšalice

folding tray (tray table)	сточић (м) на расклапање	stóčić na rasklápanje
airplane window	прозор (м)	prózor
aisle	пролаз (м)	prólaz

170. Train

train	воз (м)	voz
commuter train	електрични воз (м)	eléktrični voz
express train	брзи воз (м)	bŕzi voz
diesel locomotive	дизел локомотива (ж)	dízel lokomotíva
steam locomotive	парна локомотива (ж)	párna lokomotíva

passenger car	вагон (м)	vágon
dining car	вагон ресторан (м)	vágon restóran

rails	шине (мн)	šíne
railroad	железница (ж)	žéleznica
railway tie	праг (м)	prag

platform (railway ~)	перон (м)	péron
track (~ 1, 2, etc.)	колосек (м)	kólosek
semaphore	семафор (м)	sémafor
station	станица (ж)	stánica

engineer (train driver)	машиновођа (м)	mašinóvođa
porter (of luggage)	носач (м)	nósač
car attendant	послужитељ (м) у возу	poslúžitelj u vózu
passenger	путник (м)	pútnik
conductor (ticket inspector)	контролер (м)	kontróler

corridor (in train)	ходник (м)	hódnik
emergency brake	кочница (ж)	kóčnica

compartment	купе (м)	kúpe
berth	лежај (м)	léžaj
upper berth	горњи лежај (м)	górnji léžaj
lower berth	доњи лежај (м)	dónji léžaj
bed linen, bedding	постељина (ж)	posteljína

ticket	карта (ж)	kárta
schedule	ред (м) вожње	red vóžnje
information display	табла (ж)	tábla

to leave, to depart	одлазити (нг)	ódlaziti
departure (of train)	полазак (м)	pólazak
to arrive (ab. train)	долазити (нг)	dólaziti
arrival	долазак (м)	dólazak
to arrive by train	доћи возом	dóći vózom

to get on the train	сести у воз	sésti u voz
to get off the train	сићи с воза	síći s vóza

train wreck	железничка несрећа (ж)	žéleznička nésreća
to derail (vi)	исклизнути из шина	ískliznuti iz šína
steam locomotive	парна локомотива (ж)	párna lokomotíva
stoker, fireman	ложач (м)	lóžač
firebox	ложиште (с)	lóžište
coal	угаљ (м)	úgalj

171. Ship

ship	брод (м)	brod
vessel	брод (м)	brod

steamship	пароброд (м)	párobrod
riverboat	речни брод (м)	réčni brod
cruise ship	прекоокеански брод (м)	prekookéanski brod
cruiser	крстарица (ж)	krstárica

yacht	јахта (ж)	jáhta
tugboat	тегљач (м)	tégljač
barge	шлеп (м)	šlép
ferry	трајект (м)	trájekt

sailing ship	једрењак (м)	jedrénjak
brigantine	бригантина (ж)	brigantína

ice breaker	ледоломац (м)	ledolómac
submarine	подморница (ж)	pódmornica

boat (flat-bottomed ~)	чамац (м)	čámac
dinghy (lifeboat)	чамац (м)	čámac
lifeboat	чамац (м) за спасавање	čámac za spásavanje
motorboat	моторни брод (м)	mótorni brod

captain	капетан (м)	kapétan
seaman	морнар (м)	mórnar
sailor	поморац, морнар (м)	pómorac, mórnar
crew	посада (ж)	pósada

boatswain	вођа (м) палубе	vóđa pálube
ship's boy	бродски момак (м)	bródski mómak
cook	кувар (м)	kúvar
ship's doctor	бродски лекар (м)	bródski lékar

deck	палуба (ж)	páluba
mast	јарбол (м)	járbol
sail	једро (с)	jédro
hold	потпалубље (с)	pótpalublje

bow (prow)	прамац (м)	prámac
stern	крма (ж)	kŕma
oar	весло (с)	véslo
screw propeller	бродски пропелер (м)	bródski propéler

cabin	кабина (ж)	kabína
wardroom	официрска менза (ж)	ofícirska ménza
engine room	стројарница (ж)	strójarnica
bridge	капетански мост (м)	kapétanski most
radio room	радио кабина (ж)	rádio kabína
wave (radio)	талас (м)	tálas
logbook	бродски дневник (м)	bródski dnévnik

spyglass	дурбин (м)	dúrbin
bell	звоно (с)	zvóno
flag	застава (ж)	zástava

| hawser (mooring ~) | конопац (м) | kónopac |
| knot (bowline, etc.) | чвор (м) | čvor |

| deckrails | рукохват (м) | rúkohvat |
| gangway | рампа (ж) | rámpa |

| anchor | сидро (с) | sídro |
| to weigh anchor | дићи сидро | díći sídro |

| to drop anchor | спустити сидро | spústiti sídro |
| anchor chain | сидрени ланац (м) | sídreni lánac |

| port (harbor) | лука (ж) | lúka |
| quay, wharf | пристаниште (с) | prístanište |

| to berth (moor) | пристајати (нг) | prístajati |
| to cast off | отпловити (нг) | otplóviti |

| trip, voyage | путовање (с) | putovánje |
| cruise (sea trip) | крстарење (с) | krstárenje |

| course (route) | правац, курс (м) | právac, kurs |
| route (itinerary) | маршрута (ж) | maršrúta |

fairway (safe water channel)	пловни пут (м)	plóvni put
shallows	плићак (м)	plíćak
to run aground	насукати се	násukati se

storm	олуја (ж)	olúja
signal	сигнал (м)	sígnal
to sink (vi)	тонути (нг)	tónuti
Man overboard!	Човек у мору!	Čóvek u móru!
SOS (distress signal)	СОС	SOS
ring buoy	појас (м) за спасавање	pójas za spasávanje

172. Airport

airport	аеродром (м)	aeródrom
airplane	авион (м)	avíon
airline	авио-компанија (ж)	ávio-kompánija
air traffic controller	контролор (м) лета	kontrólor léta

departure	полазак (м)	pólazak
arrival	долазак (м)	dólazak
to arrive (by plane)	долетети (нг)	doléteti

| departure time | време (с) поласка | vréme pólaska |
| arrival time | време (с) доласка | vréme dólaska |

| to be delayed | каснити (нг) | kásniti |
| flight delay | кашњење (с) лета | kášnjenje léta |

information board	информативна табла (ж)	ínformativna tábla
information	информација (ж)	informácija
to announce (vt)	објављивати (пг)	objavljívati
flight (e.g., next ~)	лет (м)	let
customs	царина (ж)	cárina
customs officer	цариник (м)	cárinik

customs declaration	царинска декларација (ж)	cárinska deklarácija
to fill out (vt)	попунити (пг)	pópuniti
to fill out the declaration	попунити декларацију	pópuniti deklaráciju
passport control	пасошка контрола (ж)	pásoška kontróla

luggage	пртљаг (м)	pŕtljag
hand luggage	ручни пртљаг (м)	rúčni pŕtljag
luggage cart	колица (мн) за пртљаг	kolíca za pŕtljag

landing	слетање (с)	slétanje
landing strip	писта (ж) за слетање	písta za slétanje
to land (vi)	спуштати се	spúštati se
airstair (passenger stair)	степенице (мн)	stépenice

check-in	регистрација (ж), чекирање (с)	registrácija, čekíranje
check-in counter	шалтер (м) за чекирање	šálter za čekíranje
to check-in (vi)	пријавити се	prijáviti se
boarding pass	бординг карта (ж)	bórding kárta
departure gate	излаз (м)	ízlaz

transit	транзит (м)	tránzit
to wait (vt)	чекати (нг, пг)	čékati
departure lounge	чекаоница (ж)	čekaónica
to see off	пратити (пг)	prátiti
to say goodbye	опраштати се	opráštati se

173. Bicycle. Motorcycle

bicycle	бицикл (м)	bicíkl
scooter	скутер (м)	skúter
motorcycle, bike	мотоцикл (м)	motocíkl
to go by bicycle	ићи бициклом	ići bicíklom
handlebars	управљач (м)	uprávljač
pedal	педала (ж)	pedála
brakes	кочнице (мн)	kóčnice
bicycle seat (saddle)	седло, седиште (с)	sédlo, sédište
pump	пумпа (ж)	púmpa
luggage rack	пак трегер (м)	pak tréger
front lamp	фар (м)	far
helmet	шлем (м)	šlem
wheel	точак (м)	tóčak
fender	блатобран (м)	blátobran
rim	фелга (ж)	félga
spoke	жбица (ж)	žbíca

Cars

automobile, car	ауто, аутомобил (м)	áuto, automóbil
sports car	спортски ауто (м)	spórtski áuto
limousine	лимузина (ж)	limuzína
off-road vehicle	теренско возило (с)	térensko vózilo
convertible (n)	кабриолет (м)	kabriólet
minibus	минибус (м)	mínibus
ambulance	хитна помоћ (ж)	hítna pómoć
snowplow	снежни плуг (м)	snéžni plug
truck	камион (м)	kamíon
tanker truck	аутоцистерна (ж)	autocísterna
van (small truck)	комби (м)	kómbi
road tractor (trailer truck)	тегљач (м)	tégljač
trailer	приколица (ж)	príkolica
comfortable (adj)	комфоран	kómforan
used (adj)	половни	pólovni

175. Cars. Bodywork

hood	хауба (ж)	háuba
fender	блатобран (м)	blátobran
roof	кров (м)	krov
windshield	шофершајбна (ж)	šóferšajbna
rear-view mirror	ретровизор (м)	retrovízor
windshield washer	прскалица (ж)	pŕskalica
	ветробрана	vétrobrana
windshield wipers	метлице (мн) брисача	métlice brisáča
side window	бочни прозор (м)	bóčni prózor
window lift (power window)	подизач (м) прозора	pódizač prózora
antenna	антена (ж)	anténa
sunroof	отвор (м) на крову	ótvor na króvu
bumper	браник (м)	bránik
trunk	гепек (м)	gépek
roof luggage rack	пртљажник (м)	prtljážnik

door	врата (мн)	vráta
door handle	квака (ж)	kváka
door lock	брава (ж)	bráva

license plate	регистарска таблица (ж)	regístarska táblica
muffler	пригушивач (м)	prigúšivač
gas tank	резервоар (м) за гориво	rezervóar za górivo
tailpipe	ауспух (м)	áuspuh

gas, accelerator	гас (м)	gas
pedal	педала (ж)	pedála
gas pedal	папучица (ж) гаса	pápučica gása

brake	кочница (ж)	kóčnica
brake pedal	папучица (ж) кочнице	pápučica kóčnice
to brake (use the brake)	кочити (нг)	kóčiti
parking brake	ручна кочница (ж)	rúčna kóčnica

clutch	квачило (с)	kváčilo
clutch pedal	папучица (ж) квачила	pápučica kváčila
clutch disc	диск (м) квачила	disk kváčila
shock absorber	амортизер (м)	amortízer

wheel	точак (м)	tóčak
spare tire	резервни точак (м)	rézervni tóčak
tire	гума (ж)	gúma
hubcap	раткапна (ж)	rátkapna

driving wheels	погонски точкови (мн)	pógonski tóčkovi
front-wheel drive (as adj)	са предњим погоном	sa prédnjim pógonom
rear-wheel drive (as adj)	на задњи погон	na zádnji pógon
all-wheel drive (as adj)	с погоном на четири точка	s pógonom na četiri tóčka

| gearbox | мењач (м) | ménjač |
| automatic (adj) | аутоматски | autómatski |

| mechanical (adj) | механички | mehánički |
| gear shift | мењач (м) | ménjač |

| headlight | светло (с), фар (м) | svétlo, far |
| headlights | фарови (мн) | fárovi |

low beam	кратка светла (мн)	krátka svétla
high beam	дуга светла (мн)	dúga svétla
brake light	стоп светло (с)	stop svétlo

parking lights	паркинг светла (мн)	párking svétla
hazard lights	четири жмигавца (мн)	čétiri žmígavca
fog lights	светла (мн) за маглу	svétla za máglu
turn signal	мигавац (м)	mígavac
back-up light	рикверц светло (с)	ríkverc svétlo

175

176. Cars. Passenger compartment

car inside (interior)	унутрашњост (ж)	únutrašnjost
leather (as adj)	кожни	kóžni
velour (as adj)	из велура	iz velúra
upholstery	тапацирунг (м)	tapacírung

instrument (gage)	инструмент (м)	instrúment
dashboard	инструмент табла (ж)	instrúment tábla
speedometer	брзиномер (м)	brzínomer
needle (pointer)	казаљка (ж)	kázaljka

odometer	километар сат (м)	kílometar sat
indicator (sensor)	мерач (м)	mérač
level	ниво (м)	nívo
warning light	лампица (ж) упозорава	lámpica upozorava

steering wheel	волан (м)	vólan
horn	сирена (ж)	siréna
button	дугме (с)	dúgme
switch	прекидач (м)	prekídač

seat	седиште (с)	sédište
backrest	наслон (м)	náslon
headrest	наслон (м) за главу	náslon za glávu
seat belt	сигурносни појас (м)	sigúrnosni pójas
to fasten the belt	везати појас	vézati pójas
adjustment (of seats)	подешавање (с)	podešávanje

| airbag | ваздушни јастук (м) | vázdušni jástuk |
| air-conditioner | клима уређај (м) | klíma úređaj |

radio	радио (м)	rádio
CD player	ЦД плејер (м)	CD pléjer
to turn on	укључити (пг)	uključíti
antenna	антена (ж)	anténa
glove box	претинац (м)	prétinac
ashtray	пепељара (ж)	pepéljara

177. Cars. Engine

engine, motor	мотор (м)	mótor
diesel (as adj)	дизелски	dízelski
gasoline (as adj)	бензински	bénzinski

engine volume	запремина (ж) мотора	zápremina mótora
power	снага (ж)	snága
horsepower	коњска снага (ж)	kónjska snága
piston	клип (м)	klip

| cylinder | цилиндар (м) | cilíndar |
| valve | вентил (м) | véntil |

injector	инјектор (м)	ínjektor
generator (alternator)	генератор (м)	genérator
carburetor	карбуратор (м)	karburator
motor oil	моторно уље (с)	mótorno úlje

radiator	хладњак (м)	hládnjak
coolant	течност (ж) за хлађење	téčnost za hláđenje
cooling fan	вентилатор (м)	ventílator

battery (accumulator)	акумулатор (м)	akumúlator
starter	стартер (м)	stárter
ignition	паљење (с)	páljenje
spark plug	свећица (ж)	svéćica

terminal (of battery)	клема (ж)	kléma
positive terminal	плус (м)	plus
negative terminal	минус (м)	mínus
fuse	осигурач (м)	osigúrač

air filter	ваздушни филтер (м)	vázdušni fílter
oil filter	филтер (м) за уље	fílter za úlje
fuel filter	филтер (м) за гориво	fílter za górivo

178. Cars. Crash. Repair

car crash	саобраћајка (ж)	saobráćajka
traffic accident	саобраћајна несрећа (ж)	sáobraćajna nésreća
to crash (into the wall, etc.)	ударити (нг)	údariti

to get smashed up	разбити се	rázbiti se
damage	штета (ж)	štéta
intact (unscathed)	нетакнут	nétaknut

breakdown	квар (м)	kvar
to break down (vi)	покварити се	pokváriti se
towrope	уже (с) за вучу	úže za vúču

puncture	рупа, пукнута гума (ж)	rúpa, púknuta gúma
to be flat	испумпати се	ispúmpati se
to pump up	пумпати (нг)	púmpati
pressure	притисак (м)	prítisak
to check (to examine)	проверити (нг)	próveriti

repair	поправка (ж)	pópravka
auto repair shop	ауто сервис (м)	áuto sérvis
spare part	резервни део (м)	rézervni déo
part	део (м)	déo

bolt (with nut)	завртањ (м)	závrtanj
screw (fastener)	шраф (м)	šraf
nut	навртка (ж)	návrtka
washer	подлошка (ж)	pódloška
bearing (e.g., ball ~)	лежај (м)	léžaj
tube	црево (с)	crévo
gasket (head ~)	заптивка (ж)	záptivka
cable, wire	жица (ж)	žíca
jack	дизалица (ж)	dízalica
wrench	матични кључ (м)	mátični ključ
hammer	чекић (м)	čékić
pump	пумпа (ж)	púmpa
screwdriver	шрафцигер (м)	šráfciger
fire extinguisher	противпожарни апарат (м)	protivpóžarni apárat
warning triangle	безбедносни троугао (м)	bezbédnosni tróugao
to stall (vi)	гасити се	gásiti se
stall (n)	гашење (с)	gášenje
to be broken	бити покварен	biti pókvaren
to overheat (vi)	прегрејати се	prégrejati se
to be clogged up	зачепити се	začépiti se
to freeze up (pipes, etc.)	смрзнути се	smŕznuti se
to burst (vi, ab. tube)	пукнути (нг)	púknuti
pressure	притисак (м)	prítisak
level	ниво (м)	nívo
slack (~ belt)	лабав	lábav
dent	удубљење (с)	udubljénje
knocking noise (engine)	лупање (с)	lúpanje
crack	пукотина (ж)	púkotina
scratch	огреботина (ж)	ogrebótina

179. Cars. Road

road	пут (м)	put
highway	брзи пут (м)	bŕzi put
freeway	аутопут (м)	áutoput
direction (way)	правац (м)	právac
distance	раздаљина (ж)	rázdaljina
bridge	мост (м)	most
parking lot	паркиралиште (с)	parkíralište
square	трг (м)	tŕg
interchange	петља (ж)	pétlja

tunnel	тунел (м)	túnel
gas station	бензинска станица (ж)	bénzinska stánica
parking lot	паркиралиште (с)	parkíralište
gas pump (fuel dispenser)	пумпа (ж)	púmpa
auto repair shop	ауто сервис (м)	áuto sérvis
to get gas (to fill up)	напунити (пг)	nápuniti
fuel	гориво (с)	górivo
jerrycan	канта (ж) за гориво	kánta za górivo
asphalt	асфалт (м)	ásfalt
road markings	ознаке (мн) на коловозу	óznake na kólovozu
curb	ивичњак (м)	ívičnjak
guardrail	заштитна ограда (ж)	záštitna ógrada
ditch	канал (м)	kánal
roadside (shoulder)	ивица (ж) пута	ívica puta
lamppost	стуб (м)	stub
to drive (a car)	возити (пг)	vóziti
to turn (e.g., ~ left)	скретати (нг)	skrétati
to make a U-turn	окренути се	okrénuti se
reverse (~ gear)	рикверц (м)	ríkverc
to honk (vi)	трубити (нг)	trúbiti
honk (sound)	звучни сигнал (м)	zvúčni sígnal
to get stuck (in the mud, etc.)	заглавити се	zagláviti se
to spin the wheels	окретати се у месту	okrétati se u méstu
to cut, to turn off (vt)	гасити (пг)	gásiti
speed	брзина (ж)	brzína
to exceed the speed limit	прекорачити брзину	prekoráčiti brzinu
to give a ticket	кажњавати (пг)	kažnjávati
traffic lights	семафор (м)	sémafor
driver's license	возачка дозвола (ж)	vózačka dózvola
grade crossing	пружни прелаз (м)	prúžni prélaz
intersection	раскрсница (ж)	ráskrsnica
crosswalk	пешачки прелаз (м)	péšački prélaz
bend, curve	кривина (ж)	krivína
pedestrian zone	пешачка зона (ж)	péšačka zona

180. Traffic signs

rules of the road	правила (мн) саобрацаја	právila sáobracaja
road sign (traffic sign)	саобраћајни знак (м)	sáobraćajni znak
passing (overtaking)	претицање (с)	préticanje
curve	кривина (ж)	krivína
U-turn	Полукружно окретање	Pólukružno ókretanje

traffic circle	Кружни ток	Krúžni tok
No entry	Забрана саобраћаја	Zábrana sáobraćaja
No vehicles allowed	Забрана саобраћаја у оба смера	Zábrana sáobraćaja u óba sméra
No passing	Забрана претицање	Zábrana préticanje
No parking	Забрањено паркирање	Zabránjeno parkíranje
No stopping	Забрана заустављања	Zábrana zaústavljanja
dangerous bend	Опасна кривина	Opasna krivína
steep descent	Опасна низбрдица	Opasna nízbrdica
one-way traffic	Једносмерни саобраћај	Jédnosmerni sáobraćaj
crosswalk	Пешачки прелаз	Péšački prélaz
slippery road	Клизав коловоз	Klízav kólovoz
YIELD	Првенство пролаза	Prvénstvo prólaza

PEOPLE. LIFE EVENTS

181. Holidays. Event

celebration, holiday	празник (м)	práznik
national day	национални празник (м)	nacionálni práznik
public holiday	празничан дан (м)	prázničan dan
to commemorate (vt)	празновати (пг)	práznovati
event (happening)	догађај (м)	dógađaj
event (organized activity)	догађај (м)	dógađaj
banquet (party)	банкет (м)	bánket
reception (formal party)	дочек, пријем (м)	dóček, príjem
feast	гозба (ж)	gózba
anniversary	годишњица (ж)	gódišnjica
jubilee	јубилеј (м)	jubílej
to celebrate (vt)	прославити (пг)	próslaviti
New Year	Нова година (ж)	Nóva gódina
Happy New Year!	Срећна Нова година!	Srećna Nóva gódina!
Santa Claus	Деда Мраз (м)	Déda Mraz
Christmas	Божић (м)	Bóžić
Merry Christmas!	Срећан Божић!	Srećan Bóžić!
Christmas tree	Новогодишња јелка (ж)	Novogódišnja jélka
fireworks (fireworks show)	ватромет (м)	vátromet
wedding	свадба (ж)	svádba
groom	младожења (м)	mladóženja
bride	млада, невеста (ж)	mláda, névesta
to invite (vt)	позивати (пг)	pozívati
invitation card	позивница (ж)	pózivnica
guest	гост (м)	gost
to visit	ићи у госте	ići u góste
(~ your parents, etc.)		
to meet the guests	дочекивати госте	dočekívati góste
gift, present	поклон (м)	póklon
to give (sth as present)	поклањати (пг)	póklanjati
to receive gifts	добијати поклоне	dóbijati póklone
bouquet (of flowers)	букет (м)	búket
congratulations	честитка (ж)	čestitka
to congratulate (vt)	честитати (пг)	čestítati

greeting card	честитка (ж)	čestitka
to send a postcard	послати честитку	póslati čestitku
to get a postcard	добити честитку	dóbiti čestitku

toast	здравица (ж)	zdrávica
to offer (a drink, etc.)	нудити (пг)	núditi
champagne	шампањац (м)	šampánjac

to enjoy oneself	веселити се	veséliti se
merriment (gaiety)	весеље (с)	vesélje
joy (emotion)	радост (ж)	rádost

| dance | плес (м) | ples |
| to dance (vi, vt) | играти, плесати (нг) | ígrati, plésati |

| waltz | валцер (м) | válcer |
| tango | танго (м) | tángo |

182. Funerals. Burial

cemetery	гробље (с)	gróblje
grave, tomb	гроб (м)	grob
cross	крст (м)	kŕst
gravestone	надгробни споменик (м)	nádgrobni spómenik
fence	ограда (ж)	ógrada
chapel	капела (ж)	kapéla

| death | смрт (ж) | smŕt |
| to die (vi) | умрети (нг) | úmreti |

| the deceased | покојник (м) | pókojnik |
| mourning | жалост (ж) | žálost |

to bury (vt)	сахрањивати (пг)	sahranjívati
funeral home	погребно предузеће (с)	pógrebno preduzéće
funeral	сахрана (ж)	sáhrana

| wreath | венац (м) | vénac |
| casket, coffin | ковчег (м) | kóvčeg |

| hearse | погребна кола (ж) | pógrebna kóla |
| shroud | мртвачки покров (м) | mŕtvački pókrov |

funeral procession	погребна поворка (ж)	pógrebna póvorka
funerary urn	погребна урна (ж)	pógrebna úrna
crematory	крематоријум (м)	krematórijum

obituary	читуља (ж)	čítulja
to cry (weep)	плакати (нг)	plákati
to sob (vi)	јецати (пг)	jécati

183. War. Soldiers

platoon	вод (м)	vod
company	чета (ж)	četa
regiment	пук (м)	púk
army	армија (ж)	ármija
division	дивизија (ж)	divízija
section, squad	одред (м)	ódred
host (army)	војска (ж)	vójska
soldier	војник (м)	vójnik
officer	официр (м)	ofícir
private	редов (м)	rédov
sergeant	наредник (м)	nárednik
lieutenant	поручник (м)	póručnik
captain	капетан (м)	kapétan
major	мајор (м)	májor
colonel	пуковник (м)	púkovnik
general	генерал (м)	genéral
sailor	поморац, морнар (м)	pómorac, mórnar
captain	капетан (м)	kapétan
boatswain	вођа (м) палубе	vóđa pálube
artilleryman	артиљерац (м)	artiljérac
paratrooper	падобранац (м)	pádobranac
pilot	пилот (м)	pílot
navigator	навигатор (м)	navígator
mechanic	механичар (м)	meháničar
pioneer (sapper)	деминер (м)	demíner
parachutist	падобранац (м)	pádobranac
reconnaissance scout	извиђач (м)	izvíđač
sniper	снајпер (м)	snájper
patrol (group)	патрола (ж)	patróla
to patrol (vt)	патролирати (нг, пг)	patrolírati
sentry, guard	стражар (м)	strážar
warrior	војник (м)	vójnik
patriot	патриота (м)	patrióta
hero	јунак (м)	júnak
heroine	јунакиња (ж)	junákinja
traitor	издајник (м)	ízdajnik
to betray (vt)	издавати (пг)	izdávati
deserter	дезертер (м)	dezérter
to desert (vi)	дезертирати (нг)	dezertírati

mercenary	најамник (м)	nájamnik
recruit	регрут (м)	régrut
volunteer	добровољац (м)	dobrovóljac

dead (n)	убијен (м)	úbijen
wounded (n)	рањеник (м)	ránjenik
prisoner of war	заробљеник (м)	zarobljénik

184. War. Military actions. Part 1

war	рат (м)	rat
to be at war	ратовати (нг)	rátovati
civil war	грађански рат (м)	gráđanski rat

treacherously (adv)	подмукло	pódmuklo
declaration of war	објава (ж) рата	óbjava rata
to declare (~ war)	објавити (пг)	objáviti
aggression	агресија (ж)	agrésija
to attack (invade)	нападати (нг)	nápadati

to invade (vt)	инвадирати, окупирати (пг)	invadírati, okupírati
invader	освајач (м)	osvájač
conqueror	освајач (м)	osvájač

defense	одбрана (ж)	ódbrana
to defend (a country, etc.)	бранити (пг)	brániti
to defend (against ...)	бранити се	bránili se

enemy	непријатељ (м)	néprijatelj
foe, adversary	противник (м)	prótivnik
enemy (as adj)	непријатељски	neprijatéljski

| strategy | стратегија (ж) | strátegija |
| tactics | тактика (ж) | táktika |

order	наредба (ж)	náredba
command (order)	команда (ж)	kómanda
to order (vt)	наређивати (пг)	naređívati
mission	задатак (м)	zadátak
secret (adj)	тајни	tájni

| battle | битка (ж) | bítka |
| combat | бој, битка (ж) | boj, bítka |

attack	напад (м)	nápad
charge (assault)	јуриш (м)	júriš
to storm (vt)	јуришати (пг)	juríšati
siege (to be under ~)	опсада (ж)	ópsada
offensive (n)	офанзива (ж)	ofanzíva

to go on the offensive	прећи у напад	préći u nápad
retreat	повлачење (c)	povlačénje
to retreat (vi)	одступати (нг)	odstúpati
encirclement	опкољавање (c)	opkoljávanje
to encircle (vt)	опкољавати (пг)	opkoljávati
bombing (by aircraft)	бомбардовање (c)	bómbardovanje
to drop a bomb	избацити бомбу	izbáciti bómbu
to bomb (vt)	бомбардовати (пг)	bómbardovati
explosion	експлозија (ж)	eksplózija
shot	пуцањ (м)	púcanj
to fire (~ a shot)	пуцати (нг)	púcati
firing (burst of ~)	пуцање (c)	púcanje
to aim (to point a weapon)	циљати (пг)	cíljati
to point (a gun)	уперити (пг)	upériti
to hit (the target)	погодити (пг)	pogóditi
to sink (~ a ship)	потопити (пг)	potópiti
hole (in a ship)	рупа (ж)	rúpa
to founder, to sink (vi)	тонути (нг)	tónuti
front (war ~)	фронт (м)	front
evacuation	евакуација (ж)	evakuácija
to evacuate (vt)	евакуисати (пг)	evakuísati
trench	ров (м)	rov
barbwire	бодљикава жица (ж)	bódljikava žíca
barrier (anti tank ~)	препрека (ж)	prépreka
watchtower	осматрачница (ж)	osmátračnica
military hospital	војна болница (ж)	vójna bólnica
to wound (vt)	ранити (пг)	rániti
wound	рана (ж)	rána
wounded (n)	рањеник (м)	ránjenik
to be wounded	бити рањен	bíti ránjen
serious (wound)	озбиљан	ózbiljan

185. War. Military actions. Part 2

captivity	заробљеништво (c)	zarobljeníštvo
to take captive	заробити (пг)	zaróbiti
to be held captive	бити у заробљеништву	bíti u zarobljeníštvu
to be taken captive	пасти у ропство	pásti u rópstvo
concentration camp	концентрациони логор (м)	koncentracioni lógor
prisoner of war	заробљеник (м)	zarobljénik

to escape (vi)	бежати (нг)	béžati
to betray (vt)	издати (пг)	ízdati
betrayer	издајник (м)	ízdajnik
betrayal	издаја (ж)	ízdaja
to execute (by firing squad)	стрељати (пг)	stréljati
execution (by firing squad)	стрељање (с)	stréljanje
equipment (military gear)	опрема (ж)	óprema
shoulder board	еполета (ж)	epoléta
gas mask	гас маска (ж)	gas máska
field radio	покретна радио станица (ж)	pókretna rádio stánica
cipher, code	шифра (ж)	šífra
secrecy	конспирација (ж)	konspirácija
password	лозинка (ж)	lózinka
land mine	мина (ж)	mína
to mine (road, etc.)	минирати (пг)	minírati
minefield	минско поље (с)	mínsko pólje
air-raid warning	ваздушна узбуна (ж)	vázdušna úzbuna
alarm (alert signal)	узбуна (ж)	úzbuna
signal	сигнал (м)	sígnal
signal flare	сигнална ракета (ж)	sígnalna rakéta
headquarters	штаб (м)	štab
reconnaissance	извиђање (с)	izvíđanje
situation	ситуација (ж)	situácija
report	рапорт (м)	ráport
ambush	заседа (ж)	záseda
reinforcement (of army)	појачање (с)	pojačánje
target	нишан (м)	níšan
proving ground	полигон (м)	polígon
military exercise	маневри (мн)	manévri
panic	паника (ж)	pánika
devastation	рушевина (ж)	rúševina
destruction, ruins	уништења (мн)	uništénja
to destroy (vt)	разрушити (пг)	rázrušiti
to survive (vi, vt)	преживети (нг)	prežíveti
to disarm (vt)	разоружати (пг)	razorúžati
to handle (~ a gun)	обраћати се	óbraćati se
Attention!	Мирно!	Mírno!
At ease!	Вољно!	Vóljno!
feat, act of courage	подвиг (м)	pódvig
oath (vow)	заклетва (ж)	zákletva

to swear (an oath)	клети се	kléti se
decoration (medal, etc.)	награда (ж)	nágrada
to award (give medal to)	награђивати (пг)	nagrađívati
medal	медаља (ж)	médalja
order (e.g., ~ of Merit)	орден (м)	órden

victory	победа (ж)	póbeda
defeat	пораз (м)	póraz
armistice	примирје (с)	prímirje

standard (battle flag)	застава (ж)	zástava
glory (honor, fame)	слава (ж)	sláva
parade	парада (ж)	paráda
to march (on parade)	марширати (нг)	maršírati

186. Weapons

weapons	оружје (с)	óružje
firearms	ватрено оружје (с)	vátreno óružje
cold weapons (knives, etc.)	хладно оружје (с)	hládno óružje

chemical weapons	хемијско оружје (с)	hémijsko óružje
nuclear (adj)	нуклеарни	núklearni
nuclear weapons	нуклеарно оружје (с)	núklearno óružje

bomb	бомба (ж)	bómba
atomic bomb	атомска бомба (ж)	átomska bómba

pistol (gun)	пиштољ (м)	píštolj
rifle	пушка (ж)	púška
submachine gun	аутомат (м)	autómat
machine gun	митраљез (м)	mitráljez

muzzle	грло (с)	gŕlo
barrel	цев (ж)	cev
caliber	калибар (м)	kalíbar

trigger	окидач (м)	okídač
sight (aiming device)	нишан (м)	níšan
magazine	шаржер (м)	šáržer
butt (shoulder stock)	кундак (м)	kúndak

hand grenade	граната (ж)	granáta
explosive	експлозив (м)	eksplóziv

bullet	пројектил (м)	projéktil
cartridge	метак (м)	métak
charge	набој (м)	náboj
ammunition	муниција (ж)	munícija

bomber (aircraft)	бомбардер (м)	bombárder
fighter	ловачки авион (м)	lóvački avíon
helicopter	хеликоптер (м)	helikópter

anti-aircraft gun	против авионски топ (м)	prótiv avíonski top
tank	тенк (м)	tenk
tank gun	топ (м)	top

artillery	артиљерија (ж)	artiljérija
gun (cannon, howitzer)	топ (м)	top
to lay (a gun)	уперити (пг)	upériti

shell (projectile)	пројектил (м)	projéktil
mortar bomb	минобацачка мина (ж)	minobácačka mína
mortar	минобацач (м)	minobácač
splinter (shell fragment)	комадић (м)	komádić

submarine	подморница (ж)	pódmornica
torpedo	торпедо (м)	torpédo
missile	ракета (ж)	rakéta

to load (gun)	пунити (пг)	púniti
to shoot (vi)	пуцати (нг)	púcati
to point at (the cannon)	циљати (пг)	cíljati
bayonet	бајонет (м)	bajónet

rapier	мач (м)	mač
saber (e.g., cavalry ~)	сабља (ж)	sáblja
spear (weapon)	копље (с)	kóplje
bow	лук (м)	luk
arrow	стрела (ж)	stréla
musket	мускета (ж)	músketa
crossbow	самострел (м)	sámostrel

187. Ancient people

primitive (prehistoric)	првобитни	pŕvobitni
prehistoric (adj)	праисторијски	praistórijski
ancient (~ civilization)	древни	drévni

Stone Age	Камено доба (с)	Kámeno dóba
Bronze Age	Бронзано доба (с)	Brónzano dóba
Ice Age	Ледено доба (с)	Lédeno dóba

tribe	племе (с)	pléme
cannibal	људождер (м)	ljudóžder
hunter	ловац (м)	lóvac
to hunt (vi, vt)	ловити (пг)	lóviti
mammoth	мамут (м)	mámut
cave	пећина (ж)	péćina

fire	ватра (ж)	vátra
campfire	логорска ватра (ж)	lógorska vátra
cave painting	пећинска слика (ж)	pećinska slíka
tool (e.g., stone ax)	алат (м)	álat
spear	копље (с)	kóplje
stone ax	камена секира (ж)	kámena sékira
to be at war	ратовати (нг)	rátovati
to domesticate (vt)	припитомљивати (пг)	pripitomljívati
idol	идол (м)	ídol
to worship (vt)	обожавати (пг)	obožávati
superstition	сујеверје (с)	sújeverje
rite	обред (м)	óbred
evolution	еволуција (ж)	evolúcija
development	развој (м)	rázvoj
disappearance (extinction)	нестанак (м)	néstanak
to adapt oneself	прилагођавати се	prilagođávati se
archeology	археологија (ж)	arheológija
archeologist	археолог (м)	arheólog
archeological (adj)	археолошки	arheóloški
excavation site	археолошко налазиште (с)	arheóloško nálazište
excavations	ископине (мн)	ískopine
find (object)	налаз (м)	nálaz
fragment	фрагмент (м)	frágment

188. Middle Ages

people (ethnic group)	народ (м)	národ
peoples	народи (мн)	národi
tribe	племе (с)	pléme
tribes	племена (мн)	plemena
barbarians	Варвари (мн)	Várvari
Gauls	Гали (мн)	Gáli
Goths	Готи (мн)	Góti
Slavs	Славени (мн)	Slavéni
Vikings	Викинзи (мн)	Víkinzi
Romans	Римљани (мн)	Rímljani
Roman (adj)	римски	rímski
Byzantines	Византијци (мн)	Vizántijci
Byzantium	Византија (ж)	Vizántija
Byzantine (adj)	византијски	vizántijski
emperor	император (м)	imperátor

leader, chief (tribal ~)	вођа, поглавица (м)	vóđa, póglavica
powerful (~ king)	моћан	móćan
king	краљ (м)	kralj
ruler (sovereign)	владар (м)	vládar
knight	витез (м)	vítez
feudal lord	феудалац (м)	feudálac
feudal (adj)	феудалан	féudalan
vassal	вазал (м)	vázal
duke	војвода (м)	vójvoda
earl	гроф (м)	grof
baron	барон (м)	báron
bishop	епископ (м)	épiskop
armor	оклоп (м)	óklop
shield	штит (м)	štit
sword	мач (м)	mač
visor	визир (м)	vízir
chainmail	панцирна кошуља (ж)	páncirna kóšulja
Crusade	крсташки рат (м)	kŕstaški rat
crusader	крсташ (м)	kŕstaš
territory	територија (ж)	teritórija
to attack (invade)	нападати (нг)	nápadati
to conquer (vt)	освојити (нг)	osvójiti
to occupy (invade)	окупирати (нг)	okupírati
siege (to be under ~)	опсада (ж)	ópsada
besieged (adj)	опсађени	ópsađeni
to besiege (vt)	опколити (нг)	opkóliti
inquisition	инквизиција (ж)	inkvizícija
inquisitor	инквизитор (м)	inkvízitor
torture	тортура (ж)	tortúra
cruel (adj)	окрутан	ókrutan
heretic	јеретик (м)	jéretik
heresy	јерес (ж)	jéres
seafaring	морепловство (с)	moreplóvstvo
pirate	гусар (м)	gúsar
piracy	гусарство (с)	gúsarstvo
boarding (attack)	укрцај (м), укрцавање (с)	úkrcaj, ukrcávanje
loot, booty	плен (м)	plen
treasures	благо (с)	blágo
discovery	откриће (с)	otkríće
to discover (new land, etc.)	открити (нг)	ótkriti
expedition	експедиција (ж)	ekspedícija
musketeer	мускетар (м)	músketar
cardinal	кардинал (м)	kardínal

| heraldry | хералдика (ж) | heráldika |
| heraldic (adj) | хералдички | heráldički |

189. Leader. Chief. Authorities

king	краљ (м)	kralj
queen	краљица (ж)	králjica
royal (adj)	краљевски	králjevski
kingdom	краљевина (ж)	králjevina

| prince | принц (м) | princ |
| princess | принцеза (ж) | princéza |

president	председник (м)	prédsednik
vice-president	потпредседник (м)	potprédsednik
senator	сенатор (м)	sénator

monarch	монарх (м)	mónarh
ruler (sovereign)	владар (м)	vládar
dictator	диктатор (м)	diktátor
tyrant	тиранин (м)	tíranin
magnate	магнат (м)	mágnat
director	директор (м)	dírektor
chief	шеф (м)	šef
manager (director)	менаџер (м)	ménadžer
boss	газда (м)	gázda
owner	власник (м)	vlásnik

leader	вођа, лидер (м)	vóđa, líder
head (~ of delegation)	глава (ж)	gláva
authorities	власти (мн)	vlásti
superiors	руководство (с)	rúkovodstvo

governor	гувернер (м)	guvérner
consul	конзул (м)	kónzul
diplomat	дипломат (м)	diplómat
mayor	градоначелник (м)	gradonáčelnik
sheriff	шериф (м)	šérif

emperor	император (м)	imperátor
tsar, czar	цар (м)	car
pharaoh	фараон (м)	faráon
khan	кан (м)	kan

190. Road. Way. Directions

| road | пут (м) | put |
| way (direction) | пут (м) | put |

freeway	аутопут (м)	áutoput
highway	брзи пут (м)	bŕzi put
interstate	државни пут (м)	dŕžavni put

| main road | главни пут (м) | glávni put |
| dirt road | сеоски пут (м) | séoski put |

| pathway | стаза (ж), путељак (м) | stáza, putéljak |
| footpath (troddenpath) | стаза (ж) | stáza |

Where?	Где?	Gde?
Where (to)?	Куда?	Kúda?
From where?	Одакле? Откуд?	Ódakle? Ótkud?

| direction (way) | правац (м) | právac |
| to point (~ the way) | указати (пг) | ukázati |

to the left	лево	lévo
to the right	десно	désno
straight ahead (adv)	право	právo
back (e.g., to turn ~)	назад	názad

bend, curve	кривина (ж)	krivína
to turn (e.g., ~ left)	скретати (нг)	skrétati
to make a U-turn	окренути се	okrénuti se

| to be visible (mountains, castle, etc.) | бити видан | bíti vídan |
| to appear (come into view) | показати се | pokázati se |

stop, halt (e.g., during a trip)	одмор (м)	ódmor
to rest, to pause (vi)	одморити се	odmóriti se
rest (pause)	одмор (м)	ódmor

to lose one's way	залутати (нг)	zalútati
to lead to ... (ab. road)	водити до ...	vóditi dó ...
to come out (e.g., on the highway)	изаћи на ...	ízaći na ...
stretch (of road)	деоница (ж)	deónica

asphalt	асфалт (м)	ásfalt
curb	ивичњак (м)	ívičnjak
ditch	јарак (м)	járak
manhole	шахт (м)	šaht
roadside (shoulder)	ивица (ж) пута	ívica puta
pit, pothole	јама (ж)	jáma

to go (on foot)	ићи (нг)	íći
to pass (overtake)	престигнути (пг)	préstignuti
step (footstep)	корак (м)	kórak
on foot (adv)	пешке	péške

to block (road)	блокирати (пг)	blokírati
boom gate	рампа (ж)	rámpa
dead end	ћорсокак (м)	ćorsókak

191. Breaking the law. Criminals. Part 1

bandit	бандит (м)	bándit
crime	злочин (м)	zlóčin
criminal (person)	злочинац (м)	zlóčinac

thief	лопов (м)	lópov
to steal (vi, vt)	красти (нг, пг)	krásti
stealing (larceny)	крађа (ж)	kráđa
theft	крађа (ж)	kráđa

to kidnap (vt)	киднаповати (пг)	kidnapóvati
kidnapping	отмица (ж),	ótmica,
	киднаповање (с)	kidnapovanje
kidnapper	киднапер (м)	kidnáper

| ransom | откуп (м) | ótkup |
| to demand ransom | тражити откуп | trážiti ótkup |

to rob (vt)	пљачкати (пг)	pljáčkati
robbery	пљачка (ж)	pljáčka
robber	пљачкаш (м)	pljáčkaš

to extort (vt)	уцењивати (пг)	ucenjívati
extortionist	изнуђивач (м)	iznuđívač
extortion	изнуђивање (с)	iznuđívanje

to murder, to kill	убити (пг)	úbiti
murder	убиство (с)	úbistvo
murderer	убица (м)	úbica

gunshot	пуцањ (м)	púcanj
to fire (~ a shot)	пуцати (нг)	púcati
to shoot to death	устрелити (пг)	ustréliti
to shoot (vi)	пуцати (нг)	púcati
shooting	пуцњава (ж)	púcnjava

incident (fight, etc.)	инцидент (м)	incídent
fight, brawl	туча (ж)	túča
Help!	Упомоћ! У помоћ!	Upómoć! U pómoć!
victim	жртва (ж)	žŕtva

to damage (vt)	оштетити (пг)	óštetiti
damage	штета (ж)	štéta
dead body, corpse	леш (м)	leš
grave (~ crime)	тежак	téžak

to attack (vt)	нападати (нг)	nápadati
to beat (to hit)	ударати (нг)	údarati
to beat up	претући (нг)	prétući
to take (rob of sth)	отети (нг)	óteti
to stab to death	избости ножем	ízbosti nóžem
to maim (vt)	осакатити (нг)	osákatiti
to wound (vt)	ранити (нг)	ràniti
blackmail	уцењивање (с)	ucenjívanje
to blackmail (vt)	уцењивати (нг)	ucenjívati
blackmailer	уцењивач (м)	ucenjívač
protection racket	рекет (м)	réket
racketeer	рекеташ (м)	réketaš
gangster	гангстер (м)	gángster
mafia, Mob	мафија (ж)	máfija
pickpocket	џепарош (м)	džéparoš
burglar	обијач (м)	obíjač
smuggling	шверц (м)	šverc
smuggler	кријумчар (м)	kríjumčar
forgery	кривотворење (с)	krivotvórenje
to forge (counterfeit)	кривотворити (нг)	krivotvóriti
fake (forged)	лажни	lážni

192. Breaking the law. Criminals. Part 2

rape	силовање (с)	sílovanje
to rape (vt)	силовати (нг)	sílovati
rapist	силоватељ (м)	sílóvatelj
maniac	манијак (м)	mánijak
prostitute (fem.)	проститутка (ж)	próstitutka
prostitution	проституција (ж)	prostitúcija
pimp	макро (м)	mákro
drug addict	наркоман (м)	nárkoman
drug dealer	продавац (м) дроге	prodávac dróge
to blow up (bomb)	разнети (нг)	rázneti
explosion	експлозија (ж)	eksplózija
to set fire	запалити (нг)	zapáliti
arsonist	потпаљивач (м)	potpaljívač
terrorism	тероризам (м)	terorízam
terrorist	терориста (м)	terorísta
hostage	талац (м)	tálac
to swindle (deceive)	преварити (нг)	prévariti
swindle, deception	превара (ж)	prévara

swindler	варалица (м)	váralica
to bribe (vt)	потплатити (пг)	potplátiti
bribery	подмићивање (с)	podmićívanje
bribe	мито (с)	míto
poison	отров (м)	ótrov
to poison (vt)	отровати (пг)	otróvati
to poison oneself	отровати се	otróvati se
suicide (act)	самоубиство (с)	samoubístvo
suicide (person)	самоубица (м, ж)	samoubíca
to threaten (vt)	претити (нг)	prétiti
threat	претња (ж)	prétnja
to make an attempt	покушавати (пг)	pokušávati
attempt (attack)	покушај, атентат (м)	pókušaj, aténtat
to steal (a car)	украсти, отети (пг)	úkrasti, óteti
to hijack (a plane)	отети (пг)	óteti
revenge	освета (ж)	ósveta
to avenge (get revenge)	освећивати (пг)	osvećívati
to torture (vt)	мучити (пг)	múčiti
torture	тортура (ж)	tortúra
to torment (vt)	мучити (пг)	múčiti
pirate	гусар (м)	gúsar
hooligan	хулиган (м)	húligan
armed (adj)	наоружан	náoružan
violence	насиље (с)	násilje
illegal (unlawful)	илегалан	ílegalan
spying (espionage)	шпијунажа (ж)	špijunáža
to spy (vi)	шпијунирати (нг)	špijunírati

193. Police. Law. Part 1

justice	правосуђе (с)	právosuđe
court (see you in ~)	суд (м)	sud
judge	судија (м)	súdija
jurors	поротници (мн)	pórotnici
jury trial	суђење (с)	súđenje
	пред поротом	pred pórotom
to judge, to try (vt)	судити (нг)	súditi
lawyer, attorney	адвокат (м)	advókat
defendant	окривљеник (м)	ókrivljenik
dock	оптуженичка клупа (ж)	optužénička klúpa

| charge | оптужба (ж) | óptužba |
| accused | оптуженик (м) | óptuženik |

| sentence | пресуда (ж) | présuda |
| to sentence (vt) | осудити (пг) | osúditi |

guilty (culprit)	кривац (м)	krívac
to punish (vt)	казнити (пг)	kázniti
punishment	казна (ж)	kázna

fine (penalty)	новчана казна (ж)	nóvčana kázna
life imprisonment	доживотна робија (ж)	dóživotna róbija
death penalty	смртна казна (ж)	smŕtna kázna
electric chair	електрична столица (ж)	eléktrična stólica
gallows	вешала (мн)	véšala

| to execute (vt) | смакнути (пг) | smáknuti |
| execution | казна (ж) | kázna |

| prison, jail | затвор (м) | zátvor |
| cell | ћелија (ж) | ćélija |

escort (convoy)	пратња (ж)	prátnja
prison guard	чувар (м)	čúvar
prisoner	затвореник (м)	zatvorénik

| handcuffs | лисице (мн) | lísice |
| to handcuff (vt) | ставити лисице | stáviti lísice |

prison break	бекство (с)	bёkstvo
to break out (vi)	побећи (нг)	póbeći
to disappear (vi)	ишчезнути (нг)	íščeznuti
to release (from prison)	ослободити (пг)	oslobóditi
amnesty	амнестија (ж)	amnéstija

police	полиција (ж)	polícija
police officer	полицајац (м)	policájac
police station	полицијска станица (ж)	polícijska stánica
billy club	пендрек (м)	péndrek
bullhorn	мегафон (м)	mégafon

patrol car	патролна кола (ж)	pátrolna kóla
siren	сирена (ж)	siréna
to turn on the siren	укључити сирену	uključiti sirénu
siren call	звук (м) сирене	zvuk siréne

crime scene	место (с) жлочина	mésto žlóčina
witness	сведок (м)	svédok
freedom	слобода (ж)	slobóda
accomplice	саучесник (м)	sáučesnik
to flee (vi)	побећи (нг)	póbeći
trace (to leave a ~)	траг (м)	trag

194. Police. Law. Part 2

search (investigation)	потрага (ж)	pótraga
to look for …	тражити (пг)	trážiti
suspicion	сумња (ж)	súmnja
suspicious (e.g., ~ vehicle)	сумњив	súmnjiv
to stop (cause to halt)	зауставити (пг)	záustaviti
to detain (keep in custody)	задржати (пг)	zadŕžati
case (lawsuit)	кривични предмет (м)	krívični prédmet
investigation	истрага (ж)	ístraga
detective	детектив (м)	detéktiv
investigator	истражитељ (м)	istrážitelj
hypothesis	верзија (ж)	vérzija
motive	мотив (м)	mótiv
interrogation	саслушавање (с)	saslušávanje
to interrogate (vt)	саслушати (пг)	sáslušati
to question (~ neighbors, etc.)	испитивати (пг)	ispitívati
check (identity ~)	провера (ж)	próvera
round-up (raid)	рација (ж)	rácija
search (~ warrant)	претрес (м)	prétres
chase (pursuit)	потера (ж)	pótera
to pursue, to chase	гонити (пг)	góniti
to track (a criminal)	пратити (пг)	prátiti
arrest	хапшење (с)	hápšenje
to arrest (sb)	ухапсити (пг)	úhapsiti
to catch (thief, etc.)	ухватити (пг)	úhvatiti
capture	хватање, хапшење (с)	hvátanje, hápšenje
document	документ (м)	dokúmenat
proof (evidence)	доказ (м)	dókaz
to prove (vt)	доказивати (пг)	dokazívati
footprint	отисак (м) стопала	ótisak stópala
fingerprints	отисци (мн) прстију	ótisci pŕstiju
piece of evidence	доказ (м)	dókaz
alibi	алиби (м)	álibi
innocent (not guilty)	недужан	nédužan
injustice	неправда (ж)	népravda
unjust, unfair (adj)	неправедан	népravedan
criminal (adj)	криминалан	kríminalan
to confiscate (vt)	конфисковати (пг)	kónfiskovati
drug (illegal substance)	дрога (ж)	dróga
weapon, gun	оружје (с)	óružje
to disarm (vt)	разоружати (пг)	razorúžati
to order (command)	наређивати (пг)	nareðívati

to disappear (vi)	ишчезнути (нг)	íščeznuti
law	закон (м)	zákon
legal, lawful (adj)	законит	zákonit
illegal, illicit (adj)	незаконит	nezákonit
responsibility (blame)	одговорност (ж)	odgovórnost
responsible (adj)	одговоран	ódgovoran

NATURE

The Earth. Part 1

195. Outer space

space	свемир (м)	svémir
space (as adj)	космички	kósmički
outer space	свемирски простор (м)	svémirski próstor
world	свет (м)	svet
universe	универзум (м)	univérzum
galaxy	галаксија (ж)	galáksija
star	звезда (ж)	zvézda
constellation	сазвежђе (с)	sázvežđe
planet	планета (ж)	planéta
satellite	сателит (м)	satélit
meteorite	метеорит (м)	meteórit
comet	комета (ж)	kométa
asteroid	астероид (м)	asteróid
orbit	путања, орбита (ж)	pútanja, órbita
to revolve (~ around the Earth)	окретати се	okrétati se
atmosphere	атмосфера (ж)	atmosféra
the Sun	Сунце (с)	Súnce
solar system	Сунчев систем (м)	Súnčev sístem
solar eclipse	Помрачење (с) Сунца	Pomračénje Súnca
the Earth	Земља (ж)	Zémlja
the Moon	Месец (м)	Mésec
Mars	Марс (м)	Mars
Venus	Венера (ж)	Venéra
Jupiter	Јупитер (м)	Júpiter
Saturn	Сатурн (м)	Sáturn
Mercury	Меркур (м)	Mérkur
Uranus	Уран (м)	Uran
Neptune	Нептун (м)	Néptun
Pluto	Плутон (м)	Plúton
Milky Way	Млечни пут (м)	Mléčni put
Great Bear (Ursa Major)	Велики медвед (м)	Véliki médved

North Star	Северњача (ж)	Sevérnjača
Martian	марсовац (м)	marsóvac
extraterrestrial (n)	ванземаљац (м)	vanzemáljac
alien	свемирац (м)	svemírac
flying saucer	летећи тањир (м)	léteći tánjir

spaceship	свемирски брод (м)	svémirski brod
space station	орбитална станица (ж)	órbitalna stánica
blast-off	лансирање (с)	lánsiranje

engine	мотор (м)	mótor
nozzle	млазница (ж)	mláznica
fuel	гориво (с)	górivo

cockpit, flight deck	кабина (ж)	kabína
antenna	антена (ж)	anténa
porthole	бродски прозор (м)	bródski prózor
solar panel	соларни панел (м)	sólarni pánel
spacesuit	скафандар (м)	skafándar

| weightlessness | бестежинско стање (с) | béstežinsko stánje |
| oxygen | кисеоник (м) | kiseónik |

| docking (in space) | пристајање (с) | prístajanje |
| to dock (vi, vt) | спајати се (нг) | spájati se |

observatory	опсерваторија (ж)	opservatórija
telescope	телескоп (м)	téleskop
to observe (vt)	посматрати (нг)	posmátrati
to explore (vt)	истраживати (пг)	istražívati

196. The Earth

the Earth	Земља (ж)	Zémlja
the globe (the Earth)	земљина кугла (ж)	zémljina kúgla
planet	планета (ж)	planéta

atmosphere	атмосфера (ж)	atmosféra
geography	географија (ж)	geográfija
nature	природа (ж)	príroda

globe (table ~)	глобус (м)	glóbus
map	мапа (ж)	mápa
atlas	атлас (м)	átlas

Europe	Европа (ж)	Evrópa
Asia	Азија (ж)	Ázija
Africa	Африка (ж)	Áfrika
Australia	Аустралија (ж)	Austrálija
America	Америка (ж)	Amérika

| North America | Северна Америка (ж) | Séverna América |
| South America | Јужна Америка (ж) | Júžna América |

| Antarctica | Антарктик (м) | Antárktik |
| the Arctic | Арктик (м) | Árktik |

197. Cardinal directions

north	север (м)	séver
to the north	према северу	préma séveru
in the north	на северу	na séveru
northern (adj)	северни	séverni

south	југ (м)	jug
to the south	према југу	préma júgu
in the south	на југу	na júgu
southern (adj)	јужни	júžni

west	запад (м)	západ
to the west	према западу	préma západu
in the west	на западу	na západu
western (adj)	западни	západni

east	исток (м)	ístok
to the east	према истоку	préma ístoku
in the east	на истоку	na ístoku
eastern (adj)	источни	ístočni

198. Sea. Ocean

sea	море (с)	móre
ocean	океан (м)	okéan
gulf (bay)	залив (м)	záliv
straits	мореуз (м)	móreuz

land (solid ground)	копно (с)	kópno
continent (mainland)	континент (м)	kontínent
island	острво (с)	óstrvo
peninsula	полуострво (с)	poluóstrvo
archipelago	архипелаг (м)	arhipélag

bay, cove	залив (м)	záliv
harbor	лука (ж)	lúka
lagoon	лагуна (ж)	lagúna
cape	рт (м)	ŕt

| atoll | атол (м) | átol |
| reef | гребен (м) | grében |

| coral | корал (м) | kóral |
| coral reef | коралени гребен (м) | kóralni grében |

deep (adj)	дубок	dúbok
depth (deep water)	дубина (ж)	dubína
abyss	бездан (м)	bézdan
trench (e.g., Mariana ~)	ров (м)	rov

| current (Ocean ~) | струја (ж) | strúja |
| to surround (bathe) | окруживати (нг) | okružívati |

| shore | обала (ж) | óbala |
| coast | обала (ж) | óbala |

flow (flood tide)	плима (ж)	plíma
ebb (ebb tide)	осека (ж)	óseka
shoal	плићак (м)	plíćak
bottom (~ of the sea)	дно (с)	dno

wave	талас (м)	tálas
crest (~ of a wave)	гребен (м) таласа	grében talasá
spume (sea foam)	пена (ж)	péna

storm (sea storm)	морска олуја (ж)	mórska olúja
hurricane	ураган (м)	úragan
tsunami	цунами (м)	cunámi
calm (dead ~)	безветрица (ж)	bézvetrica
quiet, calm (adj)	миран	míran

| pole | пол (м) | pol |
| polar (adj) | поларни | pólarni |

latitude	ширина (ж)	širína
longitude	дужина (ж)	dužína
parallel	паралела (ж)	paraléla
equator	екватор (м)	ékvator

sky	небо (с)	nébo
horizon	хоризонт (м)	horízont
air	ваздух (м)	vázduh

lighthouse	светионик (м)	svetiónik
to dive (vi)	ронити (нг)	róniti
to sink (ab. boat)	потонути (нг)	potónuti
treasures	благо (с)	blágo

199. Seas' and Oceans' names

| Atlantic Ocean | Атлантски океан (м) | Átlantski okéan |
| Indian Ocean | Индијски океан (м) | Índijski okéan |

| Pacific Ocean | Тихи океан (м) | Tíhi okéan |
| Arctic Ocean | Северни Ледени океан (м) | Séverni Lédeni okéan |

Black Sea	Црно море (с)	Cŕno móre
Red Sea	Црвено море (с)	Cŕveno móre
Yellow Sea	Жуто море (с)	Žúto móre
White Sea	Бело море (с)	Bélo móre

Caspian Sea	Каспијско море (с)	Káspijsko móre
Dead Sea	Мртво море (с)	Mŕtvo móre
Mediterranean Sea	Средоземно море (с)	Sredózemno móre

| Aegean Sea | Егејско море (с) | Egejsko móre |
| Adriatic Sea | Јадранско море (с) | Jádransko móre |

Arabian Sea	Арабијско море (с)	Arábijsko móre
Sea of Japan	Јапанско море (с)	Jápansko móre
Bering Sea	Берингово море (с)	Béringovo móre
South China Sea	Јужно Кинеско море (с)	Južno Kinésko móre

Coral Sea	Корално море (с)	Kóralno more
Tasman Sea	Тасманово море (с)	Tasmánovo móre
Caribbean Sea	Карипско море (с)	Káripsko móre

| Barents Sea | Баренцово море (с) | Bárencovo móre |
| Kara Sea | Карско море (с) | Kársko móre |

North Sea	Северно море (с)	Séverno móre
Baltic Sea	Балтичко море (с)	Báltičko móre
Norwegian Sea	Норвешко море (с)	Nórveško móre

200. Mountains

mountain	планина (ж)	planína
mountain range	планински венац (м)	pláninski vénac
mountain ridge	планински гребен (м)	pláninski grében

summit, top	врх (м)	vŕh
peak	планиски врх (м)	plániski vŕh
foot (~ of the mountain)	подножје (с)	pódnožje
slope (mountainside)	нагиб (м), падина (ж)	nágib, pádina

volcano	вулкан (м)	vúlkan
active volcano	активни вулкан (м)	áktivni vúlkan
dormant volcano	угашени вулкан (м)	úgašeni vúlkan

eruption	ерупција (ж)	erúpcija
crater	кратер (м)	kráter
magma	магма (ж)	mágma

lava	лава (ж)	láva
molten (~ lava)	врућ	vruć
canyon	кањон (м)	kánjon
gorge	клисура (ж)	klisúra
crevice	пукотина (ж)	púkotina
abyss (chasm)	амбис, понор (м)	ámbis, pónor
pass, col	превој (м)	prévoj
plateau	висораван (ж)	vísoravan
cliff	литица (ж)	lítica
hill	брег (м)	breg
glacier	леденик (м)	ledénik
waterfall	водопад (м)	vódopad
geyser	гејзер (м)	géjzer
lake	језеро (с)	jézero
plain	равница (ж)	ravníca
landscape	пејзаж (м)	péjzaž
echo	одјек (м)	ódjek
alpinist	планинар (м)	planínar
rock climber	алпиниста (м)	alpinísta
to conquer (in climbing)	освајати (пг)	osvájati
climb (an easy ~)	пењање (с)	pénjanje

201. Mountains names

The Alps	Алпи (мн)	Álpi
Mont Blanc	Монблан (м)	Mónblan
The Pyrenees	Пиренеји (мн)	Pirenéji
The Carpathians	Карпати (мн)	Karpáti
The Ural Mountains	Уралске планине (мн)	Uralske planíne
The Caucasus Mountains	Кавказ (м)	Kávkaz
Mount Elbrus	Елбрус (м)	Elbrus
The Altai Mountains	Алтај (м)	Altaj
The Tian Shan	Тјен Шан, Тјаншан (м)	Tjen Šan, Tjánšan
The Pamir Mountains	Памир (м)	Pámir
The Himalayas	Хималаји (мн)	Himaláji
Mount Everest	Еверест (м)	Everest
The Andes	Анди (мн)	Andi
Mount Kilimanjaro	Килиманџаро (м)	Kilimandžáro

202. Rivers

river	река (ж)	réka
spring (natural source)	извор (м)	ízvor
riverbed (river channel)	корито (с)	kórito
basin (river valley)	слив (м)	sliv
to flow into …	уливати се	ulívati se
tributary	притока (ж)	prítoka
bank (of river)	обала (ж)	óbala
current (stream)	ток (м)	tok
downstream (adv)	низводно	nízvodno
upstream (adv)	узводно	úzvodno
inundation	поплава (ж)	póplava
flooding	поводањ (м)	póvodanj
to overflow (vi)	изливати се	izlívati se
to flood (vt)	преплавити (пг)	prepláviti
shallow (shoal)	плићак (м)	plíćak
rapids	брзак (м)	bŕzak
dam	брана (ж)	brána
canal	канал (м)	kánal
reservoir (artificial lake)	вештачко језеро (с)	véštačko jézero
sluice, lock	преводница (ж)	prévodnica
water body (pond, etc.)	резервоар (м)	rezervóar
swamp (marshland)	мочвара (ж)	móčvara
bog, marsh	баруштина (ж)	báruština
whirlpool	вртлог (м)	vŕtlog
stream (brook)	поток (м)	pótok
drinking (ab. water)	питка	pítka
fresh (~ water)	слатка	slátka
ice	лед (м)	led
to freeze over (ab. river, etc.)	смрзнути се	smŕznuti se

203. Rivers' names

Seine	Сена (ж)	Séna
Loire	Лоара (ж)	Loára
Thames	Темза (ж)	Témza
Rhine	Рајна (ж)	Rájna
Danube	Дунав (м)	Dúnav

Volga	**Волга** (ж)	Vólga
Don	**Дон** (м)	Don
Lena	**Лена** (ж)	Léna

Yellow River	**Хуангхе** (м)	Huánghe
Yangtze	**Јангце** (м)	Jangcé
Mekong	**Меконг** (м)	Mékong
Ganges	**Ганг** (м)	Gang

Nile River	**Нил** (м)	Nil
Congo River	**Конго** (м)	Kóngo
Okavango River	**Окаванго** (м)	Okavángo
Zambezi River	**Замбези** (м)	Zambézi
Limpopo River	**Лимпопо** (м)	Limpópo
Mississippi River	**Мисисипи** (м)	Misisípi

204. Forest

| forest, wood | **шума** (ж) | šúma |
| forest (as adj) | **шумски** | šúmski |

thick forest	**честар** (м)	čéstar
grove	**шумарак** (м)	šumárak
forest clearing	**пропланак** (м)	próplanak

| thicket | **шиpraг** (м), **шикара** (ж) | šíprag, šíkara |
| scrubland | **жбуње** (с) | žbúnje |

| footpath (troddenpath) | **стаза** (ж) | stáza |
| gully | **јаруга** (ж) | járuga |

tree	**дрво** (с)	dŕvo
leaf	**лист** (м)	list
leaves (foliage)	**лишће** (с)	líšće

fall of leaves	**листопад** (м)	lístopad
to fall (ab. leaves)	**опадати** (нг)	ópadati
top (of the tree)	**врх** (м)	vŕh

branch	**грана** (ж)	grána
bough	**грана** (ж)	grána
bud (on shrub, tree)	**пупољак** (м)	púpoljak
needle (of pine tree)	**иглица** (ж)	íglica
pine cone	**шишарка** (ж)	šíšarka

tree hollow	**дупља** (ж)	dúplja
nest	**гнездо** (с)	gnézdo
burrow (animal hole)	**јазбина, рупа** (ж)	jázbina, rúpa
trunk	**стабло** (с)	stáblo
root	**корен** (м)	kóren

| bark | кора (ж) | kóra |
| moss | маховина (ж) | máhovina |

to uproot (remove trees or tree stumps)	крчити (пг)	kŕčiti
to chop down	сећи (пг)	séći
to deforest (vt)	крчити шуму	krčiti šúmu
tree stump	пањ (м)	panj

campfire	логорска ватра (ж)	lógorska vátra
forest fire	шумски пожар (м)	šúmski póžar
to extinguish (vt)	гасити (пг)	gásiti

forest ranger	шумар (м)	šúmar
protection	заштита (ж)	záštita
to protect (~ nature)	штитити (пг)	štítiti
poacher	ловокрадица (м)	lovokrádica
steel trap	замка (ж)	zámka

| to gather, to pick (vt) | брати (пг) | bráti |
| to lose one's way | залутати (нг) | zalútati |

205. Natural resources

natural resources	природна богатства (мн)	prírodna bógatstva
minerals	рудна богатства (мн)	rúdna bógatstva
deposits	лежишта (мн)	léžišta
field (e.g., oilfield)	налазиште (с)	nálazište

to mine (extract)	добијати (пг)	dobíjati
mining (extraction)	добијање (с)	dobíjanje
ore	руда (ж)	rúda
mine (e.g., for coal)	рудник (м)	rúdnik
shaft (mine ~)	рударско окно (с)	rúdarsko ókno
miner	рудар (м)	rúdar

| gas (natural ~) | гас (м) | gas |
| gas pipeline | плиновод (м) | plínovod |

oil (petroleum)	нафта (ж)	náfta
oil pipeline	нафтовод (м)	náftovod
oil well	нафтна бушотина (ж)	náftna búšotina
derrick (tower)	нафтна платформа (ж)	náftna plátforma
tanker	танкер (м)	tánker

sand	песак (м)	pésak
limestone	кречњак (м)	kréčnjak
gravel	шљунак (м)	šljúnak
peat	тресет (м)	tréset

clay	глина (ж)	glína
coal	угаљ (м)	úgalj
iron (ore)	гвожђе (с)	gvóžđe
gold	злато (с)	zláto
silver	сребро (с)	srébro
nickel	никл (м)	nikl
copper	бакар (м)	bákar
zinc	цинк (м)	cink
manganese	манган (м)	mángan
mercury	жива (ж)	žíva
lead	олово (с)	ólovo
mineral	минерал (м)	míneral
crystal	кристал (м)	krístal
marble	мермер, мрамор (м)	mérmer, mrámor
uranium	уран (м)	úran

The Earth. Part 2

206. Weather

weather	време (c)	vréme
weather forecast	временска прогноза (ж)	vrémenska prognóza
temperature	температура (ж)	temperatúra
thermometer	термометар (м)	térmometar
barometer	барометар (м)	bárometar

humid (adj)	влажан	vlážan
humidity	влажност (ж)	vlážnost
heat (extreme ~)	врућина (ж)	vrućína
hot (torrid)	врућ	vruć
it's hot	вруће је	vrúće je

| it's warm | топло је | tóplo je |
| warm (moderately hot) | топао | tópao |

| it's cold | хладно је | hládno je |
| cold (adj) | хладан | hládan |

sun	сунце (c)	súnce
to shine (vi)	сијати (нг)	síjati
sunny (day)	сунчан	súnčan
to come up (vi)	изаћи (нг)	ízaći
to set (vi)	заћи (нг)	záći

cloud	облак (м)	óblak
cloudy (adj)	облачан	óblačan
rain cloud	кишни облак (м)	kíšni óblak
somber (gloomy)	тmuran	tmúran

rain	киша (ж)	kíša
it's raining	пада киша	páda kíša
rainy (~ day, weather)	кишовит	kišóvit
to drizzle (vi)	сипити (нг)	sípiti

pouring rain	пљусак (м)	pljúsak
downpour	пљусак (м)	pljúsak
heavy (e.g., ~ rain)	јак	jak
puddle	бара (ж)	bára
to get wet (in rain)	покиснути (нг)	pókisnuti

| fog (mist) | магла (ж) | mágla |
| foggy | магловит | maglóvit |

| snow | снег (м) | sneg |
| it's snowing | пада снег | páda sneg |

207. Severe weather. Natural disasters

thunderstorm	олуја (ж)	olúja
lightning (~ strike)	муња (ж)	múnja
to flash (vi)	севати (нг)	sévati

thunder	гром (м)	grom
to thunder (vi)	грмети (нг)	gŕmeti
it's thundering	грми	gŕmi

| hail | град (м) | grad |
| it's hailing | пада град | páda grad |

| to flood (vt) | поплавити (пг) | póplaviti |
| flood, inundation | поплава (ж) | póplava |

earthquake	земљотрес (м)	zémljotres
tremor, shoke	потрес (м)	pótres
epicenter	епицентар (м)	epicéntar
eruption	ерупција (ж)	erúpcija
lava	лава (ж)	láva

twister	вихор (м)	víhor
tornado	торнадо (м)	tórnado
typhoon	тајфун (м)	tájfun

hurricane	ураган (м)	úragan
storm	олуја (ж)	olúja
tsunami	цунами (м)	cunámi

cyclone	циклон (м)	cíklon
bad weather	невреме (с)	névreme
fire (accident)	пожар (м)	póžar
disaster	катастрофа (ж)	katastrófa
meteorite	метеорит (м)	meteórit

avalanche	лавина (ж)	lávina
snowslide	усов (м)	úsov
blizzard	мећава (ж)	méćava
snowstorm	мећава, вејавица (ж)	méćava, véjavica

208. Noises. Sounds

| silence (quiet) | тишина (ж) | tišína |
| sound | звук (м) | zvuk |

noise	бука (ж)	búka
to make noise	галамити (нг)	galamíti
noisy (adj)	бучан	búčan

loudly (to speak, etc.)	гласно	glásno
loud (voice, etc.)	гласан	glásan
constant (e.g., ~ noise)	константан	konstántan

cry, shout (n)	узвик (м)	úzvik
to cry, to shout (vi)	викати (нг)	víkati
whisper	шапат (м)	šápat
to whisper (vi, vt)	шапутати (нг, пг)	šapútati

| barking (dog's ~) | лавеж (м) | lávež |
| to bark (vi) | лајати (нг) | lájati |

groan (of pain, etc.)	стењање (с)	sténjanje
to groan (vi)	стењати (нг)	sténjati
cough	кашаљ (м)	kášalj
to cough (vi)	кашљати (нг)	kášljati

whistle	звиждук (м)	zvížduk
to whistle (vi)	звиждати (нг)	zvíždati
knock (at the door)	куцање (с)	kúcanje
to knock (on the door)	куцати (нг)	kúcati

| to crack (vi) | пуцати (нг) | púcati |
| crack (cracking sound) | пуцкање (с) | púckanje |

siren	сирена (ж)	siréna
whistle (factory ~, etc.)	сирена (ж)	siréna
to whistle (ab. train)	звиждати, трубити (нг)	zvíždati, trúbiti
honk (car horn sound)	сигнал (м)	sígnal
to honk (vi)	трубити (нг)	trúbiti

209. Winter

winter (n)	зима (ж)	zíma
winter (as adj)	зимски	zímski
in winter	зими	zími

snow	снег (м)	sneg
it's snowing	пада снег	páda sneg
snowfall	снежне падавине (мн)	snéžne pádavine
snowdrift	снежни смет (м)	snéžni smet

snowflake	пахуљица (ж)	pahúljica
snowball	грудва (ж)	grúdva
snowman	Снешко Белић (м)	Snéško Bélić
icicle	леденица (ж)	ledénica

December	децембар (м)	décembar
January	јануар (м)	jánuar
February	фебруар (м)	fébruar
frost (severe ~, freezing cold)	мраз (м)	mraz
frosty (weather, air)	мразни	mrázni
below zero (adv)	испод нуле	íspod núle
first frost	мразеви (мн)	mrázevi
hoarfrost	иње (с)	ínje
cold (cold weather)	хладноћа (ж)	hladnóća
it's cold	хладно	hládno
fur coat	бунда (ж)	búnda
mittens	рукавице (мн)	rukávice
to get sick	разболети се	razbóleti se
cold (illness)	прехлада (ж)	préhlada
to catch a cold	прехладити се	prehláditi se
ice	лед (м)	led
black ice	лед (м)	led
to freeze over (ab. river, etc.)	заледити се	zaléditi se
ice floe	ледена санта (ж)	lédena sánta
skis	скије (мн)	skíje
skier	скијаш (м)	skíjaš
to ski (vi)	скијати (нг)	skíjati
to skate (vi)	клизати (нг)	klízati

Fauna

predator	предатор, грабљивац (м)	prédator, grábljivac
tiger	тигар (м)	tígar
lion	лав (м)	lav
wolf	вук (м)	vuk
fox	лисица (ж)	lísica
jaguar	јагуар (м)	jáguar
leopard	леопард (м)	léopard
cheetah	гепард (м)	gépard
black panther	пантер (м)	pánter
puma	пума (ж)	púma
snow leopard	снежни леопард (м)	snéžni léopard
lynx	рис (м)	ris
coyote	којот (м)	kójot
jackal	шакал (м)	šákal
hyena	хијена (ж)	hijéna

animal	животиња (ж)	živótinja
beast (animal)	звер (м)	zver
squirrel	веверица (ж)	véverica
hedgehog	јеж (м)	jež
hare	зец (м)	zec
rabbit	кунић (м)	kúnić
badger	јазавац (м)	jázavac
raccoon	ракун (м)	rákun
hamster	хрчак (м)	hŕčak
marmot	мрмот (м)	mŕmot
mole	кртица (ж)	kŕtica
mouse	миш (ж)	miš
rat	пацов (м)	pácov
bat	слепи миш (м)	slépi miš
ermine	хермелин (м)	hérmelin

sable	самур (м)	sámur
marten	куна (ж)	kúna
weasel	ласица (ж)	lásica
mink	нерц, визон (м)	nerc, vízon
beaver	дабар (м)	dábar
otter	видра (ж)	vídra
horse	коњ (м)	konj
moose	лос (м)	los
deer	јелен (м)	jélen
camel	камила (ж)	kámila
bison	бизон (м)	bízon
wisent	зубар (м)	zúbar
buffalo	бивол (м)	bívol
zebra	зебра (ж)	zébra
antelope	антилопа (ж)	antilópa
roe deer	срна (ж)	sŕna
fallow deer	јелен лопатар (м)	jélen lópatar
chamois	дивокоза (ж)	dívokoza
wild boar	вепар (м)	vépar
whale	кит (м)	kit
seal	фока (ж)	fóka
walrus	морж (м)	morž
fur seal	фока (ж)	fóka
dolphin	делфин (м)	délfin
bear	медвед (м)	médved
polar bear	бели медвед (м)	béli médved
panda	панда (ж)	pánda
monkey	мајмун (м)	májmun
chimpanzee	шимпанза (ж)	šimpánza
orangutan	орангутан (м)	orangútan
gorilla	горила (ж)	goríla
macaque	макаки (м)	makáki
gibbon	гибон (м)	gíbon
elephant	слон (м)	slon
rhinoceros	носорог (м)	nósorog
giraffe	жирафа (ж)	žiráfa
hippopotamus	нилски коњ (м)	nílski konj
kangaroo	кенгур (м)	kéngur
koala (bear)	коала (ж)	koála
mongoose	мунгос (м)	múngos
chinchilla	чинчила (ж)	čínčila
skunk	твор (м)	tvor
porcupine	дикобраз (м)	díkobraz

212. Domestic animals

cat	мачка (ж)	máčka
tomcat	мачак (м)	máčak
dog	пас (м)	pas
horse	коњ (м)	konj
stallion (male horse)	ждребац (м)	ždrébac
mare	кобила (ж)	kóbila
cow	крава (ж)	kráva
bull	бик (м)	bik
ox	во (м)	vo
sheep (ewe)	овца (ж)	óvca
ram	ован (м)	óvan
goat	коза (ж)	kóza
billy goat, he-goat	јарац (м)	járac
donkey	магарац (м)	mágarac
mule	мазга (ж)	mázga
pig, hog	свиња (ж)	svínja
piglet	прасе (с)	práse
rabbit	кунић, домаћи зец (м)	kúnić, dómaći zec
hen (chicken)	кокош (ж)	kókoš
rooster	певац (м)	pévac
duck	патка (ж)	pátka
drake	патак (м)	pátak
goose	гуска (ж)	gúska
tom turkey, gobbler	ћуран (м)	ćúran
turkey (hen)	ћурка (ж)	ćúrka
domestic animals	домаће животиње (мн)	domáće živótinje
tame (e.g., ~ hamster)	питом	pítom
to tame (vt)	припитомљивати (пг)	pripitomljívati
to breed (vt)	узгајати (пг)	uzgájati
farm	фарма (ж)	fárma
poultry	живина (ж)	živína
cattle	стока (ж)	stóka
herd (cattle)	стадо (с)	stádo
stable	штала (ж)	štála
pigpen	свињац (м)	svínjac
cowshed	стаја (ж)	stája
rabbit hutch	зечињак (м)	zéčinjak
hen house	кокошињац (м)	kókošinjac

213. Dogs. Dog breeds

dog	пас (м)	pas
sheepdog	овчар (м)	óvčar
German shepherd	немачки овчар (м)	némački óvčar
poodle	пудла (ж)	púdla
dachshund	јазавичар (м)	jázavičar
bulldog	булдог (м)	búldog
boxer	боксер (м)	bókser
mastiff	мастиф (м)	mástif
Rottweiler	ротвајлер (м)	rótvajler
Doberman	доберман (м)	dóberman
basset	басет (м)	báset
bobtail	бобтејл (м)	bóbtejl
Dalmatian	далматинац (м)	dalmatínac
cocker spaniel	кокер шпанијел (м)	kóker špánijel
Newfoundland	њуфаундленд (м)	njufáundlend
Saint Bernard	бернардинац (м)	bernardínac
husky	хаски (м)	háski
Chow Chow	чау-чау (м)	čáu-čáu
spitz	шпиц (м)	špic
pug	мопс (м)	mops

214. Sounds made by animals

barking (n)	лавеж (м)	lávež
to bark (vi)	лајати (нг)	lájati
to meow (vi)	маукати (нг)	maúkati
to purr (vi)	прести (нг)	présti
to moo (vi)	мукати (нг)	múkati
to bellow (bull)	рикати (нг)	ríkati
to growl (vi)	режати (нг)	réžati
howl (n)	завијање (с)	zavijanje
to howl (vi)	завијати (нг)	zavijati
to whine (vi)	цвилети (нг)	cvíleti
to bleat (sheep)	блејати (нг)	bléjati
to oink, to grunt (pig)	гроктати (нг)	gróktati
to squeal (vi)	вриштати (нг)	vríštati
to croak (vi)	крекетати (нг)	krekétati
to buzz (insect)	зујати (нг)	zújati
to chirp (crickets, grasshopper)	цврчати (нг)	cvŕčati

215. Young animals

cub	младунче (c)	mladúnče
kitten	маче (c)	máče
baby mouse	мишић (м)	míšić
puppy	штене (c)	šténe
leveret	зеко (м)	zéko
baby rabbit	зеко, зечић (м)	zéko, zéčić
wolf cub	вучић (м)	vúčić
fox cub	лисичић (м)	lísičić
bear cub	медведић (м)	médvedić
lion cub	лавић (м)	lávić
tiger cub	тигрић (м)	tígrić
elephant calf	слонче (c)	slónče
piglet	прасе (c)	práse
calf (young cow, bull)	теле (c)	téle
kid (young goat)	jape (c)	járe
lamb	jarње (c)	jágnje
fawn (young deer)	лане (c)	láne
young camel	младунче камиле (c)	mladúnče kámile
snakelet (baby snake)	змијче (c)	zmíjče
froglet (baby frog)	жабица (ж)	žábica
baby bird	пиле (c)	píle
chick (of chicken)	пиле (c)	píle
duckling	паче (c)	páče

216. Birds

bird	птица (ж)	ptíca
pigeon	голуб (м)	gólub
sparrow	врабац (м)	vrábac
tit (great tit)	сеница (ж)	sénica
magpie	сврака (ж)	svráka
raven	гавран (м)	gávran
crow	врана (ж)	vrána
jackdaw	чавка (ж)	čávka
rook	гачац (м)	gáčac
duck	патка (ж)	pátka
goose	гуска (ж)	gúska
pheasant	фазан (м)	fázan
eagle	орао (м)	órao
hawk	jастреб (м)	jástreb

falcon	соко (м)	sóko
vulture	суп (м)	sup
condor (Andean ~)	кондор (м)	kóndor

swan	лабуд (м)	lábud
crane	ждрал (м)	ždral
stork	рода (ж)	róda

parrot	папагај (м)	papágaj
hummingbird	колибри (м)	kolíbri
peacock	паун (м)	páun

ostrich	ној (м)	noj
heron	чапља (ж)	čáplja
flamingo	фламинго (м)	flamíngo
pelican	пеликан (м)	pelíkan

| nightingale | славуј (м) | slávuj |
| swallow | ластавица (ж) | lástavica |

thrush	дрозд (м)	drozd
song thrush	дрозд певач (м)	drozd peváč
blackbird	кос (м)	kos

swift	брегуница (ж)	brégunica
lark	шева (ж)	šéva
quail	препелица (ж)	prépelica

woodpecker	детлић (м)	détlić
cuckoo	кукавица (ж)	kúkavica
owl	сова (ж)	sóva
eagle owl	совуљага (ж)	sovúljaga
wood grouse	велики тетреб (м)	véliki tétreb
black grouse	мали тетреб (м)	máli tétreb
partridge	јаребица (ж)	jarébica

starling	чворак (м)	čvórak
canary	канаринац (м)	kanarínac
hazel grouse	лештарка (ж)	léštarka
chaffinch	зеба (ж)	zéba
bullfinch	зимовка (ж)	zímovka

seagull	галеб (м)	gáleb
albatross	албатрос (м)	álbatros
penguin	пингвин (м)	píngvin

217. Birds. Singing and sounds

| to sing (vi) | певати (нг, пг) | pévati |
| to call (animal, bird) | викати (нг) | víkati |

to crow (rooster)	кукурикати (нг)	kukuríkati
cock-a-doodle-doo	кукурику	kukuríku
to cluck (hen)	кокодакати (нг)	kokodákati
to caw (crow call)	грактати (нг)	gráktati
to quack (duck call)	гакати (нг)	gákati
to cheep (vi)	пиштати (нг)	píštati
to chirp, to twitter	цвркутати (нг)	cvrkútati

218. Fish. Marine animals

bream	деверика (ж)	devérika
carp	шаран (м)	šáran
perch	гргеч (м)	gŕgeč
catfish	сом (м)	som
pike	штука (ж)	štúka
salmon	лосос (м)	lósos
sturgeon	јесетра (ж)	jésetra
herring	харинга (ж)	háringa
Atlantic salmon	атлантски лосос (м)	átlantski lósos
mackerel	скуша (ж)	skúša
flatfish	лист (м)	list
zander, pike perch	смуђ (м)	smuđ
cod	бакалар (м)	bakálar
tuna	туна (ж), туњ (м)	tuna, tunj
trout	пастрмка (ж)	pástrmka
eel	јегуља (ж)	jégulja
electric ray	ража (ж)	ráža
moray eel	мурина (ж)	múrina
piranha	пирана (ж)	pirána
shark	ајкула (ж)	ájkula
dolphin	делфин (м)	délfin
whale	кит (м)	kit
crab	краба (ж)	krába
jellyfish	медуза (ж)	medúza
octopus	хоботница (ж)	hóbotnica
starfish	морска звезда (ж)	mórska zvézda
sea urchin	морски јеж (м)	mórski jež
seahorse	морски коњић (м)	mórski kónjić
oyster	острига (ж)	óstriga
shrimp	шкамп (м)	škamp
lobster	хлап (м)	hlap
spiny lobster	јастог (м)	jástog

219. Amphibians. Reptiles

snake	змија (ж)	zmíja
venomous (snake)	отрован	ótrovan
viper	шарка (ж)	šárka
cobra	кобра (ж)	kóbra
python	питон (м)	píton
boa	удав (м)	údav
grass snake	белоушка (ж)	beloúška
rattle snake	звечарка (ж)	zvéčarka
anaconda	анаконда (ж)	anakónda
lizard	гуштер (м)	gúšter
iguana	игуана (ж)	iguána
monitor lizard	варан (м)	váran
salamander	даждевњак (м)	daždévnjak
chameleon	камелеон (м)	kameléon
scorpion	шкорпија (ж)	škórpija
turtle	корњача (ж)	kórnjača
frog	жаба (ж)	žába
toad	крастача (ж)	krástača
crocodile	крокодил (м)	krokódil

220. Insects

insect, bug	инсект (м)	ínsekt
butterfly	лептир (м)	léptir
ant	мрав (м)	mrav
fly	мува (ж)	múva
mosquito	комарац (м)	komárac
beetle	буба (ж)	búba
wasp	оса (ж)	ósa
bee	пчела (ж)	pčéla
bumblebee	бумбар (м)	búmbar
gadfly (botfly)	обад (м)	óbad
spider	паук (м)	páuk
spiderweb	паучина (ж)	páučina
dragonfly	вилин коњиц (м)	vílin kónjic
grasshopper	скакавац (м)	skákavac
moth (night butterfly)	мољац (м)	móljac
cockroach	бубашваба (ж)	bubašvába
tick	крпељ (м)	kŕpelj

| flea | бува (ж) | búva |
| midge | мушица (ж) | múšica |

locust	миграторни скакавац (м)	mígratorni skákavac
snail	пуж (м)	puž
cricket	цврчак (м)	cvŕčak
lightning bug	свитац (м)	svítac
ladybug	бубамара (ж)	bubamára
cockchafer	гундељ (м)	gúndelj

leech	пијавица (ж)	píjavica
caterpillar	гусеница (ж)	gúsenica
earthworm	црв (м)	cŕv
larva	ларва (ж)	lárva

221. Animals. Body parts

beak	кљун (м)	kljun
wings	крила (мн)	kríla
foot (of bird)	нога (ж)	nóga

feathers (plumage)	перје (с)	pérje
feather	перо (с)	péro
crest	креста (ж)	krésta

gills	шкрге (мн)	škŕge
spawn	икра (ж)	íkra
larva	личинка (ж)	líčinka

| fin | пераје (ж) | peráje |
| scales (of fish, reptile) | крљушт (ж) | kŕljušt |

fang (canine)	очњак (м)	óčnjak
paw (e.g., cat's ~)	шапа (ж)	šápa
muzzle (snout)	њушка (ж)	njúška
maw (mouth)	чељуст (ж)	čéljust

| tail | реп (м) | rep |
| whiskers | бркови (мн) | bŕkovi |

| hoof | копито (с) | kópito |
| horn | рог (м) | rog |

carapace	оклоп (м)	óklop
shell (of mollusk)	шкољка (ж)	škóljka
eggshell	љуска (ж)	ljúska

| animal's hair (pelage) | вуна (ж) | vúna |
| pelt (hide) | кожа (ж) | kóža |

222. Actions of animals

to fly (vi)	летети (нг)	léteti
to fly in circles	кружити (нг)	krúžiti
to fly away	одлетети (нг)	odléteti
to flap (~ the wings)	махати (нг)	máhati
to peck (vi)	кљуцати (нг)	kljúcati
to sit on eggs	лећи јаја	léći jája
to hatch out (vi)	излазити напоље	ízlaziti nápolje
to build a nest	вити гнездо	víti gnézdo
to slither, to crawl	пузити (нг)	púziti
to sting, to bite (insect)	бости (пг)	bósti
to bite (ab. animal)	ујед̦ати (пг)	ujédati
to sniff (vt)	њушити (пг)	njúšiti
to bark (vi)	лајати (нг)	lájati
to hiss (snake)	шиштати (нг)	šíštati
to scare (vt)	плашити (пг)	plášiti
to attack (vt)	нападати (нг)	nápadati
to gnaw (bone, etc.)	гристи (пг)	grísti
to scratch (with claws)	гребати, грепсти (пг)	grébati, grépsti
to hide (vi)	крити се	kríti se
to play (kittens, etc.)	играти се	ígrati se
to hunt (vi, vt)	ловити (пг)	lóviti
to hibernate (vi)	бити у зимском сну	bíti u zímskom snu
to go extinct	изумрети (нг)	izúmreti

223. Animals. Habitats

habitat	станиште (с)	stánište
migration	миграција (ж)	migrácija
mountain	планина (ж)	planína
reef	гребен (м)	grében
cliff	литица (ж)	lítica
forest	шума (ж)	šúma
jungle	џунгла (ж)	džúngla
savanna	савана (ж)	savána
tundra	тундра (ж)	túndra
steppe	степа (ж)	stépa
desert	пустиња (ж)	pústinja
oasis	оаза (ж)	oáza
sea	море (с)	móre

lake	језеро (c)	jézero
ocean	океан (м)	okéan
swamp (marshland)	мочвара (ж)	móčvara
freshwater (adj)	слатководни	slátkovodni
pond	језерце (c)	jézerce
river	река (ж)	réka
den (bear's ~)	брлог (м)	bŕlog
nest	гнездо (c)	gnézdo
tree hollow	дупља (ж)	dúplja
burrow (animal hole)	јазбина, рупа (ж)	jázbina, rúpa
anthill	мравињак (м)	mrávinjak

224. Animal care

zoo	зоолошки врт (м)	zoóloški vŕt
nature preserve	природни резерват (м)	prírodni rezérvat
breeder (cattery, kennel, etc.)	одгајивачница (ж)	odgajiváčnica
open-air cage	волијера (ж)	volijera
cage	кавез (м)	kávez
doghouse (kennel)	штенара (ж)	šténara
dovecot	голубињак (м)	golubínjak
aquarium (fish tank)	акваријум (м)	akvárijum
dolphinarium	делфинаријум (м)	delfinárijum
to breed (animals)	гајити (пг)	gájiti
brood, litter	потомство (c)	pótomstvo
to tame (vt)	припитомљивати (пг)	pripitomljívati
to train (animals)	дресирати (пг)	dresírati
feed (fodder, etc.)	храна (ж)	hrána
to feed (vt)	хранити (пг)	hrániti
pet store	пет шоп (м)	pet šop
muzzle (for dog)	брњица (ж)	bŕnjica
collar (e.g., dog ~)	огрлица (ж)	ógrlica
name (of animal)	надимак (м), име (c)	nádimak, íme
pedigree (of dog)	педигре (м)	pedígre

225. Animals. Miscellaneous

pack (wolves)	чопор (м)	čópor
flock (birds)	јато (c)	játo
shoal, school (fish)	јато (c)	játo
herd (horses)	крдо (c)	kŕdo

| male (n) | мужјак (м) | múžjak |
| female (n) | женка (ж) | žénka |

hungry (adj)	гладан	gládan
wild (adj)	дивљи	dívlji
dangerous (adj)	опасан	ópasan

226. Horses

| horse | коњ (м) | konj |
| breed (race) | раса (ж) | rása |

| foal | ждребе (с) | ždrébe |
| mare | кобила (ж) | kóbila |

mustang	мустанг (м)	mústang
pony	пони (м)	póni
draft horse	товарни коњ (м)	tóvarni konj

| mane | грива (ж) | gríva |
| tail | реп (м) | rep |

hoof	копито (с)	kópito
horseshoe	потковица (ж)	pótkovica
to shoe (vt)	потковати (пг)	potkóvati
blacksmith	ковач (м)	kóvač

saddle	седло (с)	sédlo
stirrup	стреме (с)	stréme
bridle	узда (ж)	úzda
reins	дизгине (мн)	dízgine
whip (for riding)	корбач (м)	kórbač

rider	јахач (м)	jáhač
to saddle up (vt)	оседлати (пг)	ósedlati
to mount a horse	сести у седло	sésti u sédlo

gallop	галоп (м)	gálop
to gallop (vi)	галопирати (нг)	galopírati
trot (n)	кас (м)	kas
at a trot (adv)	касом	kásom
to go at a trot	ићи касом	íći kásom

| racehorse | тркачки коњ (м) | tŕkački konj |
| horse racing | коњске трке (мн) | kónjske tŕke |

stable	штала (ж)	štála
to feed (vt)	хранити (пг)	hrániti
hay	сено (с)	séno
to water (animals)	појити (пг)	pójiti

to wash (horse)	чистити (пг)	čístiti
horse-drawn cart	коњска запрега (ж)	kónjska záprega
to graze (vi)	пасти (нг)	pásti
to neigh (vi)	рзати (нг)	ŕzati
to kick (to buck)	ударити (пг)	údariti

Flora

tree	дрво (c)	dŕvo
deciduous (adj)	листопадно	lístopadno
coniferous (adj)	четинарско	čétinarsko
evergreen (adj)	зимзелено	zímzeleno

apple tree	јабука (ж)	jábuka
pear tree	крушка (ж)	krúška
sweet cherry tree	трешња (ж)	tréšnja
sour cherry tree	вишња (ж)	víšnja
plum tree	шљива (ж)	šljíva

birch	бреза (ж)	bréza
oak	храст (м)	hrast
linden tree	липа (ж)	lípa
aspen	јасика (ж)	jásika
maple	јавор (м)	jávor

spruce	јела (ж)	jéla
pine	бор (м)	bor
larch	ариш (м)	áriš
fir tree	јела (ж)	jéla
cedar	кедар (м)	kédar

poplar	топола (ж)	topóla
rowan	јаребика (ж)	járebika
willow	врба (ж)	vŕba
alder	јова (ж)	jóva

| beech | буква (ж) | búkva |
| elm | брест (м) | brest |

| ash (tree) | јасен (м) | jásen |
| chestnut | кестен (м) | késten |

magnolia	магнолија (ж)	magnólija
palm tree	палма (ж)	pálma
cypress	чемпрес (м)	čémpres

mangrove	мангрово дрво (c)	mángrovo dŕvo
baobab	баобаб (м)	báobab
eucalyptus	еукалиптус (м)	eukalíptus
sequoia	секвоја (ж)	sekvója

228. Shrubs

bush	грм, жбун (м)	gŕm, žbun
shrub	жбун (м)	žbun
grapevine	винова лоза (ж)	vínova lóza
vineyard	виноград (м)	vínograd
raspberry bush	малина (ж)	málina
blackcurrant bush	црна рибизла (ж)	cŕna ríbizla
redcurrant bush	црвена рибизла (ж)	crvéna ríbizla
gooseberry bush	огрозд (м)	ógrozd
acacia	багрем (м)	bágrem
barberry	жутика, шимширика (ж)	žútika, šimšírika
jasmine	јасмин (м)	jásmin
juniper	клека (ж)	kléka
rosebush	ружин грм (м)	rúžin gŕm
dog rose	шипак (м)	šípak

229. Mushrooms

mushroom	гљива, печурка (ж)	gljíva, péčurka
edible mushroom	јестива гљива, печурка (ж)	jéstiva gljíva, péčurka
poisonous mushroom	отровна гљива (ж)	ótrovna gljíva
cap (of mushroom)	шешир (м)	šéšir
stipe (of mushroom)	ножица (ж)	nóžica
cep (Boletus edulis)	вргањ (м)	vŕganj
orange-cap boletus	јасикин турчин (м)	jásikin túrčin
birch bolete	брезов дед (м)	brézov ded
chanterelle	лисичарка (ж)	lísičarka
russula	красница (ж)	krásnica
morel	смрчак (м)	smŕčak
fly agaric	мухара (ж)	múhara
death cap	отровна гљива (ж)	ótrovna gljíva

230. Fruits. Berries

fruit	воћка (ж)	vóćka
fruits	воће, плодови (мн)	vóće, plódovi
apple	јабука (ж)	jábuka
pear	крушка (ж)	krúška
plum	шљива (ж)	šljíva

strawberry (garden ~)	јагода (ж)	jágoda
sour cherry	вишња (ж)	víšnja
sweet cherry	трешња (ж)	tréšnja
grape	грожђе (с)	gróžđe
raspberry	малина (ж)	málina
blackcurrant	црна рибизла (ж)	cŕna ríbizla
redcurrant	црвена рибизла (ж)	crvéna ríbizla
gooseberry	огрозд (м)	ógrozd
cranberry	брусница (ж)	brúsnica
orange	наранџа (ж)	nárandža
mandarin	мандарина (ж)	mandarína
pineapple	ананас (м)	ánanas
banana	банана (ж)	banána
date	урма (ж)	úrma
lemon	лимун (м)	límun
apricot	кајсија (ж)	kájsija
peach	бресква (ж)	bréskva
kiwi	киви (м)	kívi
grapefruit	грејпфрут (м)	gréjpfrut
berry	бобица (ж)	bóbica
berries	бобице (мн)	bóbice
cowberry	брусница (ж)	brúsnica
wild strawberry	шумска јагода (ж)	šúmska jágoda
bilberry	боровница (ж)	boróvnica

231. Flowers. Plants

flower	цвет (м)	cvet
bouquet (of flowers)	букет (м)	búket
rose (flower)	ружа (ж)	rúža
tulip	тулипан (м)	tulípan
carnation	каранфил (м)	karánfil
gladiolus	гладиола (ж)	gladióla
cornflower	различак (м)	razlíčak
harebell	звонце (с)	zvónce
dandelion	маслачак (м)	maslàčak
camomile	камилица (ж)	kamílica
aloe	алоја (ж)	áloja
cactus	кактус (м)	káktus
rubber plant, ficus	фикус (м)	fíkus
lily	љиљан (м)	ljíljan
geranium	гераниум, здравац (м)	geránium, zdrávac

hyacinth	зумбул (м)	zúmbul
mimosa	мимоза (ж)	mimóza
narcissus	нарцис (м)	nárcis
nasturtium	драгољуб (м)	drágoljub
orchid	орхидеја (ж)	orhidéja
peony	божур (м)	bóžur
violet	љубичица (ж)	ljubičíca
pansy	дан и ноћ	dan i noć
forget-me-not	споменак (м)	spoménak
daisy	красуљак (м)	krasúljak
poppy	мак (м)	mak
hemp	конопља (ж)	kónoplja
mint	нана, метвица (ж)	nána, métvica
lily of the valley	ђурђевак (м)	đurđévak
snowdrop	висибаба (ж)	vísibaba
nettle	коприва (ж)	kópriva
sorrel	кисељак (м)	kiséljak
water lily	локвањ (м)	lókvanj
fern	папрат (ж)	páprat
lichen	лишај (м)	líšaj
conservatory (greenhouse)	стакленик (м)	stáklenik
lawn	травњак (м)	trávnjak
flowerbed	цветна леја (ж)	cvétna léja
plant	биљка (ж)	bíljka
grass	трава (ж)	tráva
blade of grass	травчица (ж)	trávčica
leaf	лист (м)	list
petal	латица (ж)	lática
stem	стабљика (ж)	stábljika
tuber	гомољ (м)	gómolj
young plant (shoot)	изданак (м)	ízdanak
thorn	трн (м)	trn
to blossom (vi)	цветати (нг)	cvétati
to fade, to wither	венути (нг)	vénuti
smell (odor)	мирис (м)	míris
to cut (flowers)	одсећи (пг)	ódseći
to pick (a flower)	убрати (пг)	ubráti

232. Cereals, grains

grain	зрно (с)	zŕno
cereal crops	житарице (мн)	žitárice

ear (of barley, etc.)	клас (м)	klas
wheat	пшеница (ж)	pšénica
rye	раж (ж)	raž
oats	овас (м)	óvas
millet	просо (с)	próso
barley	јечам (м)	jéčam

corn	кукуруз (м)	kukúruz
rice	пиринач (м)	pírinač
buckwheat	хељда (ж)	héljda

pea plant	грашак (м)	grášak
kidney bean	пасуљ (м)	pásulj
soy	соја (ж)	sója
lentil	сочиво (с)	sóčivo
beans (pulse crops)	махунарке (мн)	mahúnarke

233. Vegetables. Greens

| vegetables | поврће (с) | póvrće |
| greens | зелен (ж) | zélen |

tomato	парадајз (м)	parádajz
cucumber	краставац (м)	krástavac
carrot	шаргарепа (ж)	šargarépa
potato	кромпир (м)	krómpir
onion	црни лук (м)	cŕni luk
garlic	бели лук (м)	béli luk

cabbage	купус (м)	kúpus
cauliflower	карфиол (м)	karfíol
Brussels sprouts	прокељ (м)	prókelj
broccoli	брокуле (мн)	brókule

beet	цвекла (ж)	cvékla
eggplant	патлиџан (м)	patlidžán
zucchini	тиквица (ж)	tíkvica
pumpkin	тиква (ж)	tíkva
turnip	репа (ж)	répa

parsley	першун (м)	péršun
dill	мирођија (ж)	miróđija
lettuce	зелена салата (ж)	zélena saláta
celery	целер (м)	céler
asparagus	шпаргла (ж)	špárgla
spinach	спанаћ (м)	spánać

pea	грашак (м)	grášak
beans	махунарке (мн)	mahúnarke
corn (maize)	кукуруз (м)	kukúruz

kidney bean	пасуљ (м)	pásulj
pepper	паприка (ж)	páprika
radish	ротквица (ж)	rótkvica
artichoke	артичока (ж)	artičóka

REGIONAL GEOGRAPHY

234. Western Europe

Europe	Европа (ж)	Evrópa
European Union	Европска унија (ж)	Evrópska únija
European (n)	Европљанин (м)	Evrópljanin
European (adj)	европски	évropski
Austria	Аустрија (ж)	Áustrija
Austrian (masc.)	Аустријанац (м)	Austrijánac
Austrian (fem.)	Аустријанка (ж)	Austríjanka
Austrian (adj)	аустријски	áustrijski
Great Britain	Велика Британија (ж)	Vélika Brítanija
England	Енглеска (ж)	Engleska
British (masc.)	Енглез (м)	Englez
British (fem.)	Енглескиња (ж)	Engléskinja
English, British (adj)	енглески	éngleski
Belgium	Белгија (ж)	Bélgija
Belgian (masc.)	Белгијанац (м)	Belgijánac
Belgian (fem.)	Белгијанка (ж)	Belgíjanka
Belgian (adj)	белгијски	bélgijski
Germany	Немачка (ж)	Némačka
German (masc.)	Немац (м)	Némac
German (fem.)	Немица (ж)	Némica
German (adj)	немачки	némački
Netherlands	Низоземска (ж)	Nízozemska
Holland	Холандија (ж)	Holándija
Dutch (masc.)	Холанђанин (м)	Holánđanin
Dutch (fem.)	Холанђанка (ж)	Holánđanka
Dutch (adj)	холандски	hólandski
Greece	Грчка (ж)	Gŕčka
Greek (masc.)	Грк (м)	Gŕk
Greek (fem.)	Гркиња (ж)	Gŕkinja
Greek (adj)	грчки	gŕčki
Denmark	Данска (ж)	Dánska
Dane (masc.)	Данац (м)	Dánac
Dane (fem.)	Данкиња (ж)	Dánkinja
Danish (adj)	дански	dánski
Ireland	Ирска (ж)	Irska

Irish (masc.)	Ирац (м)	Irac
Irish (fem.)	Иркиња (ж)	Irkinja
Irish (adj)	ирски	írski

Iceland	Исланд (м)	Island
Icelander (masc.)	Исланђанин (м)	Islánđanin
Icelander (fem.)	Исланђанка (ж)	Islánđanka
Icelandic (adj)	исландски	íslandski

Spain	Шпанија (ж)	Špánija
Spaniard (masc.)	Шпанац (м)	Špánac
Spaniard (fem.)	Шпанкиња (ж)	Špánkinja
Spanish (adj)	шпански	špánski

Italy	Италија (ж)	Itálija
Italian (masc.)	Италијан (м)	Italíjan
Italian (fem.)	Италијанка (ж)	Italíjanka
Italian (adj)	италијански	italíjanski

Cyprus	Кипар (м)	Kípar
Cypriot (masc.)	Кипранин (м)	Kípranin
Cypriot (fem.)	Кипранка (ж)	Kípranka
Cypriot (adj)	кипарски	kíparski

Malta	Малта (ж)	Málta
Maltese (masc.)	Малтежанин (м)	Maltéžanin
Maltese (fem.)	Малтежанка (ж)	Maltéžanka
Maltese (adj)	малтешки	málteški

Norway	Норвешка (ж)	Nórveška
Norwegian (masc.)	Норвежанин (м)	Norvéžanin
Norwegian (fem.)	Норвежанка (ж)	Norvéžanka
Norwegian (adj)	норвешки	nórveški

Portugal	Португалија (ж)	Portugálija
Portuguese (masc.)	Португалац (м)	Portugálac
Portuguese (fem.)	Португалка (ж)	Portugálka
Portuguese (adj)	португалски	portugálski

Finland	Финска (ж)	Fínska
Finn (masc.)	Финац (м)	Fínac
Finn (fem.)	Финкиња (ж)	Fínkinja
Finnish (adj)	фински	fínski

France	Француска (ж)	Fráncuska
French (masc.)	Француз (м)	Fráncuz
French (fem.)	Францускиња (ж)	Fráncuskinja
French (adj)	француски	fráncuski

Sweden	Шведска (ж)	Švédska
Swede (masc.)	Швеђанин (м)	Švéđanin
Swede (fem.)	Швеђанка (ж)	Švéđanka

Swedish (adj)	шведски	švédski
Switzerland	Швајцарска (ж)	Švájcarska
Swiss (masc.)	Швајцарац (м)	Švájcarac
Swiss (fem.)	Швајцаркиња (ж)	Švájcarkinja
Swiss (adj)	швајцарски	švájcarski

Scotland	Шкотска (ж)	Škótska
Scottish (masc.)	Шкот (м)	Škot
Scottish (fem.)	Шкоткиња (ж)	Škótkinja
Scottish (adj)	шкотски	škótski

Vatican	Ватикан (м)	Vátikan
Liechtenstein	Лихтенштајн (м)	Líhtenštajn
Luxembourg	Луксембург (м)	Lúksemburg
Monaco	Монако (м)	Mónako

235. Central and Eastern Europe

Albania	Албанија (ж)	Albánija
Albanian (masc.)	Албанац (м)	Albánac
Albanian (fem.)	Албанка (ж)	Álbanka
Albanian (adj)	албански	álbanski

Bulgaria	Бугарска (ж)	Búgarska
Bulgarian (masc.)	Бугарин (м)	Búgarin
Bulgarian (fem.)	Бугарка (ж)	Búgarka
Bulgarian (adj)	бугарски	búgarski

Hungary	Мађарска (ж)	Máđarska
Hungarian (masc.)	Мађар (м)	Máđar
Hungarian (fem.)	Мађарица (ж)	Mađárica
Hungarian (adj)	мађарски	máđarski

Latvia	Летонија (ж)	Létonija
Latvian (masc.)	Летонац (м)	Letónac
Latvian (fem.)	Летонка (ж)	Letonka
Latvian (adj)	летонски	létonski

Lithuania	Литванија (ж)	Litvánija
Lithuanian (masc.)	Литванац (м)	Litvánac
Lithuanian (fem.)	Литванка (ж)	Litvanka
Lithuanian (adj)	литвански	litvánski

Poland	Пољска (ж)	Póljska
Pole (masc.)	Пољак (м)	Póljak
Pole (fem.)	Пољакиња (ж)	Poljákinja
Polish (adj)	пољски	póljski

| Romania | Румунија (ж) | Rúmunija |
| Romanian (masc.) | Румун (м) | Rúmun |

| Romanian (fem.) | Румунка (ж) | Rumunka |
| Romanian (adj) | румунски | rúmunski |

Serbia	Србија (ж)	Sŕbija
Serbian (masc.)	Србин (м)	Sŕbin
Serbian (fem.)	Српкиња (ж)	Sŕpkinja
Serbian (adj)	српски	sŕpski

Slovakia	Словачка (ж)	Slóvačka
Slovak (masc.)	Словак (м)	Slóvak
Slovak (fem.)	Словакиња (ж)	Slovákinja
Slovak (adj)	словачки	slóvački

Croatia	Хрватска (ж)	Hrvátska
Croatian (masc.)	Хрват (м)	Hŕvat
Croatian (fem.)	Хрватица (ж)	Hrvática
Croatian (adj)	хрватски	hŕvatski

Czech Republic	Чешка република (ж)	Čéška repúblika
Czech (masc.)	Чех (м)	Čeh
Czech (fem.)	Чехиња (ж)	Čéhinja
Czech (adj)	чешки	čéški

Estonia	Естонија (ж)	Estonija
Estonian (masc.)	Естонац (м)	Estónac
Estonian (fem.)	Естонка (ж)	Estónka
Estonian (adj)	естонски	éstonski

Bosnia and Herzegovina	Босна и Херцеговина (ж)	Bósna i Hércegovina
Macedonia (Republic of ~)	Македонија (ж)	Mákedonija
Slovenia	Словенија (ж)	Slóvenija
Montenegro	Црна Гора (ж)	Cŕna Góra

236. Former USSR countries

Azerbaijan	Азербејџан (м)	Azerbéjdžan
Azerbaijani (masc.)	Азербејџанац (м)	Azerbejdžánac
Azerbaijani (fem.)	Азербејџанка (ж)	Azerbejdžánka
Azerbaijani, Azeri (adj)	азербејџански	azerbejdžánski

Armenia	Јерменија (ж)	Jérmenija
Armenian (masc.)	Јерменин (м)	Jermenin
Armenian (fem.)	Јерменка (ж)	Jermenka
Armenian (adj)	јермենски	jermenski

Belarus	Белорусија (ж)	Belorúsija
Belarusian (masc.)	Белорус (м)	Bélorus
Belarusian (fem.)	Белорускиња (ж)	Beloruskinja
Belarusian (adj)	белоруски	béloruski
Georgia	Грузија (ж)	Grúzija

Georgian (masc.)	Грузијанац (м)	Gruzijanac
Georgian (fem.)	Грузијанка (ж)	Gruzijanka
Georgian (adj)	грузијски	grúzijski

Kazakhstan	Казахстан (м)	Kázahstan
Kazakh (masc.)	Казах (м)	Kázah
Kazakh (fem.)	Казахиња (ж)	Kázahinja
Kazakh (adj)	казашки	kázaški

Kirghizia	Киргистан (м)	Kírgistan
Kirghiz (masc.)	Киргиз (м)	Kírgiz
Kirghiz (fem.)	Киргискиња (ж)	Kirgiskinja
Kirghiz (adj)	киргиски	kírgiski

Moldova, Moldavia	Молдавија (ж)	Moldávija
Moldavian (masc.)	Молдавац (м)	Móldavac
Moldavian (fem.)	Молдавка (ж)	Móldavka
Moldavian (adj)	молдавски	móldavski

Russia	Русија (ж)	Rúsija
Russian (masc.)	Рус (м)	Rus
Russian (fem.)	Рускиња (ж)	Rúskinja
Russian (adj)	руски	rúski

Tajikistan	Таџикистан (м)	Tadžikístan
Tajik (masc.)	Таџик (м)	Tadžik
Tajik (fem.)	Таџикиња (ж)	Tadžikinja
Tajik (adj)	таџички	tádžički

Turkmenistan	Туркменистан (м)	Turkménıstan
Turkmen (masc.)	Туркмен (м)	Túrkmen
Turkmen (fem.)	Туркменка (ж)	Turkmenka
Turkmenian (adj)	туркменски	túrkmenski

Uzbekistan	Узбекистан (м)	Uzbekistan
Uzbek (masc.)	Узбек (м)	Uzbek
Uzbek (fem.)	Узбекиња (ж)	Uzbekinja
Uzbek (adj)	узбечки	úzbečki

Ukraine	Украјина (ж)	Úkrajina
Ukrainian (masc.)	Украјинац (м)	Ukrajinac
Ukrainian (fem.)	Украјинка (ж)	Ukrajinka
Ukrainian (adj)	украјински	úkrajinski

237. Asia

Asia	Азија (ж)	Ázija
Asian (adj)	азијски	ázijski
Vietnam	Вијетнам (м)	Víjetnam
Vietnamese (masc.)	Вијетнамац (м)	Vijetnamac

| Vietnamese (fem.) | Вијетнамка (ж) | Vijetnamka |
| Vietnamese (adj) | вијетнамски | víjetnamski |

India	Индија (ж)	Índija
Indian (masc.)	Индијац (м)	Indijac
Indian (fem.)	Индијка (ж)	Indijka
Indian (adj)	индијски	índijski

Israel	Израел (м)	Izrael
Israeli (masc.)	Израелац (м)	Izraélac
Israeli (fem.)	Израелка (ж)	Izraélka
Israeli (adj)	израелски	ízraelski

Jew (n)	Јеврејин (м)	Jévrejin
Jewess (n)	Јеврејка (ж)	Jévrejka
Jewish (adj)	јеврејски	jévrejski

China	Кина (ж)	Kína
Chinese (masc.)	Кинез (м)	Kínez
Chinese (fem.)	Кинескиња (ж)	Kinéskinja
Chinese (adj)	кинески	kíneski

Korean (masc.)	Корејац (м)	Koréjac
Korean (fem.)	Корејка (ж)	Koréjka
Korean (adj)	корејски	koréjski

Lebanon	Либан (м)	Líban
Lebanese (masc.)	Либанац (м)	Libánac
Lebanese (fem.)	Либанка (ж)	Libánka
Lebanese (adj)	либански	libánski

Mongolia	Монголија (ж)	Móngolija
Mongolian (masc.)	Монгол (м)	Móngol
Mongolian (fem.)	Монголка (ж)	Móngolka
Mongolian (adj)	монголски	móngolski

Malaysia	Малезија (ж)	Malézija
Malaysian (masc.)	Малајац (м)	Malájac
Malaysian (fem.)	Малајка (ж)	Málajka
Malaysian (adj)	малајски	malájski

Pakistan	Пакистан (м)	Pákistan
Pakistani (masc.)	Пакистанац (м)	Pakistánac
Pakistani (fem.)	Пакистанка (ж)	Pakistánka
Pakistani (adj)	пакистански	pákistanski

Saudi Arabia	Саудијска Арабија (ж)	Sáudijska Árabija
Arab (masc.)	Арапин (м)	Árapin
Arab (fem.)	Арапкиња (ж)	Árapkinja
Arab, Arabic (adj)	арапски	árapski
Thailand	Тајланд (м)	Tájland
Thai (masc.)	Тајланђанин (м)	Tajlánđanin

Thai (fem.)	Тајланђанка (ж)	Tajlánđanka
Thai (adj)	тајландски	tájlandski
Taiwan	Тајван (м)	Tájvan
Taiwanese (masc.)	Тајванац (м)	Tajvánac
Taiwanese (fem.)	Тајванка (ж)	Tájvanka
Taiwanese (adj)	тајвански	tájvanski
Turkey	Турска (ж)	Túrska
Turk (masc.)	Турчин (м)	Túrčin
Turk (fem.)	Туркиња (ж)	Túrkinja
Turkish (adj)	турски	túrski
Japan	Јапан (м)	Jápan
Japanese (masc.)	Јапанац (м)	Japánac
Japanese (fem.)	Јапанка (ж)	Japánka
Japanese (adj)	јапански	jápanski
Afghanistan	Авганистан (м)	Avganístan
Bangladesh	Бангладеш (м)	Bángladeš
Indonesia	Индонезија (ж)	Indonezija
Jordan	Јордан (м)	Jórdan
Iraq	Ирак (м)	Irak
Iran	Иран (м)	Iran
Cambodia	Камбоџа (ж)	Kambódža
Kuwait	Кувајт (м)	Kúvajt
Laos	Лаос (м)	Láos
Myanmar	Мјанмар (м)	Mjánmar
Nepal	Непал (м)	Népal
United Arab Emirates	Уједињени Арапски Емирати	Ujedínjeni Árapski Emiráti
Syria	Сирија (ж)	Sírija
Palestine	Палестина (ж)	Palestína
South Korea	Јужна Кореја (ж)	Júžna Koréja
North Korea	Северна Кореја (ж)	Séverna Koréja

238. North America

United States of America	Сједињене Америчке Државе	Sjédinjene Américke Države
American (masc.)	Американац (м)	Amerikánac
American (fem.)	Американка (ж)	Amerikánka
American (adj)	амерички	américki
Canada	Канада (ж)	Kanada
Canadian (masc.)	Канађанин (м)	Kanáđanin
Canadian (fem.)	Канађанка (ж)	Kanáđanka

Canadian (adj)	канадски	kánadski
Mexico	Мексико (м)	Méksiko
Mexican (masc.)	Мексиканац (м)	Meksikánac
Mexican (fem.)	Мексиканка (ж)	Meksikánka
Mexican (adj)	мексикански	meksíkanski

239. Central and South America

Argentina	Аргентина (ж)	Argentína
Argentinian (masc.)	Аргентинац (м)	Argentínac
Argentinian (fem.)	Аргентинка (ж)	Argentínka
Argentinian (adj)	аргентински	argéntinski

Brazil	Бразил (м)	Brázil
Brazilian (masc.)	Бразилац (м)	Brazílac
Brazilian (fem.)	Бразилка (ж)	Brazílka
Brazilian (adj)	бразилски	brázilski

Colombia	Колумбија (ж)	Kolúmbija
Colombian (masc.)	Колумбијац (м)	Kolumbíjac
Colombian (fem.)	Колумбијка (ж)	Kolúmbijka
Colombian (adj)	колумбијски	kolúmbijski

Cuba	Куба (ж)	Kúba
Cuban (masc.)	Кубанац (м)	Kubánac
Cuban (fem.)	Кубанка (ж)	Kubánka
Cuban (adj)	кубански	kubánski

Chile	Чиле (м)	Číle
Chilean (masc.)	Чилеанац (м)	Čileánac
Chilean (fem.)	Чилеанка (ж)	Čileánka
Chilean (adj)	чилеански	čileánski

| Bolivia | Боливија (ж) | Bolívija |
| Venezuela | Венецуела (ж) | Venecuéla |

| Paraguay | Парагвај (м) | Páragvaj |
| Peru | Перу (м) | Péru |

Suriname	Суринам (м)	Surínam
Uruguay	Уругвај (м)	Urugvaj
Ecuador	Еквадор (м)	Ekvador

| The Bahamas | Бахами (мн) | Bahámi |
| Haiti | Хаити (м) | Haiti |

Dominican Republic	Доминиканска република (ж)	Dominikanska repúblika
Panama	Панама (ж)	Pánama
Jamaica	Јамајка (ж)	Jamájka

240. Africa

Egypt	**Египат** (м)	Egipat
Egyptian (masc.)	**Египћанин** (м)	Egipćanin
Egyptian (fem.)	**Египћанка** (ж)	Egipćanka
Egyptian (adj)	**египатски**	égipatski

Morocco	**Мароко** (м)	Maróko
Moroccan (masc.)	**Мароканац** (м)	Marokánac
Moroccan (fem.)	**Мароканка** (ж)	Marokánka
Moroccan (adj)	**марокански**	marokánski

Tunisia	**Тунис** (м)	Túnis
Tunisian (masc.)	**Тунижанин** (м)	Tunížanin
Tunisian (fem.)	**Тунижанка** (ж)	Tunížanka
Tunisian (adj)	**туниски**	túniski

Ghana	**Гана** (ж)	Gána
Zanzibar	**Занзибар** (м)	Zanzibar
Kenya	**Кенија** (ж)	Kénija
Libya	**Либија** (ж)	Líbija
Madagascar	**Мадагаскар** (м)	Madagáskar

Namibia	**Намибија** (ж)	Námibija
Senegal	**Сенегал** (м)	Sénegal
Tanzania	**Танзанија** (ж)	Tánzanija
South Africa	**Јужноафричка република** (ж)	Južnoáfrička repúblika

African (masc.)	**Африканац** (м)	Afrikánac
African (fem.)	**Африканка** (ж)	Afrikánka
African (adj)	**афрички, африкански**	áfrički, afríkanski

241. Australia. Oceania

Australia	**Аустралија** (ж)	Austrálija
Australian (masc.)	**Аустралијанац** (м)	Australijánac
Australian (fem.)	**Аустралијанка** (ж)	Australíjanka
Australian (adj)	**аустралијски**	aústralijski

| New Zealand | **Нови Зеланд** (м) | Nóvi Zéland |
| New Zealander (masc.) | **Новозеланђанин** (м) | Novozelánđanin |

| New Zealander (fem.) | **Новозеланђанка** (ж) | Novozelánđanka |
| New Zealand (as adj) | **новозеландски** | novozélandski |

| Tasmania | **Тасманија** (ж) | Tásmanija |
| French Polynesia | **Француска Полинезија** (ж) | Fráncuska Polinézija |

242. Cities

Amsterdam	Амстердам (м)	Ámsterdam
Ankara	Анкара (ж)	Ánkara
Athens	Атина (ж)	Atína
Baghdad	Багдад (м)	Bágdad
Bangkok	Бангкок (м)	Bángkok
Barcelona	Барселона (ж)	Barselóna
Beijing	Пекинг (м)	Péking
Beirut	Бејрут (м)	Béjrut
Berlin	Берлин (м)	Bérlin
Mumbai (Bombay)	Бомбај (м)	Bómbaj
Bonn	Бон (м)	Bon
Bordeaux	Бордо (м)	Bordó
Bratislava	Братислава (ж)	Brátislava
Brussels	Брисел (м)	Brísel
Bucharest	Букурешт (м)	Búkurešt
Budapest	Будимпешта (ж)	Búdimpešta
Cairo	Каиро (м)	Káiro
Kolkata (Calcutta)	Калкута (ж)	Kalkúta
Chicago	Чикаго (м)	Čikágo
Copenhagen	Копенхаген (м)	Kopenhágen
Dar-es-Salaam	Дар ес Салам (м)	Dar es Salám
Delhi	Делхи (м)	Délhi
Dubai	Дубаи (м)	Dubái
Dublin	Даблин (м)	Dáblin
Düsseldorf	Диселдорф (м)	Díseldorf
Florence	Фиренца (ж)	Firénca
Frankfurt	Франкфурт (м)	Fránkfurt
Geneva	Женева (ж)	Ženéva
The Hague	Хаг (м)	Hag
Hamburg	Хамбург (м)	Hámburg
Hanoi	Ханој (м)	Hánoj
Havana	Хавана (ж)	Havána
Helsinki	Хелсинки (м)	Hélsinki
Hiroshima	Хирошима (ж)	Hirošíma
Hong Kong	Хонгконг (м)	Hóngkong
Istanbul	Истанбул (м)	Istanbul
Jerusalem	Јерусалим (м)	Jerusálim
Kyiv	Кијев (м)	Kíjev
Kuala Lumpur	Куала Лумпур (м)	Kuála Lúmpur
Lisbon	Лисабон (м)	Lísabon
London	Лондон (м)	Lóndon
Los Angeles	Лос Анђелес (м)	Los Anđeles

Lyons	Лион (м)	Líon
Madrid	Мадрид (м)	Mádrid
Marseille	Марсеј (м)	Marséj
Mexico City	Мексико (м)	Méksiko
Miami	Мајами (м)	Majámi
Montreal	Монтреал (м)	Móntreal
Moscow	Москва (ж)	Móskva
Munich	Минхен (м)	Mínhen
Nairobi	Најроби (м)	Najróbi
Naples	Напуљ (м)	Nápulj
New York	Њујорк (м)	Njújork
Nice	Ница (ж)	Níca
Oslo	Осло (с)	Oslo
Ottawa	Отава (ж)	Otava
Paris	Париз (м)	Páriz
Prague	Праг (м)	Prag
Rio de Janeiro	Рио де Жанеиро (м)	Río de Žanéiro
Rome	Рим (м)	Rim
Saint Petersburg	Санкт Петербург (м)	Sankt Péterburg
Seoul	Сеул (м)	Séul
Shanghai	Шангај (м)	Šángaj
Singapore	Сингапур (м)	Síngapur
Stockholm	Стокхолм (м)	Stókholm
Sydney	Сиднеј (м)	Sídnej
Taipei	Тајпеј (м)	Tájpej
Tokyo	Токио (м)	Tókio
Toronto	Торонто (м)	Torónto
Venice	Венеција (ж)	Vénecija
Vienna	Беч (м)	Beč
Warsaw	Варшава (ж)	Váršava
Washington	Вашингтон (м)	Vášington

243. Politics. Government. Part 1

politics	политика (ж)	polítika
political (adj)	политички	polítički
politician	политичар (м)	polítičar
state (country)	држава (ж)	država
citizen	држављанин (м)	državljanin
citizenship	држављанство (с)	državljánstvo
national emblem	државни грб (м)	državni grb
national anthem	државна химна (ж)	državna hímna
government	влада (ж)	vláda

head of state	шеф (м) државе	šef držáve
parliament	парламент (м)	parláment
party	странка (ж)	stránka

| capitalism | капитализам (м) | kapitalízam |
| capitalist (adj) | капиталистички | kapitalístički |

| socialism | социјализам (м) | socijalízam |
| socialist (adj) | социјалистички | socijalístički |

communism	комунизам (м)	komunízam
communist (adj)	комунистички	komunístički
communist (n)	комуниста (м)	komunísta

democracy	демократија (ж)	demokrátija
democrat	демократа (м)	demókrata
democratic (adj)	демократски	demókratski
Democratic party	демократска странка (ж)	demókratska stránka

liberal (n)	либерал (м)	libéral
liberal (adj)	либералан	líberalan
conservative (n)	конзерватор (м)	konzervátor
conservative (adj)	конзервативни	kónzervativni

republic (n)	република (ж)	repúblika
republican (n)	републиканац (м)	republikánac
Republican party	републиканска странка (ж)	republíkanska stránka

| elections | избори (мн) | ízbori |
| to elect (vt) | изабирати (нг) | izábirati |

| elector, voter | бирач (м) | bírač |
| election campaign | изборна кампања (ж) | ízborna kampánja |

voting (n)	гласање (с)	glásanje
to vote (vi)	гласати (нг)	glásati
suffrage, right to vote	право (с) гласа	právo glása

candidate	кандидат (м)	kandídat
to be a candidate	кандидовати се	kandidovati se
campaign	кампања (ж)	kampánja

| opposition (as adj) | опозициони | opozícioni |
| opposition (n) | опозиција (ж) | opozícija |

visit	посета (ж)	póseta
official visit	званична посета (ж)	zvánična póseta
international (adj)	међународни	međunárodni

| negotiations | преговори (мн) | prégovori |
| to negotiate (vi) | преговарати (нг) | pregovárati |

244. Politics. Government. Part 2

society	друштво (с)	drúštvo
constitution	устав (м)	ústav
power (political control)	власт (ж)	vlast
corruption	корупција (ж)	korúpcija
law (justice)	закон (м)	zákon
legal (legitimate)	законит	zákonit
justice (fairness)	правда (ж)	právda
just (fair)	праведан	právedan
committee	комитет (м)	komítet
bill (draft law)	нацрт (м) закона	nacrt zákona
budget	буџет (м)	búdžet
policy	политика (ж)	polítika
reform	реформа (ж)	réforma
radical (adj)	радикалан	rádikalan
power (strength, force)	снага (ж)	snága
powerful (adj)	моћан	móćan
supporter	присталица (м)	prístalica
influence	утицај (м)	úticaj
regime (e.g., military ~)	режим (м)	réžim
conflict	конфликт (м)	kónflikt
conspiracy (plot)	завера (ж)	závera
provocation	провокација (ж)	provokácija
to overthrow (regime, etc.)	оборити (пг)	obóriti
overthrow (of government)	свргавање (с)	svrgávanje
revolution	револуција (ж)	revolúcija
coup d'état	државни удар (м)	dŕžavni údar
military coup	војни удар (м)	vójni údar
crisis	криза (ж)	kríza
economic recession	економски пад (м)	ekónomski pad
demonstrator (protester)	демонстрант (м)	demónstrant
demonstration	демонстрација (ж)	demonstrácija
martial law	ванредно стање (с)	vánredno stánje
military base	војна база (ж)	vójna báza
stability	стабилност (ж)	stabílnost
stable (adj)	стабилан	stábilan
exploitation	експлоатација (ж)	eksploatácija
to exploit (workers)	експлоатисати (пг)	eksploatísati
racism	расизам (м)	rasízam
racist	расиста (м)	rásista

| fascism | фашизам (м) | fašízam |
| fascist | фашиста (м) | fašísta |

245. Countries. Miscellaneous

foreigner	странац (м)	stránac
foreign (adj)	стран	stran
abroad (in a foreign country)	у иностранству	u inostránstvu

emigrant	емигрант (м)	emígrant
emigration	емиграција (ж)	emigrácija
to emigrate (vi)	емигрирати (нг)	emigrírati

the West	Запад (м)	Západ
the East	Исток (м)	Ístok
the Far East	Далеки Исток (м)	Dáleki Ístok

civilization	цивилизација (ж)	civilizácija
humanity (mankind)	човечанство (с)	čovečánstvo
the world (earth)	свет (м)	svet
peace	мир (м)	mir
worldwide (adj)	светски	svétski

homeland	отаџбина (ж)	ótadžbina
people (population)	народ (м)	národ
population	становништво (с)	stanovníštvo

people (a lot of ~)	људи (мн)	ljúdi
nation (people)	нација (ж)	nácija
generation	генерација (ж)	generácija

territory (area)	територија (ж)	teritórija
region	регион (м)	región
state (part of a country)	држава (ж)	dŕžava

tradition	традиција (ж)	trádicija
custom (tradition)	обичај (м)	óbičaj
ecology	екологија (ж)	ekológija

Indian (Native American)	Индијанац (м)	Indijánac
Gypsy (masc.)	Циганин (м)	Cíganin
Gypsy (fem.)	Циганка (ж)	Cíganka
Gypsy (adj)	цигански	cíganski

empire	империја (ж)	impérija
colony	колонија (ж)	kólonija
slavery	ропство (с)	rópstvo
invasion	инвазија (ж)	ínvazija
famine	глад (ж)	glád

246. Major religious groups. Confessions

religion	религија (ж)	réligija
religious (adj)	религиозан	réligiozan
faith, belief	вера (ж)	véra
to believe (in God)	веровати (нг)	vérovati
believer	верник (м)	vérnik
atheism	атеизам (м)	ateízam
atheist	атеиста (м)	ateísta
Christianity	хришћанство (с)	hríśćanstvo
Christian (n)	хришћанин (м)	hríśćanin
Christian (adj)	хришћански	hríśćanski
Catholicism	католицизам (м)	katolicízam
Catholic (n)	католик (м)	kátolik
Catholic (adj)	католички	kátolički
Protestantism	протестантизам (м)	protestantízam
Protestant Church	протестантска црква (ж)	protestántska cŕkva
Protestant (n)	протестант (м)	protéstant
Orthodoxy	православље (с)	právoslavlje
Orthodox Church	православна црква (с)	právoslavna cŕkva
Orthodox (n)	православни (м)	právoslavni
Presbyterianism	презвитеријанство (с)	prezviterijánstvo
Presbyterian Church	презвитеријанска црква (ж)	prezviterijánska cŕkva
Presbyterian (n)	презвитеријанац (м)	prezviterijánac
Lutheranism	лутеранска црква (ж)	lutéranska cŕkva
Lutheran (n)	лутеранац (м)	lutéranac
Baptist Church	баптизам (м)	baptízam
Baptist (n)	баптиста (м)	baptísta
Anglican Church	англиканска црква (ж)	anglíkanska cŕkva
Anglican (n)	англиканац (м)	anglikánac
Mormonism	мормонизам (м)	mormonízam
Mormon (n)	мормон (м)	mórmon
Judaism	јудаизам (м)	judaízam
Jew (n)	Јеврејин (м)	Jévrejin
Buddhism	будизам (м)	budízam
Buddhist (n)	будиста (м)	budísta
Hinduism	хиндуизам (м)	hinduízam
Hindu (n)	хиндуиста (м)	hinduísta

Islam	ислам (м)	islam
Muslim (n)	муслиман (м)	muslíman
Muslim (adj)	муслимански	muslímanski

Shiah Islam	шиизам (м)	šíízam
Shiite (n)	шиит (м)	šíit
Sunni Islam	сунизам (м)	sunízam
Sunnite (n)	сунит (м)	súnit

247. Religions. Priests

| priest | свештеник (м) | svéštenik |
| the Pope | Римски Папа (м) | Rímski Pápa |

monk, friar	монах (м)	mónah
nun	монахиња (ж)	monáhinja
pastor	пастор (м)	pástor

abbot	опат (м)	ópat
vicar (parish priest)	викар (м)	víkar
bishop	епископ (м)	épiskop
cardinal	кардинал (м)	kardínal

preacher	проповедник (м)	propovédnik
preaching	проповед (ж)	própoved
parishioners	парохијани (мн)	parohíjani

| believer | верник (м) | vérnik |
| atheist | атеиста (м) | ateísta |

248. Faith. Christianity. Islam

| Adam | Адам (м) | Ádam |
| Eve | Ева (ж) | Eva |

God	Бог (м)	Bog
the Lord	Господ (м)	Góspod
the Almighty	Свемоћни (м)	Svémoćni

sin	грех (м)	greh
to sin (vi)	грешити (нг)	gréšiti
sinner (masc.)	грешник (м)	gréšnik
sinner (fem.)	грешница (ж)	gréšnica

hell	пакао (м)	pákao
paradise	рај (м)	raj
Jesus	Исус (м)	Isus
Jesus Christ	Исус Христос (м)	Isus Hrístos

the Holy Spirit	Свети Дух (м)	Svéti Duh
the Savior	Спаситељ (м)	Spásitelj
the Virgin Mary	Богородица (ж)	Bogoródica

the Devil	Ђаво (м)	Ðávo
devil's (adj)	ђаволски	đávolski
Satan	Сатана (м)	Satána
satanic (adj)	сатански	satánski

angel	анђео (м)	ánđeo
guardian angel	анђео чувар (м)	ánđeo čúvar
angelic (adj)	анђеоски	ánđeoski

apostle	апостол (м)	ápostol
archangel	арханђео (м)	arhánđeo
the Antichrist	Антихрист (м)	Antíhrist

Church	Црква (ж)	Cŕkva
Bible	Библија (ж)	Bíblija
biblical (adj)	библијски	bíblijski

Old Testament	Стари Завет (м)	Stári Závet
New Testament	Нови Завет (м)	Nóvi Závet
Gospel	јеванђеље (с)	jevánđelje
Holy Scripture	Свето Писмо (с)	Svéto Písmo
Heaven	Царство (с) небеско	Cárstvo nébesko

Commandment	заповест (ж)	zápovest
prophet	пророк (м)	prórok
prophecy	пророчанство (с)	proročánstvo

Allah	Алах (м)	Álah
Mohammed	Мухамед (м)	Muhámed
the Koran	Куран (м)	Kúran

mosque	џамија (ж)	džámija
mullah	хоџа (м)	hódža
prayer	молитва (ж)	mólitva
to pray (vi, vt)	молити се	móliti se

pilgrimage	ходочашће (с)	hodóčašće
pilgrim	ходочасник (м)	hodóčasnik
Mecca	Мека (ж)	Méka

church	црква (ж)	cŕkva
temple	храм (м)	hram
cathedral	катедрала (ж)	katedrála
Gothic (adj)	готички	gótički
synagogue	синагога (ж)	sinagóga
mosque	џамија (ж)	džámija
chapel	капела (ж)	kapéla
abbey	опатија (ж)	opátija

convent	женски манастир (м)	žénski mánastir
monastery	мушки манастир (м)	múški mánastir
bell (church ~s)	звоно (с)	zvóno
bell tower	звоник (м)	zvónik
to ring (ab. bells)	звонити (нг)	zvóniti
cross	крст (м)	kŕst
cupola (roof)	купола (ж)	kúpola
icon	икона (ж)	íkona
soul	душа (ж)	dúša
fate (destiny)	судбина (ж)	súdbina
evil (n)	зло (с)	zlo
good (n)	добро (с)	dóbro
vampire	вампир (м)	vámpir
witch (evil ~)	вештица (ж)	véštica
demon	демон (м)	démon
spirit	дух (м)	duh
redemption (giving us ~)	искупљење (с)	iskúplenje
to redeem (vt)	искупити (нг)	iskúpiti
church service, mass	служба (ж)	slúžba
to say mass	служити (нг)	slúžiti
confession	исповест (ж)	íspovest
to confess (vi)	исповедати се	ispovédati se
saint (n)	светац (м)	svétac
sacred (holy)	свет	svet
holy water	света вода (ж)	svéta vóda
ritual (n)	ритуал (м)	ritúal
ritual (adj)	ритуалан	rítualan
sacrifice	приношење (с) жртве	prinóšenje žŕtve
superstition	сујеверје (с)	sújeverje
superstitious (adj)	сујеверан	sújeveran
afterlife	загробни живот (м)	zágrobni žívot
eternal life	вечни живот (м)	véčni žívot

MISCELLANEOUS

background (green ~)	позадина (ж)	pózadina
balance (of situation)	равнотежа (ж)	ravnotéža
barrier (obstacle)	преграда (ж)	prégrada
base (basis)	база (ж)	báza
beginning	почетак (м)	počétak
category	категорија (ж)	kategórija
cause (reason)	узрок (м)	úzrok
choice	избор (м)	ízbor
coincidence	коинциденција (ж)	koincidéncija
comfortable (~ chair)	комфоран	kómforan
comparison	поређење (с)	póređenje
compensation	компензација (ж)	kompenzácija
degree (extent, amount)	степен (м)	stépen
development	развој (м)	rázvoj
difference	разлика (ж)	rázlika
effect (e.g., of drugs)	ефекат (м)	éfekat
effort (exertion)	напор (м)	nápor
element	елеменат (м)	elémenat
end (finish)	крај (м)	kraj
example (illustration)	пример (м)	prímer
fact	чињеница (ж)	čínjenica
frequent (adj)	чест	čest
growth (development)	раст (м)	rast
help	помоћ (ж)	pómoć
ideal	идеал (м)	idéal
kind (sort, type)	врста (ж)	vŕsta
labyrinth	лавиринт (м)	lavírint
mistake, error	грешка (ж)	gréška
moment	моменат (м)	mómenat
object (thing)	објекат, предмет (м)	óbjekat, prédmet
obstacle	препрека (ж)	prépreka
original (original copy)	оригинал (м)	origínal
part (~ of sth)	део (м)	déo
particle, small part	делић (м)	délić
pause (break)	пауза (ж)	páuza

position	позиција (ж)	pózicija
principle	принцип (м)	príncip
problem	проблем (м)	próblem
process	процес (м)	próces
progress	прогрес (м)	prógres
property (quality)	својство (с)	svójstvo
reaction	реакција (ж)	reákcija
risk	ризик (м)	rízik
secret	тајна (ж)	tájna
series	серија (ж)	sérija
shape (outer form)	облик (м)	óblik
situation	ситуација (ж)	situácija
solution	решење (с)	rešénje
standard (adj)	стандардни	standárdni
standard (level of quality)	стандард (м)	stándard
stop (pause)	пауза, станка (ж)	páuza, stánka
style	стил (м)	stil
system	систем (м)	sístem
table (chart)	таблица (ж)	táblica
tempo, rate	темпо (м)	témpo
term (word, expression)	термин (м)	términ
thing (object, item)	ствар (ж)	stvar
truth (e.g., moment of ~)	истина (ж)	ístina
turn (please wait your ~)	ред (м)	red
type (sort, kind)	тип (м)	tip
urgent (adj)	хитан	hítan
urgently (adv)	хитно	hítno
utility (usefulness)	корист (ж)	kórist
variant (alternative)	варијанта (ж)	varijánta
way (means, method)	начин (м)	náčin
zone	зона (ж)	zóna

250. Modifiers. Adjectives. Part 1

additional (adj)	додатан	dódatan
ancient (~ civilization)	древни	drévni
artificial (adj)	вештачки	véštački
back, rear (adj)	задњи	zádnji
bad (adj)	лош	loš
beautiful (~ palace)	прекрасан	prékrasan
beautiful (person)	леп	lep
big (in size)	велик	vélik

bitter (taste)	горак	górak
blind (sightless)	слеп	slep
calm, quiet (adj)	спокојан	spókojan
careless (negligent)	немаран	némaran
caring (~ father)	брижан	brížan
central (adj)	централни	céntralni
cheap (low-priced)	јефтин	jéftin
cheerful (adj)	весео	véseo
children's (adj)	дечји	déčji
civil (~ law)	грађански	grádanski
clandestine (secret)	илегалан	ílegalan
clean (free from dirt)	чист	čist
clear (explanation, etc.)	јасан	jásan
clever (smart)	паметан	pámetan
close (near in space)	близак	blízak
closed (adj)	затворен	zátvoren
cloudless (sky)	ведар	védar
cold (drink, weather)	хладан	hládan
compatible (adj)	компатибилан	kómpatibilan
contented (satisfied)	задовољан	zádovoljan
continuous (uninterrupted)	непрекидан	néprekidan
cool (weather)	прохладан	próhladan
dangerous (adj)	опасан	ópasan
dark (room)	мрачан	mráčan
dead (not alive)	мртав	mȑtav
dense (fog, smoke)	густ	gust
destitute (extremely poor)	сиромашан	sirómašan
different (not the same)	разан	razan
difficult (decision)	тежак	téžak
difficult (problem, task)	тежак	téžak
dim, faint (light)	слаб	slab
dirty (not clean)	прљав	pȑljav
distant (in space)	далек	dálek
dry (clothes, etc.)	сув	suv
easy (not difficult)	лак (м)	lak
empty (glass, room)	празан	prázan
even (e.g., ~ surface)	раван	rávan
exact (amount)	тачан	táčan
excellent (adj)	одличан	ódličan
excessive (adj)	прекомеран	prékomeran
expensive (adj)	скуп	skup
exterior (adj)	спољашњи	spóljašnji
far (the ~ East)	далек	dálek

fast (quick)	брз	br̂z
fatty (food)	мастан	mástan
fertile (land, soil)	плодан	plódan
flat (~ panel display)	пљоснат	pljósnat
foreign (adj)	стран	stran
fragile (china, glass)	ломљив	lómljiv
free (at no cost)	бесплатан	bésplatan
free (unrestricted)	слободан	slóbodan
fresh (~ water)	слатка	slátka
fresh (e.g., ~ bread)	свеж	svež
frozen (food)	замрзнут	zámrznut
full (completely filled)	пун	pun
gloomy (house, forecast)	мрачан	mráčan
good (book, etc.)	добар	dóbar
good, kind (kindhearted)	добар	dóbar
grateful (adj)	захвалан	záhvalan
happy (adj)	срећан	sréćan
hard (not soft)	тврд	tvr̂d
heavy (in weight)	тежак	téžak
hostile (adj)	непријатељски	neprijatéljski
hot (adj)	врућ	vruć
huge (adj)	огроман	ógroman
humid (adj)	влажан	vlážan
hungry (adj)	гладан	gládan
ill (sick, unwell)	болестан	bólestan
immobile (adj)	непокретан	népokretan
important (adj)	важан	vážan
impossible (adj)	немогућ	némoguć
incomprehensible	неразумљив	nerazúmljiv
indispensable (adj)	неопходан	néophodan
inexperienced (adj)	неискусан	néiskusan
insignificant (adj)	безначајан	béznačajan
interior (adj)	унутрашњи	únutrašnji
joint (~ decision)	заједнички	zájednički
last (e.g., ~ week)	прошли	próšli
last (final)	последњи	póslednji
left (e.g., ~ side)	леви	lévi
legal (legitimate)	законит	zákonit
light (in weight)	лак (м)	lak
light (pale color)	светао	svétao
limited (adj)	ограничен	ográničen
liquid (fluid)	течан	téčan
long (e.g., ~ hair)	дуг, дугачак	dug, dúgačak

| loud (voice, etc.) | гласан | glásan |
| low (voice) | тих | tih |

251. Modifiers. Adjectives. Part 2

main (principal)	главни	glávni
matt, matte	мат	mat
meticulous (job)	уредан	úredan
mysterious (adj)	загонетан	zágonetan
narrow (street, etc.)	узак	úzak

native (~ country)	родни	ródni
nearby (adj)	ближњи	óbližnji
nearsighted (adj)	кратковид	kratkóvid
needed (necessary)	потребан	pótreban
negative (~ response)	негативан	négativan

neighboring (adj)	суседни	súsedni
nervous (adj)	нервозан	nérvozan
new (adj)	нов	nov
next (e.g., ~ week)	следећи	slédeći

nice (agreeable)	мио	mío
pleasant (voice)	пријатан	príjatan
normal (adj)	нормалан	nórmalan
not big (adj)	невелик	névelik
not difficult (adj)	једноставан	jédnostavan

obligatory (adj)	обавезан	óbavezan
old (house)	стар	star
open (adj)	отворен	ótvoren
opposite (adj)	супротан	súprotan

ordinary (usual)	обичан	óbičan
original (unusual)	оригиналан	óriginalan
past (recent)	прошли	próšli
permanent (adj)	сталан	stálan
personal (adj)	персонални	pérsonalni

polite (adj)	учтив	účtiv
poor (not rich)	сиромашан	sirómašan
possible (adj)	могућ	móguć
present (current)	садашњи	sádašnji
previous (adj)	претходан	préthodan

principal (main)	основни	ósnovni
private (~ jet)	приватни	prívatni
probable (adj)	вероватни	vérovatni
prolonged (e.g., ~ applause)	дуготрајан	dúgotrajan

public (open to all)	јавни	jávni
punctual (person)	тачан	táčan
quiet (tranquil)	тих	tih
rare (adj)	редак	rédak
raw (uncooked)	сиров	sírov
right (not left)	десни	désni
right, correct (adj)	правилан	právilan
ripe (fruit)	зрео	zréo
risky (adj)	ризичан	rízičan
sad (~ look)	тужан	túžan
sad (depressing)	тужан	túžan
safe (not dangerous)	безбедан	bézbedan
salty (food)	слан	slan
satisfied (customer)	задовољан	zádovoljan
second hand (adj)	половни	pólovni
shallow (water)	плитак	plítak
sharp (blade, etc.)	оштар	óštar
short (in length)	кратак	krátak
short, short-lived (adj)	краткотрајан	krátkotrajan
significant (notable)	значајан	znáčajan
similar (adj)	сличан	slíčan
simple (easy)	прост	prost
skinny	мршав	mŕšav
small (in size)	мали	máli
smooth (surface)	гладак	gládak
soft (~ toys)	мек, мекан	mek, mékan
solid (~ wall)	чврст	čvŕst
sour (flavor, taste)	кисео	kíseo
spacious (house, etc.)	просторан	próstoran
special (adj)	специјалан	spécijalan
straight (line, road)	прав	prav
strong (person)	снажан	snážan
stupid (foolish)	глуп	glup
suitable (e.g., ~ for drinking)	погодан	pógodan
sunny (day)	сунчан	súnčan
superb, perfect (adj)	изврсни	ízvrsni
swarthy (adj)	тамнопут, гарав	támnoput, gárav
sweet (sugary)	сладак	sládak
tan (adj)	преплануо	preplánuo
tasty (delicious)	укусан	úkusan
tender (affectionate)	нежан	néžan
the highest (adj)	највиши	nájviši
the most important	најважнији	nájvažniji

the nearest	најближи	nájbliži
the same, equal (adj)	једнак	jédnak
thick (e.g., ~ fog)	густ	gust
thick (wall, slice)	дебео	débeo

thin (person)	танак, мршав	tának, mŕšav
tight (~ shoes)	тесан	tésan
tired (exhausted)	уморан	úmoran
tiring (adj)	заморан	zámoran

transparent (adj)	providан	próvidan
unclear (adj)	нејасан	néjasan
unique (exceptional)	јединствен	jedínstven
various (adj)	различит	rázličit

warm (moderately hot)	топао	tópao
wet (e.g., ~ clothes)	мокар	mókar
whole (entire, complete)	цео	céo
wide (e.g., ~ road)	широк	šírok
young (adj)	млад	mlad

MAIN 500 VERBS

to accompany (vt)	пратити (пг)	prátiti
to accuse (vt)	оптуживати (пг)	optužívati
to acknowledge (admit)	признавати (пг)	priznávati
to act (take action)	деловати (нг)	délovati
to add (supplement)	додавати (пг)	dodávati
to address (speak to)	обраћати се	óbraćati se
to admire (vi)	дивити се	díviti se
to advertise (vt)	рекламирати (пг)	reklamírati
to advise (vt)	саветовати (пг)	sávetovati
to affirm (assert)	утврђивати (пг)	utvrđívati
to agree (say yes)	слагати се	slágati se
to aim (to point a weapon)	циљати (пг)	cíljati
to allow (sb to do sth)	дозвољавати (нг)	dozvoljávati
to amputate (vt)	ампутирати (пг)	amputírati
to answer (vi, vt)	одговарати (нг, пг)	odgovárati
to apologize (vi)	извињавати се	izvinjávati se
to appear (come into view)	појављивати се	pojavljívati se
to applaud (vi, vt)	аплаудирати (нг)	aplaudírati
to appoint (assign)	именовати (пг)	ímenovati
to approach (come closer)	приближити се	priblížiti se
to arrive (ab. train)	стићи (нг)	stíći
to ask (~ sb to do sth)	тражити, молити (пг)	trážiti, móliti
to aspire to …	тежити (нг)	téžiti
to assist (help)	асистирати (пг)	asistírati
to attack (mil.)	нападати (нг)	nápadati
to attain (objectives)	постизати (пг)	póstizati
to avenge (get revenge)	освећивати се	osvećívati se
to avoid (danger, task)	избегавати (пг)	izbegávati
to award (give medal to)	наградити (пг)	nagráditi
to battle (vi)	бити се	bíti se
to be (vi)	бити (нг, пг)	bíti
to be a cause of …	узроковати (пг)	úzrokovati
to be afraid	плашити се	plášiti se
to be angry (with …)	љутити се на …	ljútiti se na …

to be at war	ратовати (нг)	rátovati
to be based (on ...)	базирати се на ...	bazírati se na ...
to be bored	досађивати се	dosađívati se
to be convinced	бити убеђен	bíti ubeđen
to be enough	достајати (нг)	dóstajati
to be envious	завидети (нг)	závideti
to be indignant	бунити се	búniti se
to be interested in ...	интересовати се	ínteresovati se
to be lost in thought	замислити се	zámisliti se
to be lying (~ on the table)	лежати (нг)	léžati
to be needed	бити потребан	bíti pótreban
to be perplexed (puzzled)	бити збуњен	biti zbúnjen
to be preserved	очувати се	očúvati se
to be required	бити тражен	bíti trážen
to be surprised	чудити се	čúditi se
to be worried	бринути се	brínuti se
to beat (to hit)	ударати (пг)	údarati
to become (e.g., ~ old)	постати (пг)	póstati
to behave (vi)	понашати се	ponášati se
to believe (think)	веровати (нг)	vérovati
to belong to ...	припадати (нг)	prípadati
to berth (moor)	пристајати (нг)	prístajati
to blind (other drivers)	ослепљавати (пг)	oslepljávati
to blow (wind)	дувати (нг)	dúvati
to blush (vi)	црвенити (нг)	crvéniti
to boast (vi)	хвалисати се	hválisati se
to borrow (money)	позајмити (пг)	pozájmiti
to break (branch, toy, etc.)	ломити (пг)	lómiti
to breathe (vi)	дисати (нг)	dísati
to bring (sth)	доносити (пг)	donósiti
to burn (paper, logs)	палити (пг)	páliti
to buy (purchase)	куповати (пг)	kupóvati
to call (~ for help)	звати (пг)	zváti
to call (yell for sb)	позвати (пг)	pózvati
to calm down (vt)	смиривати (пг)	smirívati
can (v aux)	моћи (нг)	móći
to cancel (call off)	отказати (пг)	otkázati
to cast off (of a boat or ship)	отпловити (нг)	otplóviti
to catch (e.g., ~ a ball)	ловити (пг)	lóviti
to change (~ one's opinion)	променити (пг)	proméniti
to change (exchange)	мењати (пг)	ménjati
to charm (vt)	очаравати (пг)	očarávati
to choose (select)	бирати (пг)	bírati

to chop off (with an ax)	одсећи (nr)	ódseći
to clean (e.g., kettle from scale)	чистити (nr)	čístiti
to clean (shoes, etc.)	чистити (nr)	čístiti
to clean up (tidy)	поспремати (nr)	posprémati
to close (vt)	затварати (nr)	zatvárati
to comb one's hair	чешљати се	čéšljati se
to come down (the stairs)	спуштати се	spúštati se
to come out (book)	изаћи (нr)	ízaći
to compare (vt)	упоређивати (nr)	upoređívati
to compensate (vt)	компензирати (nr)	kompenzírati
to compete (vi)	конкурисати (nr)	konkúrisati
to compile (~ a list)	састављати (nr)	sástavljati
to complain (vi, vt)	жалити се	žáliti se
to complicate (vt)	компликовати (nr)	kómplikovati
to compose (music, etc.)	компоновати (nr)	komponóvati
to compromise (reputation)	компромитовати (nr)	komprómitovati
to concentrate (vi)	концентрисати се	koncéntrisati se
to confess (criminal)	признавати (nr)	priznávati
to confuse (mix up)	бркати (nr)	bŕkati
to congratulate (vt)	честитати (nr)	čestítati
to consult (doctor, expert)	консултовати се	kónsultovati se
to continue (~ to do sth)	настављати (nr)	nástavljati
to control (vt)	контролисати (nr)	kontrólisati
to convince (vt)	убеђивати (nr)	ubeđívati
to cooperate (vi)	сарађивати (нr)	sarađívati
to coordinate (vt)	координирати (nr)	koordinírati
to correct (an error)	исправљати (nr)	íspravljati
to cost (vt)	коштати (нr)	kóštati
to count (money, etc.)	бројати (nr)	brójati
to count on ...	рачунати на ...	račúnati na ...
to crack (ceiling, wall)	пуцати (нr)	púcati
to create (vt)	створити (nr)	stvóriti
to crush, to squash (~ a bug)	смрскати (nr)	smŕskati
to cry (weep)	плакати (нr)	plákati
to cut off (with a knife)	одсећи (nr)	ódseći

253. Verbs D-G

to dare (~ to do sth)	усуђивати се	usuđívati se
to date from ...	датира (нr)	dátira

| to deceive (vi, vt) | обмањивати (nr) | obmanjívati |
| to decide (~ to do sth) | одлучивати (nr) | odlučívati |

to decorate (tree, street)	украшавати (nr)	ukrašávati
to dedicate (book, etc.)	посвећивати (nr)	posvećívati
to defend (a country, etc.)	штитити (nr)	štítiti
to defend oneself	бранити се	brániti se

to demand (request firmly)	захтевати, тражити	zahtévati, trážiti
to denounce (vt)	потказивати (нг)	potkazívati
to deny (vt)	порећи (nr)	póreći
to depend on …	зависити од …	závisiti od …

to deprive (vt)	лишавати (nr)	lišávati
to deserve (vt)	заслуживати (nr)	zaslužívati
to design (machine, etc.)	пројектовати (nr)	projéktovati
to desire (want, wish)	желети (nr)	žéleti

to despise (vt)	презирати (nr)	prézirati
to destroy (documents, etc.)	уништавати (nr)	uništávati
to differ (from sth)	разликовати се	rázlikovati se
to dig (tunnel, etc.)	копати (nr)	kópati
to direct (point the way)	упутити (nr)	upútiti

to disappear (vi)	ишчезнути (нг)	íščeznuti
to discover (new land, etc.)	откривати (nr)	otkrívati
to discuss (vt)	расправљати (nr)	ráspravljati
to distribute (leaflets, etc.)	делити (nr)	déliti

to disturb (vt)	сметати (iii)	smétati
to dive (vi)	ронити (нг)	róniti
to divide (math)	делити (nr)	déliti
to do (vt)	радити (nr)	ráditi

to do the laundry	прати (nr)	práti
to double (increase)	удвостручити (nr)	udvóstručiti
to doubt (have doubts)	сумњати (нг)	súmnjati
to draw a conclusion	изводити закључак	ízvoditi zákljúčak

to dream (daydream)	маштати (нг)	máštati
to dream (in sleep)	сањати (нг)	sánjati
to drink (vi, vt)	пити (нг, nr)	píti
to drive a car	возити ауто	vóziti áuto

to drive away (scare away)	отерати (nr)	óterati
to drop (let fall)	испуштати (nr)	ispúštati
to drown (ab. person)	удавити се	udáviti se
to dry (clothes, hair)	сушити (nr)	súšiti

| to eat (vi, vt) | јести (нг, nr) | jésti |
| to eavesdrop (vi) | прислушкивати (нг, nr) | prisluškívati |

to emit (diffuse - odor, etc.)	ширити (пг)	šíriti
to enjoy oneself	уживати (нг)	užívati
to enter (on the list)	уписати (пг)	upísati
to enter (room, house, etc.)	ући, улазити (нг)	úći, úlaziti
to entertain (amuse)	забављати (пг)	zábavljati
to equip (fit out)	опремати (пг)	oprémati
to examine (proposal)	размотрити (пг)	razmótriti
to exchange (sth)	размењивати се	razmenjívati se
to excuse (forgive)	извињавати (пг)	izvinjávati
to exist (vi)	постојати (нг)	póstojati
to expect (anticipate)	очекивати (пг)	očekívati
to expect (foresee)	предвиђати (пг)	predvídati
to expel (from school, etc.)	избацити (пг)	izbáciti
to explain (vt)	објашњавати (пг)	objašnjávati
to express (vt)	изразити (пг)	izráziti
to extinguish (a fire)	гасити (пг)	gásiti
to fall in love (with …)	заљубити (нг)	zaljúbiti
to feed (provide food)	хранити (пг)	hrániti
to fight (against the enemy)	борити се	bóriti se
to fight (vi)	тући се	túći se
to fill (glass, bottle)	пунити (пг)	púniti
to find (~ lost items)	наћи, налазити (пг)	náći, nálaziti
to finish (vt)	завршавати (пг)	završávati
to fish (angle)	пецати (нг)	pécati
to fit (ab. dress, etc.)	пристајати (нг)	prístajati
to flatter (vt)	ласкати (нг)	láskati
to fly (bird, plane)	летети (нг)	léteti
to follow … (come after)	пратити (пг)	prátiti
to forbid (vt)	забрањивати (пг)	zabranjívati
to force (compel)	принуђавати (пг)	prinuđávati
to forget (vi, vt)	заборавити (нг, пг)	zabóraviti
to forgive (pardon)	опраштати (пг)	opráštati
to form (constitute)	формирати (пг)	formírati
to get dirty (vi)	испрљати се	ispŕljati se
to get infected (with …)	заразити се	zaráziti se
to get irritated	раздраживати се	razdražívati se
to get married	женити се	žéniti se
to get rid of …	избављати се	izbavljati se
to get tired	умарати се	umárati se
to get up (arise from bed)	устајати (нг)	ústajati

| to give (vt) | давати (пг) | dávati |
| to give a bath (to bath) | купати (пг) | kúpati |

to give a hug, to hug (vt)	грлити (пг)	gŕliti
to give in (yield to)	уступати (пг)	ustúpati
to glimpse (vt)	приметити (пг)	primétiti
to go (by car, etc.)	ићи (нг)	íći

to go (on foot)	ићи (нг)	íći
to go for a swim	купати се	kúpati se
to go out (for dinner, etc.)	изаћи (нг)	ízaći
to go to bed (go to sleep)	ићи на спавање	íći na spávanje

to greet (vt)	поздрављати (пг)	pózdravljati
to grow (plants)	гајити (пг)	gájiti
to guarantee (vt)	гарантовати (пг)	gárantovati
to guess (the answer)	погодити (пг)	pogóditi

254. Verbs H-M

to hand out (distribute)	раздати (пг)	rázdati
to hang (curtains, etc.)	вешати (пг)	véšati
to have (vt)	имати (пг)	ímati
to have a try	покушати (пг)	pókušati
to have breakfast	доручковати (нг)	dóručkovati

to have dinner	вечерати (нг)	véčerati
to have lunch	ручати (нг)	rúčati
to head (group, etc.)	бити на челу	bítl na čélu
to hear (vt)	чути (нг, пг)	čúti
to heat (vt)	загрејавати (пг)	zagrejávati

to help (vt)	помагати (пг)	pomágati
to hide (vt)	крити (пг)	kríti
to hire (e.g., ~ a boat)	изнајмити (пг)	iznájmiti
to hire (staff)	запослити (пг)	zapósliti
to hope (vi, vt)	надати се	nádati se

to hunt (for food, sport)	ловити (пг)	lóviti
to hurry (vi)	журити се	žúriti se
to imagine (to picture)	замишљати (пг)	zamíšljati
to imitate (vt)	имитирати (пг)	imitírati
to implore (vt)	умољавати (пг)	umoljávati
to import (vt)	импортирати, увозити	importírati, uvóziti
to increase (vi)	повећавати се	povećávati se
to increase (vt)	повећавати (пг)	povećávati
to infect (vt)	заразити (пг)	zaráziti
to influence (vt)	утицати (нг)	úticati
to inform (e.g., ~ the police about ...)	саопштавати (пг)	saopštávati

to inform (vt)	информисати (пг)	infórmisati
to inherit (vt)	наслеђивати (пг)	nasleđívati
to inquire (about …)	распитати се	raspítati se
to insert (put in)	убацивати (пг)	ubacívati
to insinuate (imply)	наговештавати (нг)	nagoveštávati
to insist (vi, vt)	инсистирати (нг)	insistírati
to inspire (vt)	одушевљавати (пг)	oduševljávati
to instruct (teach)	давати инструкције	dávati instrúkcije
to insult (offend)	вређати (пг)	vréđati
to interest (vt)	интересовати (пг)	ínteresovati
to intervene (vi)	интервенисати (нг)	intervénisati
to introduce (sb to sb)	упознавати (пг)	upoznávati
to invent (machine, etc.)	проналазити (пг)	pronálaziti
to invite (vt)	позивати (пг)	pozívati
to iron (clothes)	пеглати (пг)	péglati
to irritate (annoy)	раздраживати (пг)	razdražívati
to isolate (vt)	изолирати (пг)	izolírati
to join (political party, etc.)	припајати се	pripájati se
to joke (be kidding)	шалити се	šáliti se
to keep (old letters, etc.)	чувати (пг)	čúvati
to keep silent, to hush	ћутати (нг)	ćútati
to kill (vt)	убијати (нг)	ubíjati
to knock (on the door)	куцати (нг)	kúcati
to know (sb)	знати (пг)	znáti
to know (sth)	знати (пг)	znáti
to laugh (vi)	смејати се	sméjati se
to launch (start up)	започети (пг)	zapóčeti
to leave (~ for Mexico)	одлазити (нг)	ódlaziti
to leave (forget sth)	остављати (пг)	óstavljati
to leave (spouse)	напуштати (пг)	napuštati
to liberate (city, etc.)	ослобађати (пг)	oslobáđati
to lie (~ on the floor)	лежати (нг)	léžati
to lie (tell untruth)	лагати (нг)	lágati
to light (campfire, etc.)	запалити (пг)	zapáliti
to light up (illuminate)	осветљавати (пг)	osvetljávati
to like (I like …)	свиђати се	svíđati se
to limit (vt)	ограничавати (пг)	ograničávati
to listen (vi)	слушати (пг)	slúšati
to live (~ in France)	живети (нг)	žíveti
to live (exist)	живети (нг)	žíveti
to load (gun)	пунити (пг)	púniti
to load (vehicle, etc.)	товарити (пг)	tóvariti
to look (I'm just ~ing)	гледати (пг)	glédati
to look for … (search)	тражити (пг)	trážiti

to look like (resemble)	личити (нг)	líčiti
to lose (umbrella, etc.)	губити (пг)	gúbiti
to love (e.g., ~ dancing)	волети (пг)	vóleti
to love (sb)	волети (пг)	vóleti
to lower (blind, head)	спуштати (пг)	spúštati
to make (~ dinner)	кувати (пг)	kúvati
to make a mistake	грешити (нг)	gréšiti
to make angry	љутити (пг)	ljútiti
to make easier	олакшати (пг)	olákšati
to make multiple copies	направити копије	nápraviti kópije
to make the acquaintance	упознавати се	upoznávati se
to make use (of …)	користити (пг)	kóristiti
to manage, to run	руководити (пг)	rukovóditi
to mark (make a mark)	обележити (пг)	obéležiti
to mean (signify)	значити (нг)	znáčiti
to memorize (vt)	запамтити (пг)	zápamtiti
to mention (talk about)	спомињати (пг)	spóminjati
to miss (school, etc.)	пропуштати (пг)	propúštati
to mix (combine, blend)	смешати (пг)	sméšati
to mock (make fun of)	подсмевати се	podsmévati se
to move (to shift)	мицати (пг)	mícati
to multiply (math)	множити (пг)	mnóžiti
must (v aux)	морати	mórati

255. Verbs N-R

to name, to call (vt)	називати (пг)	nazívati
to negotiate (vi)	преговарати (нг)	pregovárati
to note (write down)	забележити (пг)	zabéležiti
to notice (see)	запажати (пг)	zapážati
to obey (vi, vt)	подчињавати се	podčinjávati se
to object (vi, vt)	приговарати (нг)	prigovárati
to observe (see)	посматрати (нг)	posmátrati
to offend (vt)	вређати (пг)	vréđati
to omit (word, phrase)	пропуштати (пг)	propúštati
to open (vt)	отварати (пг)	otvárati
to order (in restaurant)	наручивати (пг)	naručívati
to order (mil.)	наређивати (пг)	naređívati
to organize (concert, party)	направити (пг)	nápraviti
to overestimate (vt)	преценити (пг)	precéniti
to own (possess)	поседовати (пг)	pósedovati
to participate (vi)	учествовати (нг)	účestvovati
to pass through (by car, etc.)	пролазити кроз …	prólaziti kroz …

to pay (vi, vt)	платити (нг, пг)	plátiti
to peep, spy on	шпијунирати	špijunírati
to penetrate (vt)	пробијати (нг)	probíjati
to permit (vt)	допуштати (нг)	dopúštati
to pick (flowers)	брати (пг)	bráti
to place (put, set)	смештати (пг)	sméštati
to plan (~ to do sth)	планирати (пг)	planírati
to play (actor)	глумити (пг)	glúmiti
to play (children)	играти се	ígrati se
to point (~ the way)	указати (пг)	ukázati
to pour (liquid)	сипати (пг)	sípati
to pray (vi, vt)	молити се	móliti se
to prefer (vt)	преферирати (пг)	preferírati
to prepare (~ a plan)	припремити (пг)	priprémiti
to present (sb to sb)	представљати (пг)	prédstavljati
to preserve (peace, life)	очувати (пг)	očúvati
to prevail (vt)	превлађивати (нг)	prevlađívati
to progress (move forward)	напредовати (нг)	nápredovati
to promise (vt)	обећати (пг)	obéćati
to pronounce (vt)	изговарати (пг)	izgovárati
to propose (vt)	предлагати (пг)	predlágati
to protect (e.g., ~ nature)	штитити (пг)	štítiti
to protest (vi)	протестовати (нг)	prótestovati
to prove (vt)	доказивати (пг)	dokazívati
to provoke (vt)	изазивати (пг)	izazívati
to pull (~ the rope)	вући (пг)	vúći
to punish (vt)	кажњавати (пг)	kažnjávati
to push (~ the door)	гурати (пг)	gúrati
to put away (vt)	склонити (пг)	slóniti
to put in order	сређивати (пг)	sređívati
to put, to place	ставити (пг)	stáviti
to quote (cite)	цитирати (пг)	citírati
to reach (arrive at)	доћи (пг)	dóći
to read (vi, vt)	читати (нг, пг)	čítati
to realize (a dream)	остваривати (пг)	ostvarívati
to recognize (identify sb)	препознавати (пг)	prepoznávati
to recommend (vt)	препоручивати (пг)	preporučívati
to recover (~ from flu)	оздрављати (нг)	ódzdravljati
to redo (do again)	поново урадити	pónovo uráditi
to reduce (speed, etc.)	смањивати (пг)	smanjívati
to refuse (~ sb)	одбијати (пг)	odbíjati
to regret (be sorry)	жалити (нг)	žáliti

to reinforce (vt)	учвршћивати (пг)	učvršćívati
to remember (Do you ~ me?)	сећати се	sećati se
to remember (I can't ~ her name)	сетити се	sétiti se
to remind of …	подсећати (пг)	pódsećati
to remove (~ a stain)	уклањати (пг)	úklanjati
to remove (~ an obstacle)	уклањати (пг)	úklanjati
to rent (sth from sb)	изнајмити (пг)	iznájmiti
to repair (mend)	поправити (пг)	pópraviti
to repeat (say again)	понављати (пг)	ponávljati
to report (make a report)	извештавати (нг)	izveštávati
to reproach (vt)	корити (пг)	kóriti
to reserve, to book	резервисати (пг)	rezervísati
to restrain (hold back)	спречавати (пг)	sprečávati
to return (come back)	враћати се	vráćati se
to risk, to take a risk	ризиковати (нг)	rízikovati
to rub out (erase)	избрисати (пг)	ízbrisati
to run (move fast)	трчати (нг)	tŕčati
to rush (hurry sb)	журити (пг)	žúriti

to satisfy (please)	задовољавати (пг)	zadovoljávati
to save (rescue)	спасавати (ш)	spasávatl
to say (~ thank you)	казати (пг)	kázati
to scold (vt)	грдити (пг)	gŕditi
to scratch (with claws)	гребати, грепсти (пг)	grébati, grépsti
to select (to pick)	одабрати (пг)	odábrati
to sell (goods)	продавати (пг)	prodávati
to send (a letter)	слати (пг)	sláti
to send back (vt)	вратити (пг)	vrátiti
to sense (~ danger)	осећати (пг)	ósećati
to sentence (vt)	осуђивати (пг)	osuđívati
to serve (in restaurant)	послуживати (пг)	poslužívati
to settle (a conflict)	решавати (пг)	rešávati
to shake (vt)	трести (пг)	trésti
to shave (vi)	бријати се	bríjati se
to shine (gleam)	сијати (нг)	síjati
to shiver (with cold)	дрхтати (нг)	dŕhtati
to shoot (vi)	пуцати (нг)	púcati
to shout (vi)	викати (нг)	víkati

to show (to display)	показивати (пг)	pokazívati
to shudder (vi)	дрхтати (нг)	dŕhtati
to sigh (vi)	уздахнути (нг)	uzdáhnuti
to sign (document)	потписивати (пг)	potpisívati
to signify (mean)	значити (нг)	znáčiti
to simplify (vt)	упрошћавати (пг)	uprošćávati
to sin (vi)	грешити (нг)	gréšiti
to sit (be sitting)	седети (нг)	sédeti
to sit down (vi)	сести (нг)	sésti
to smell (emit an odor)	мирисати (нг)	mirísati
to smell (inhale the odor)	мирисати, њушити (пг)	mirísati, njúšiti
to smile (vi)	осмехивати се	osmehívati se
to snap (vi, ab. rope)	пукнути (нг)	púknuti
to solve (problem)	решити (пг)	réšiti
to sow (seed, crop)	сејати (нг, пг)	séjati
to spill (liquid)	пролити (пг)	próliti
to spill out, scatter (flour, etc.)	просути се	prósuti se
to spit (vi)	пљувати (нг)	pljúvati
to stand (toothache, cold)	трпети (нг)	tŕpeti
to start (begin)	почињати (нг, пг)	póčinjati
to steal (money, etc.)	красти (пг)	krásti
to stop (for pause, etc.)	заустављати се	zaústavljati se
to stop (please ~ calling me)	прекидати (пг)	prekídati
to stop talking	заћутати (нг)	zaćútati
to stroke (caress)	гладити (пг)	gláditi
to study (vt)	студирати (пг)	studírati
to suffer (feel pain)	патити (нг)	pátiti
to support (cause, idea)	подржати (пг)	podŕžati
to suppose (assume)	претпостављати (пг)	pretpóstavljati
to surface (ab. submarine)	испливати (нг)	ísplivati
to surprise (amaze)	чудити (пг)	čúditi
to suspect (vt)	сумњати (нг, пг)	súmnjati
to swim (vi)	пливати (нг)	plívati
to take (get hold of)	узети (пг)	úzeti
to take a bath	купати се	kúpati se
to take a rest	одмарати се	odmárati se
to take away (e.g., about waiter)	односити (пг)	odnósiti
to take off (airplane)	полетати (нг)	polétati
to take off (painting, curtains, etc.)	скидати (пг)	skídati

to take pictures	сликати (nr)	slíkati
to talk to ...	говорити са ...	govóriti sa ...
to teach (give lessons)	обучавати (nr)	obučávati
to tear off, to rip off (vt)	откинути (nr)	ótkinuti
to tell (story, joke)	причати (nr)	príčati
to thank (vt)	захваљивати (nr)	zahvaljívati
to think (believe)	мислити (нr)	mísliti
to think (vi, vt)	мислити (нr)	mísliti
to threaten (vt)	претити (нr)	prétiti
to throw (stone, etc.)	бацати (nr)	bácati
to tie to ...	привезивати (nr)	privezívati
to tie up (prisoner)	свезивати (nr)	svezívati
to tire (make tired)	умарати (nr)	umárati
to touch (one's arm, etc.)	тицати (nr)	tícati
to tower (over ...)	уздизати се	úzdizati se
to train (animals)	дресирати (nr)	dresírati
to train (sb)	тренирати (nr)	trenírati
to train (vi)	тренирати (нr)	trenírati
to transform (vt)	трансформисати (nr)	transfórmisati
to translate (vt)	преводити (nr)	prevóditi
to treat (illness)	лечити (nr)	léčiti
to trust (vt)	веровати (nr)	vérovati
to try (attempt)	покушавати (нr)	pokušávati
to turn (e.g., ~ left)	скретати (нr)	skrétati
to turn away (vi)	окретати се	okrétati se
to turn off (the light)	гасити (nr)	gásiti
to turn on (computer, etc.)	укључивати (nr)	uključívati
to turn over (stone, etc.)	преврнути (nr)	prevŕnuti
to underestimate (vt)	подцењивати (nr)	podcenjívati
to underline (vt)	подвући (nr)	pódvući
to understand (vt)	разумевати (nr)	razumévati
to undertake (vt)	предузети (nr)	préduzeti
to unite (vt)	уједињавати (nr)	ujedinjávati
to untie (vt)	одрешити (nr)	ódrešiti
to use (phrase, word)	употребити (nr)	upotrébiti
to vaccinate (vt)	вакцинисати (nr)	vakcinísati
to vote (vi)	гласати (нr)	glásati
to wait (vt)	чекати (нr, nr)	čékati
to wake (sb)	будити (nr)	búditi
to want (wish, desire)	хтети (nr)	htéti
to warn (of the danger)	упозоравати (nr)	upozorávati
to wash (clean)	прати (nr)	práti

to water (plants)	заливати (пг)	zalívati
to wave (the hand)	махати (нг)	máhati
to weigh (have weight)	тежити (нг)	téžiti
to work (vi)	радити (нг)	ráditi
to worry (make anxious)	узнемиравати (пг)	uznemirávati
to worry (vi)	бринути се	brínuti se
to wrap (parcel, etc.)	завијати (пг)	zavijati
to wrestle (sport)	рвати се	rvati se
to write (vt)	писати (пг)	písati
to write down	записивати (пг)	zapisívati

Made in the USA
Middletown, DE
09 February 2025